Other AUSA Books

Matthews & Brown   THE CHALLENGE OF MILITARY LEADERSHIP

Matthews & Brown   THE PARAMETERS OF MILITARY ETHICS

Smith   ASSIGNMENT: PENTAGON—THE INSIDER'S GUIDE TO THE POTOMAC PUZZLE PALACE

Titles of Related Interest

Baynes   SOLDIERS OF SCOTLAND

Clayton   FRANCE, SOLDIERS & AFRICA

Laffin   BRASSEY'S BATTLES: 3500 YEARS OF CONFLICT, CAMPAIGNS & WARS FROM A-Z

Liddle   GALLIPOLI: 1915

Liddle   HOME FIRES & FOREIGN FIELDS

Vaux   TAKE THAT HILL!: ROYAL MARINES IN THE FALKLANDS WAR

Related Periodicals*

Armed Forces Journal International

Defense Analysis

*Specimen copies available upon request.

An AUSA Book

Gen. John R. Galvin, U.S. Army
Supreme Allied Commander, Europe

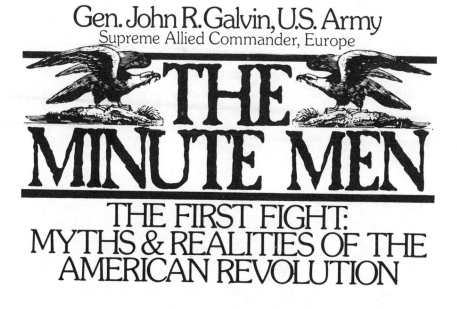

THE MINUTE MEN

THE FIRST FIGHT: MYTHS & REALITIES OF THE AMERICAN REVOLUTION

Second Edition, Revised

A Pergamon-Brassey's Classic

Published with the
Institute of Land Warfare
Association of the U.S. Army

PERGAMON-BRASSEY'S
International Defense Publishers, Inc.

Washington · New York · London · Oxford · Beijing
Frankfurt · São Paulo · Sydney · Tokyo · Toronto

U.S.A.	Pergamon-Brassey's International Defense Publishers,
(Editorial)	8000 Westpark Drive, Fourth Floor, McLean,
	Virginia 22102, U.S.A.
(Orders)	Pergamon Press, Maxwell House, Fairview Park, Elmsford, New York 10523, U.S.A.
U.K. (Editorial)	Brassey's Defence Publishers, 24 Gray's Inn Road, London WC1X 8HR
(Orders)	Brassey's Defence Publishers, Headington Hill Hall, Oxford OX3 0BW, England
PEOPLE'S REPUBLIC OF CHINA	Pergamon Press, Room 4037, Qianmen Hotel, Beijing, People's Republic of China
FEDERAL REPUBLIC OF GERMANY	Pergamon Press, Hammerweg 6, D-6242 Kronberg, Federal Republic of Germany
BRAZIL	Pergamon Editora, Rua Eça de Queiros, 346, CEP 04011, Paraiso, São Paulo, Brazil
AUSTRALIA	Pergamon-Brassey's Defence Publishers, P.O. Box 544, Potts Point, N.S.W. 2011, Australia
JAPAN	Pergamon Press, 8th Floor, Matsuoka Central Building, 1-7-1 Nishishinjuku, Shinjuku-ku, Tokyo 160, Japan
CANADA	Pergamon Press Canada, Suite No. 271, 253 College Street, Toronto, Ontario, Canada M5T 1R5

First Pergamon-Brassey's printing 1989
First published by Hawthorn Books, Inc., 1967

Library of Congress Cataloging-in-Publication Data

Galvin, John R., 1929-
  The minute men.

  (An AUSA book)
  "A Pergamon-Brassey's classic."
  "Published with the Institute of Land Warfare Association of the U.S. Army."
  Includes index.
  1. Minutemen (Militia)--History.   2. United States--History--Revolution, 1775-1783--Campaigns.   3. United States--Militia--History--17th century.   4. United States--Militia--History--18th century. 5. Lexington, Battle of, 1775. 6. Concord, Battle of, 1775.
I. Title. II. Series.
E255.G35   1989   973.3'3   88-34496
ISBN 0-08-036733-X

AN AUSA INSTITUTE OF LAND WARFARE BOOK

The Association of the United States Army, or AUSA, was founded in 1950 as a not-for-profit organization dedicated to education concerning the role of the U.S. Army, to providing material for military professional development, and to the promotion of proper recognition and appreciation of the profession of arms. Its constituencies include those who serve in the Army today, including Army National Guard, Army Reserve, and Army civilians, and the retirees and veterans who have served in the past, and all their families. A large number of public-minded citizens and business leaders are also an important constituency. The Association seeks to educate the public, elected and appointed officials, and leaders of defense industry on crucial issues involving the adequacy of our national defense, particularly those issues affecting land warfare.

In 1988 AUSA established within its existing organization a new entity known as the Institute of Land Warfare. Its purpose is to extend the educational work of AUSA by sponsoring scholarly publications, to include books, monographs and essays on key defense issues, as well as workshops and symposia. Among the volumes chosen for designation as "An AUSA Institute of Land Warfare Book" are both new texts and reprints of titles of enduring value which are no longer in print. Topics include history, policy issues, strategy and tactics. Publication as an AUSA Book does not indicate that the Association of United States Army and the publishers agree with everything in the book, but does suggest that the AUSA and the publisher believe this book will stimulate the thinking of AUSA members and others concerned about important issues.

ABOUT THE AUTHOR

General John R. Galvin, USA, is the Supreme Allied Commander, Europe (SACEUR), and the Commander-in-Chief, United States European Command (CINCEUR).

A native of Wakefield, Massachusetts, General Galvin earned a bachelors degree at the U.S. Military Academy, holds a master of arts in English from Columbia University, did additional graduate work at the University of Pennsylvania, and was a fellow at the Fletcher School of Law and Diplomacy. He is a graduate of the U.S. Army Command and General Staff College and the Army War College.

General Galvin has held a wide variety of command staff positions in Europe, Puerto Rico, Colombia, Vietnam, and Panama. Although much of his service has been outside the United States, General Galvin has served as an assistant professor at the U.S. Military Academy and as military assistant to the Secretary of the Army.

General Galvin's other published works include *Air Assault*, an analysis of the development of air mobility in twentieth century warfare, and *Three Men of Boston*, a study of the political events that led up to the American Revolution.

Preface

The Minute Men was fun to write; over the years it has been a source of many good moments for me. In reading the book again I relived some of those memorable times: the days with Leo Flaherty in the Massachusetts archives—which were then in the basement of the State House—going over the rolls of companies that marched to battle; working through the old newspapers like the *Massachusetts Spy* and the *Massachusetts Gazette*, which at that time had not yet been microfilmed and were slowly oxidizing and falling to pieces; reading fragile letters in the Massachusetts Historical Society rooms on Boyleston Street; talking with local historians; and searching through dusty town records where plain men had recorded their thoughts with homespun eloquence as they saw events of vast importance crowding in on them. Best of all, I remember as a young lieutenant in the South American Andes exchanging letters on the Minute Men with my father—part of a conversation by mail that began when I left home and lasted for 38 years. Those are great memories.

For historians the first battle in our war of independence has been hard to categorize and define: it began in peacetime as a British march to Lexington and Concord and ended in war as rebels and regulars fought back to Boston. What meaning does it have today? What is its place in all that came before and after? Those are important questions, yet historians have given them scant attention and few words. At the time I wrote *The Minute Men*, there had been little research or writing that dealt with the early organization of military opposition to the Crown. Since the book's publication in 1967, Robert Gross (*The Minutemen and their World*), Thomas Fleming (*The First Stroke*), and John Shy (*A People Numerous and Armed*) have addressed the question of the Minute Men. Nonetheless, most Americans still know surprisingly little about the men who fought the first engagement of our revolutionary struggle, even though the uniqueness of that extraordinary event—a spontaneous attack on the British Regulars by local colonial soldiers—has inspired a wealth of speculation and controversy.

A kind of mythology, embellished over the years, tends to obscure what took place in April 1775. The result is considerable confusion as to what wisdom the battle should hold for Americans, and indeed what it should mean to the world. As a schoolboy I was always proud that the Minute Men and militia from my home town (Wakefield, formerly South Reading) marched to Concord and fought the British all the way to Boston. I read everything I could find on these local soldiers. At some point, however, I became skeptical about the way the story was told: the Minute Men didn't appear to have been real people. Instead they seemed to explode into battle out of nowhere, fully trained and organized, well-equipped, knowing what to do, skillful and brave in combat, able to take on the formidable British Regulars and drive them into a long and costly retreat. It was a strange story; I thought about it for years.

When Arthur Tourtellot wrote *William Diamond's Drum*, I read it as soon as it was published and found myself in a kind of historical vertigo. Tourtellot said that the battle of Lexington was understandable if you concluded that Sam Adams convinced militia Captain John Parker and his seventy-seven men to make a suicidal stand against five hundred British soldiers in order to get the Revolutionary War started. For me, that did not ring true. Thus began my personal effort to arrive at an understanding of the Minute Men and their one great day.

Coming to some idea of what actually took place turned out to be more difficult than I had expected. The biggest obstacles were the countless legends and stories that obscured the historical facts. Accounts of the battle at Lexington had evolved over time, as Americans changed the way they wanted to depict the actions of the Minute Men and the colonial militia.

The drawings reproduced on these pages—collected and published by Houghton Mifflin Company in 1923 by the great local historian Harold Murdock in *The Nineteenth of April 1775*—illustrate this process. The first print was engraved by Doolittle in the fall of 1775 and illustrates the story of Lexington as it was accepted in colonial America at that time. It depicts well-organized British troops firing on a rapidly dispersing Lexington company. Murdock described it with brilliant understatement. "Even the magnifying glass fails to reveal any member of that company in an attitude of resistance," he wrote. There is, he continued, "no suggestion of a return fire, or even of loading. One wonders why the title was not engraved, the 'massacre,' instead of the 'battle of Lexington'." The Doolittle print left no doubt that the British were the aggressors.

Over the decades that followed, the citizens of Massachusetts began to take more pride in their ancestors who had fought the first battles against the British. A lithograph by Pendleton done about 1830 still shows the British firing by platoons and most of the Minute Men dispersing. Now, however, eight hearty defenders are facing the enemy—six firing and two loading. The reinterpretation of the battle was under way.

The Battle of Lexington
From a lithograph after an original by M. Swett

By the time of the sketch by Billings, which was printed in the first edition of Hudson's *Lexington* in 1868, nearly a century of speculation—and patriotic pride—had changed even more the idea of what happened. In Billings' sketch over half of the Americans are firing; only a handful are dispersing, and they are shrouded by the smoke at the far left of the print. The painting done by Sandham in 1886 completed the evolution. "Here at least is a battle," Murdock noted. "The line holds firm from end to end, while, unterrified by the running blaze of British musketry and the sight of stricken comrades, the minute men stand grimly to their work."

As time went by we built the mythology of the Minute Men even further. We depicted them as a small but courageous band of farmers who responded to a spontaneous call to arms, an untrained and poorly armed rabble. The truth, of course, was very different. There were actually 14,000 colonials under arms in the militia and Minute Man regiments. They were alerted by organized alarm riders via a system that dated back to the 17th century wars. They had trained intensively for a year and were armed with the same type weapons as the British.

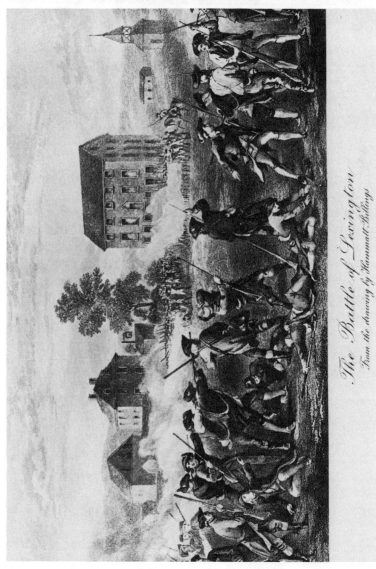

The Battle of Lexington
From the drawing by Hammatt Billings

The Dawn of Liberty
From a painting by Henry Sandham

Lexington was an important battle in the history of the United States, not only because it was the opening moment of the war that created our country but also because it provides us a microcosm of the drift to war—with all the tensions, the misinterpretations, the fears and the posturings, the courageous and the foolish acts that augur the clash of arms. The distortion of this historical event has kept us from some vital insights concerning the way that wars begin—as I think you will see when you read this story.

John R. Galvin

Acknowledgments

This book was first suggested and later encouraged by my father, John J. Galvin, a local historian of eastern Massachusetts with an abiding interest in the soldiers of that area and all the wars they have fought. My analysis of the minute man concept and the regimental organization was greatly assisted by the advice of several U.S. Army officers, among them Colonel Donald J. Delaney (editor of the *Military Review*), Colonel Shirley M. Castle, Lieutenant Colonel John M. Dunn, and Major Harold B. Birch, all of whom read and discussed with me the early chapters, and Major Lewis S. Sorley III, who helped with the analysis of the state of training in the British regiments. Several people who have intimate knowledge of the area where the battle was fought as well as the history of those scenes contributed their advice: Edwin B. Worthen of Lexington, Laurence E. Richardson and Mrs. Ruth R. Wheeler of Concord, and Robert Ronsheim, historian of the Minute Man National Park. I owe thanks also to Edwin B. Small, project coordinator of the Boston Park Service Group; to Mr. and Mrs. Leo Flaherty of the Massachusetts Archives, to Mrs. Langdon Wales, town historian of Lincoln; and to the many town clerks and librarians I have bothered. Needless to say, the errors I claim as my own.

The libraries that provided me space to work at various times were those of Columbia University, the United States Military Academy, and the Command and General Staff College; others that helped were the William L. Clements Library, the New York Public, the Boston Public, and of course, all the town libraries of the battle area. The most efficient interlibrary loan desk I have seen is run by Mrs. Betty Bohannon at the Staff College.

A number of well-known earlier studies of this battle are still valid and readable, and I am indebted to nearly all of them in one way or another, especially to the objective and sympathetic Harold Murdock, to the authoritative trail-breaker Richard Frothingham, Jr., and to Warren Coburn, a man who did his best to seek out every last detail of the battle. Allen French is still the most competent historian who has studied the battle in detail. French, in *The First Year of the American Revolution*, written a decade after his book on the battle itself, made the comment "Much romance attaches to the minutemen and rightly; but the wide spontaneity of their origin, their extralegal status, and their sudden and complete disappearance have never been thoroughly traced." His intriguing challenge was one of the spurs that started the research for this present book.

My wife, Virginia Lee Galvin, was my typist, proofreader, and consultant through all the drafts of this book, which would not now be finished without her help.

The Minute Men is dedicated to my father, John J. Galvin.

Contents

List of Illustrations

Prologue
The Men and the Myth

The mere mention of the 19th of April, 1775, evokes at once a flood of the half-legendary vignettes that have captured our imagination. We see Paul Revere riding hard for the Mistick Road to avoid a galloping patrol of British Regulars; angry farmers with muskets in their field-hardened fists hurrying across dark furrows; a ragged line of proud men facing the tide of on-coming red-and-white ranks at Lexington Green; brave Captain Isaac Davis, marked for death, striding down the causeway to the North Bridge at Concord; and stubborn, cantankerous old Sam Whittemore staggering under the weight of his musket, pistols, and saber to plant himself directly in the path of Lord Percy's hard-pressed, hard-fighting 1st Brigade coming in full retreat back down the road to Boston. The fury of the hundreds of minor clashes and the courageous performance of many of the combatants always tend to draw attention away from the story of the minute men as a unit, but the true history—the birth and growth of the minute man idea—is worth knowing in full, not only for the further understanding of the great effort these men made, but also because the problems they faced are in a great many ways analogous to our own.

The 19th of April certainly was the greatest day in the history of the minute men, but it was not their debut by any means.

1

They had been called out earlier on a number of minor alerts caused by Gage's practice marches and his raids on Charlestown and Salem, but also they were well organized and in some ways as well prepared as the regulars in Boston.

Still more important, not only the minute men themselves, but also the whole countryside understood the "minute man concept," which was to them no new thing: beginning with the earliest colonial military companies under Patrick, Underhill, and Standish, the organizational and tactical concept (alarm riders, alerts, inter-town cooperation, rapid assembly of special units detached from the militia) had begun to develop. On August 12, 1645, the Massachusetts Council ordered the commander of every militia company to appoint thirty percent of the soldiers "who shall be ready at half an hour's warning upon any service they shall be put by their chief military officers." The preparations and campaigns of the half dozen wars before 1763 illustrate a continuing refinement of this concept right up to the end of the Revolution.

Any attempt to tell the story of the battle of Lexington and Concord is handicapped by the inordinate number of legends and anecdotes that over the years have become associated with the events of the day's fighting. This historical embroidery grew up because the battle has never received the analytical attention given to most of the other actions fought by this country's soldiers. Into the vacuum left by this neglect has crept many a local myth. The story of the fight often has been passed over with a light touch in the histories, suffering a variety of rather hasty interpretations: it has been dismissed as an accident that occurred only once and, happily, with good results; or explained away as the spontaneous combustion of a smouldering rabble; or, worst of all, given as a proof of the conviction that not much training is necessary to build an army.

The difficulties in analyzing the battle of April 19 arise not in following the actions that took place, but in understanding the participants. Who were the minute men? How were they organized, trained, equipped, and led? How did they manage to march from distant towns in time to strike the fast-moving British column before it could get back to Boston? What relationship existed between the minute men and the militia? How did the minute man and militia soldier compare to his opponent, the British regular in Gage's army at Boston?

It is a distortion of the facts to say that the battle of April 19 was a spontaneous uprising of loosely organized "embattled farmers"—it was much more than that. The battle can better be seen as the final clash of arms of the old Massachusetts militia, in which forty-seven regiments, containing over 14,000 men, marched against the British regulars (over 4,000 men from fourteen of the regiments actually struck the column) and employed concepts of organization and methods of command and control that had been forged during a century and a half of nearly constant warfare.

In the progressive transition of this fighting force from a crude miniature replica of Elizabethan militias to a state of near-completion as a powerful army, some factors can be isolated as not only contributory to a very important degree but also quite unique. First, the militia organization, though strongly based on the English Muster Law of 1572 and later regulations, was continually revamped by the super-imposition of requirements such as the levy system for the provisional expeditionary forces and the concept of alert and rapid response by a designated portion of the regiments. The combination of these and other requirements produced several precursors of the minute man-militia structure of 1774, among these the "snow shoe men" of 1702-1743 and the "picket guards" of 1755, both to be discussed in later chapters. Second, the system of command and control also quickly departed from English tradition under the new pressures of the North American military and political situation and continually showed a realistic evaluation of the possibilities and limits in areas such as weaponry, tactics, supply systems, and training. Third, the individual towns of the province, from the earliest days, provided a degree of discipline and an environment of cooperation which would have been impossible except in the political, social, and spiritual atmosphere under which these communities chose to live. The close mutual association of these towns and the influence of the town meetings, the clergy, and later the newspapers created a matrix in which the cooperative spirit of the province was nurtured; thus when the Committees of Correspondence were created in 1773, they had a profound effect, galvanizing the province into the collective action that created the famous minute men.

There is no way to separate the story of the minute men from the story of the militia. The minute men were drawn from the militia and the men of both units fought side by side in the April 19 battle. But the tactical concept under which the minute men were created can be isolated and studied by itself, and it is the history of the development of the minute man concept that can provide the answer to many of the questions relating to the battle. We will trace that story, following the thread of the minute man concept through a century and a half of the life of Massachusetts.

While many of the details are new here, the fact that a minute man concept existed was recognized at least as early as 1890, when Samuel Abbot Green, comparing in *Groton During the Revolution* the military activities of several of the earlier wars to the organization of the minute men, noted that "these various instances all contain the germ of the system," meaning that there were minute men in fact if not in name from the earliest days of the province. Other historians have seen parallels between the minute men and earlier military units, but only Green and Allen French seem to have recognized the long development of the minute man over many years of fighting in the province.

The concept becomes easy to trace once the essence of the minute men—what it is that makes them different from other units—is brought to light. The minute man was a member of a unit drawn from the regular militia and comprising a set percentage of that militia, specially trained, specially equipped, and required to assemble very rapidly and to be prepared at all times to march immediately into combat. A system of decentralized tactical control allowed officers at very low levels, usually company commanders, to exercise extraordinary authority, being permitted to assemble and march their men in time of danger without any orders from a higher command. The instant readiness of the units was supplemented by a wide net of inter-town alarm signals and messengers.

In addition to an application of the minute man concept to the study of the battle, this book attempts to bring to light several other considerations that to the present time have not been given much weight in the analysis of the action. An examination of the experience and organization of the British regular regiments vis-à-vis the provincial units brings out the fact that the provincials were not at much disadvantage either in training or equipment, and had far more battle-proven small-unit leaders than did the British. The marches and raids made by Gage's troops into the countryside during the fall and winter preceding the battle, when studied in terms of their effects on the tactical thinking of the provincial leaders, provide some new light on several important decisions made by such men as Lexington's

Captain John Parker and Concord's Colonel James Barrett. General Gage's failure to march to Worcester, with the impetus this gave to the creation of a provincial congress and a rebel army, is seen as a major incident in the trend of events toward April 19. Some of the chief characters on the stage that day have been passed over without much evaluation in the previous works; Major Mitchell, of the British patrol that captured Revere (and later had a strong effect on the frame of mind of the British leaders in the column approaching Lexington), is one example; Major Loammi Baldwin of the Woburn militia is another; General William Heath is a third—and there are several more, including John Brooks of Reading, John Nixon of Framingham, and Gideon Foster of Danvers. It is not widely known that the story of the minute man continued after April 19, and that the minute man concept, after the successes of the battle, was put to use again in Massachusetts and in other states during the war years that followed.

In the past, very little work has been done in reconstructing the provincial regiments, and the organization as it is set forth in these pages (forty-seven regiments of militia and minute men) may not be entirely without error. There may have been fifty regiments, or forty-five; much on this question may still come to light. The important point, for the purposes of this book, is that the story of the battle is told against a background of the minute man concept and the regimental organization of the militia and the minute men. Seen against this background, the battle of April 19 becomes the culmination and final proving ground of the Massachusetts provincial militia system, as well as the first step in the creation of the Continental Army.

In view of the persistent and nearly universal reluctance of able historians to see the battle that opened the Revolution as more than a farmers' uprising, or at best the ragged but surprisingly effective response of an unorganized and leaderless bumpkin militia, it is not hard to sympathize with the bullet-ridden ghosts of redcoat grenadiers and light infantry who (the legends tell us) still walk the old road to Lexington and Concord, lost in dumbfounded amazement.

Chapter 1

The Minute Man Concept

The colonies of Plymouth and Massachusetts Bay were confronted from the beginning with the almost insurmountable problems of scratching out a living from the boulder-strewn land while at the same time protecting themselves from upwards of 10,000 Indians roaming nearby forests. Much of the credit for the success of the settlements in the face of such imposing difficulties must be given to the leaders of both the Massachusetts and the Plymouth expeditions, who had the foresight to include in each group several very good soldiers. The stalwart Miles Standish of Plymouth with his well-thumbed copy of Caesar's *Commentaries* was a veteran of several campaigns in the Low Countries, as were Daniel Patrick and John Underhill, the two soldiers who became the first military tacticians of Massachusetts Bay. Nor were these the only men of military experience in the settlements; a good many of the early militia company commanders had been members of London's Ancient and Honorable Artillery Company or of other militia units in the old country, and several had fought in Holland or Spain.

It is no wonder, then, that the first military organizations in both Plymouth and the Bay Colony were simply crude replicas in miniature of the English arrangement. Every man was required to have a weapon (those not able to buy one outright could buy

one on credit), and all males over sixteen automatically became
members of the militia. Each time a new town sprang up, a new
company of militia was organized, and as the town expanded, the
number of its companies also grew. Musters were frequent and
mandatory, punishments were assessed for absence or for not being properly outfitted, and the governor maintained the sole right
to call out the militia. These earliest regulations laid down for
the militia were reflections of the laws governing the English
militia of the day.

Almost immediately, however, the governor and his council, in
cooperation with the experienced soldiers, began to modify the
old system to fit their own local requirements. In England the
musters were for training only, because there was no immediate
threat to the individual English towns; but in the New World all
soldiers had to be ready to assemble on short notice as ready to
fight as to train. This was the first variation from the old
muster laws. Adding to the requirement for "watch and ward"
in the towns, the governors ordered a signal (either the beating
of a drum or the firing of a musket) to be given in case of
Indian attack; at this signal all the men of the threatened town
were required to assemble immediately with their weapons.

This simple system of alarm and muster was sufficient to meet
the dangers of the first few years, but both colonies soon out-
grew it. By 1635 Massachusetts Bay contained three counties,
with a regiment in each, and Plymouth had militia companies in
eight towns. The informal relationship between the governor's
councils and the town began to prove unwieldy, and Massachusetts therefore created a council of war, an eleven-man committee presided over by the governor—actually the first military
staff in the New World. The council was empowered to supervise
training, to call musters, and to march the militia out to war;
with these new powers the concept of static defense of individual
towns was replaced by a new, more flexible arrangement.

In the years that followed, the council of war in Massachusetts had its ups and downs, sometimes being dissolved in favor
of the governor's council, only to be reinstituted later. Plymouth
continued to follow the older system, probably because Miles
Standish was such a powerful figure and able to control the
growing militia (the first council of war in Plymouth was formed
in 1658, two years after his death).

The continuing rapid expansion of the colonies, driving the
Indians away from their hunting grounds, resulted in an increas-

ing number of hostile encounters between the settlers and the Indians in the no man's land along the frontier. The first sporadic skirmishes began in Connecticut in 1636 when Massachusetts sent Colonel John Endicott with four companies on an unsuccessful campaign against the Pequot Indians. According to one account, the expedition killed one Indian and burned some wigwams.

The problems of the expedition had been many. Weeks elapsed between the incidents that caused the march and the arrival of Endicott's column in the area. Then there was confusion as to which Indians to fight and why, and the Indians themselves did not deduce that the column was intended as a punitive force. The Massachusetts soldiers, improperly supplied and poorly equipped, were not able to keep to the field long enough to force the Pequots into a fight. This feeble response encouraged the Indians, and attacks on the settlers in the Connecticut Valley increased.

In the following year Massachusetts again put a force in the field in collaboration with the Plymouth and Connecticut colonies. Plymouth agreed to send out fifty men, Connecticut ninety, and Massachusetts one hundred fifty. By mutual agreement the highest ranking officer of the Connecticut contingent was placed in command, since the fighting was to take place in that colony. The Massachusetts men were raised, as they had been before, by levy from the three regiments. The major incident of the campaign was a skirmish near the present Fairfield, Connecticut, where the Pequots were finally defeated and scattered, the survivors (about 200) being absorbed by other tribes.

The men from Plymouth, fifty volunteers under a Lieutenant Holmes, were so slow in mustering and preparing for the expedition that by the time they were ready to march the campaign was over.

For Massachusetts the Pequot War was the first test of the militia system. In each of the two principal expeditions, the council formed provisional fighting teams by drafting men from the various militia regiments, a process that uncovered problems that were not forgotten at the end of hostilities—the hastily arranged joint operations were not well coordinated, the soldiers were slow in assembling and getting to the critical area after the call was sent out for them, and the men impressed from the regiments were poorly trained and poorly equipped for the kind of combat they had to face.

For the colonials, perhaps the most valuable lesson of this

first Indian war was a realization that trained units and the new war councils were not enough. Four of the New England colonies—Plymouth, Connecticut, New Haven, and Massachusetts—exchanged views on the possibility of forming a joint council, and in May of 1643 they published the articles of a New England confederation, in which a board of eight commissioners, two from each colony, would meet annually (or more often if necessary) to insure "a firm and perpetual league of friendship . . . for offense and defense . . . and for their own mutual safety and welfare." The board was empowered to coordinate all military activities and to deal with intercolonial disputes, the return of fugitives, Indian affairs, and migration. This confederation was to be called The United Colonies of New England. The real power of the confederation was the agreement under which each of the four colonies promised to contribute soldiers to an alert force that would fight anywhere in the colonies. Massachusetts was to give a hundred men and the other three colonies were to meet quotas of forty-five men each.

The Pequot War and the resulting confederation also inspired a reorganization in the military structures of the Bay Colony and, to some extent, Plymouth. Massachusetts provided its council with stronger powers for alerting, assembling, and distributing the militia of the colony and created the rank of sergeant major general to command the whole militia, organize and lead expeditions, impress supplies and transport, and levy troops. The sergeant major general was to be given the deciding vote in the council of war and complete tactical control of all expeditions, without interference from the governor or the rest of the council. Plymouth gave the governor a four-man military staff, including, of course, Miles Standish.

With arrangements completed for a coordinated defense of New England and with the military command and staff structure greatly improved, the council of Massachusetts turned to the problem of creating a force responsive enough to meet the possibility of a strong and sudden Indian attack on any one of the towns; an attack that, in view of the activities of the increasingly hostile Narragansetts, could not be too far off. It was at this time that the alarm system and the levy system, the two tried-and-true concepts that had by now become part of the military heritage of the colonies, began to fuse together under the influence of the council of war.

First, the council took a hard look at the towns, and realizing that the strength and readiness of the town militia companies was the key to a successful defense of the colony, decided to decentralize the tactical control of the colony's armed forces. On September 7, 1643, new regulations were put in effect. The first law provided that any town "upon any sudden exigent or assault" could defend itself without orders from the council, and reiterated the authority given to the council of war "in all cases of danger and assault, to raise the whole force of the country, or any part thereof, and to draw them together to one or more places within this jurisdiction, or otherwise to dispose of them in the best manner for the necessary defense of the country."

Another rule provided for a shire lieutenant, the equivalent of a regimental commander, who was empowered to assemble any portion of the shire's militia regiment and march to defend any part of his county against a surprise attack. This arrangement was soon revised, giving these responsibilities to the sergeant major and eliminating the office of shire lieutenant, but the principle remained the same. The rules further permitted any company commander to call up his company "to make any just and necessary defense" in the absence of orders to the contrary. These new regulations increased the power and responsibility not only of the junior commanders but also of the individual towns.

It was the attack of the Narragansetts on the Mohegan tribe in 1644 that brought about the rapid completion of the new military refinements. The Mohegans had maintained a loose alliance with the colonists, and this attack could mean only that a new war was unavoidable. This increased the possibility of an assault against one of the outlying towns and made the need for rapid response even more imperative. The council, under this pressure, decided to combine alarm and muster with the familiar system of levying soldiers for expeditions, and to create a kind of permanent levy in a continual state of readiness. The result was a new regulation, on August 12, 1645, ordering the company commanders "to appoint out and to make choice of thirty soldiers of their companies in ye hundred, who shall be ready at half an hour's warning upon any service they shall be put upon by their chief military officers." The law also required all soldiers "to be ready, with their arms ready fixed, and that they have powder, bullets, match, and bandoliers always ready, according to former order; as also that every soldier provide himself a knapsack to be in a readiness upon any service they shall be called to."

With the coming together of these rules of muster and march only a few years after the arrival of the colonists, the rudimentary elements of the minute man concept were created: the council of war (later to be the Committee of Safety); a specific portion of the miltia, well trained, well equipped, and set aside as a ready force; command and control decentralized to the extent that individual militia company commanders could put their troops into defensive battle if necessary; an alarm system of riders and signals in which each town was required to participate. All of these basic elements were departures from the old militia system the colonists had known in England.

Chapter 2

The Concept in Practice:

King Philip's War

When the commissioners of the United Colonies of New England met in Hartford in the fall of 1650, all-out war with the Narragansetts seemed just around the corner. Looking at the growing list of incidents between the settlers and the Indians, the council decided to prepare a very strong expedition, more than a thousand men, to deal with the Narragansetts once and for all—but such preparations would take time. While the men were being mustered and trained, a small column under Captain Humphrey Atherton was sent out to keep the Indians on the defensive.

Preparations for the new war were well under way, with a number of infantry companies organized and training in Boston, when the Narragansett chiefs, who were not anxious to see a powerful force of colonists take the field against them, came to Boston to negotiate with the council and avert a war. Peace was reestablished after the Narragansetts were forced into many concessions, including the payment of an indemnity to cover the cost of the preparations for war in the colonies. This arrangement did not solve any problems either for the Indians or for the colonists. The Narragansett chiefs returned to the forests of the Connecticut Valley, but the settlers, who were never to be reconciled with this tribe, generally agreed that the war was merely postponed.

This trouble smouldered for another two decades, always seeming on the point of flaming up into full war. During this period the council came to see that to fight the Narragansetts with any success the colonies would have to defend along their perimeter of outlying towns and settlements, and at the same time seek out and attack the Indians in their wilderness villages. Plans for defense and plans for raiding had to be in operation at the same time, and the success of one would be to a great degree dependent on the other—as it turned out, the same force was sometimes called on to do both jobs when the expedition became a relief force for some beleaguered town. On May 14, 1653, the council of Massachusetts issued a new order referring to the "necessities of being in readiness in these times of danger" and called for one eighth of the men in each trained band to be "in a readiness to march in a day's warning should the Lord call us to war." Once more the minute man concept was restated, interweaving the old ideas of levy and alarm.

When the Narragansetts suddenly attacked the Indians of Long Island, Massachusetts moved to join Connecticut in an attempt to destroy them once and for all. The council issued an order raising forty men, with horses, to be "in a readiness at an hour's warning on command," and these men were sent to join forty raised by Connecticut, the whole under the command of Simon Willard of Massachusetts. Willard scouted the forest trails but was unable to make contact with the main body of the Narragansetts, who retreated before his column; he did manage to meet the chief of the tribe and get a signed agreement promising peace. With this paper he returned to Boston.

The war with the Narragansetts was postponed another few years by Willard's show of force, but as settlers continued to pour into the Connecticut Valley from the coastal towns, forcing the now desperate Indians westward until they were hopelessly hemmed in between the new farms on the east and other strong tribes to the west and south, the prospect of violence dominated every meeting of the New England confederation and of the individual councils.

In 1672 the Massachusetts council decided to form a military committee to control the militia in each town in order to insure cooperation between the various companies. Each committee was to consist of "the magistrate living in the town, the chief officer of the horse, if living in the town, and the chief officer of each company of foot," and was empowered to act independently in case of alarm. This new regulation further emphasized the moves toward decentralization begun in 1643 by providing an embryo staff for the creation of small defense units of two or three companies each. By placing a civil official of the town on the committee it again increased the responsibility and the influence of the individual town in the conduct of its own militia.

On June 24, 1675, a marauding Wampanoag was shot by a settler at Swansea, near the border between Massachusetts and Connecticut, and the conflict later to be called King Philip's War began with sharp skirmishes around that town. The United Colonies council immediately mustered troops to be sent against the Wampanoags, who were allies of the Narragansetts. The Massachusetts council ordered one hundred men impressed from the regiments "to be ready at an hour's warning from Captain Daniel Henchman who is appointed captain and commander of the Foot Company and that each soldier shall have his arms complete and knapsack ready to march and not fail to be at the rendezvous." This was to be the first test of the minute man concept.

A second company under Captain Thomas Prentice was formed by reinforcing the Middlesex Regiment's cavalry troop, and a third company was made up of an unbelievable but very effective conglomeration of "volunteers"—transients, sailors, vagrants, adventurers, and even jailbirds released under the promise of enlisting. These were assembled and turned over to Captain Samuel Moseley, the unsung hero who not only held this gang together but led it successfully in many combat actions. All three companies arrived at Swansea on the 28th, only four days after the first shot had been fired, and there they were joined by two companies from Plymouth. The rest of the Massachusetts militia was told to stand by. The Suffolk and Middlesex regiments were ordered "to gather the troopers together in their complete arms, and be ready to march on a moment's warning, to prevent such danger as may seem to threaten us. . . ."

The Indians, under the leadership of the Wampanoag King Philip, were forced back into Pocasset Swamp near what is now Tiverton, Rhode Island, but King Philip managed to elude the colonists and move westward to join forces with the Nipmucks and Narragansetts who were already harassing the towns in the upper Connecticut Valley. The battle thus shifted to western Massachusetts, around Springfield, and while Captains Henchman and Moseley marched west with their foot troops to garrison the river towns, new companies were drafted from the Massachusetts militia to reinforce them. The Suffolk Regiment sent out a company under Captain Beers and the Essex Regiment sent one commanded by Captain Lathrop. Connecticut reinforced the garrisons with two companies under Captain Watts. Major Pynchon of Massachusetts was picked by the council to lead this force.

In terms of the preparations for the war, the new system had worked very well. The ready force of the United Colonies was assembled and marched to the battlefield, fifty miles away, in four days (supplemented, of course, by the cavalry and by Moseley's conglomerate company). The second expedition, which reinforced the earlier group after the battle shifted westward, had time to impress men proportionately from the regiments, equip and supply them, and move to the battle area.

If the minute man idea worked well, the success was somewhat dimmed by the tactical failures that followed. During the fall of 1675, the expedition took heavy losses and learned some hard lessons. The towns of Deerfield and Northfield were raided; Captain Beers was ambushed and killed with twenty of his men at Saw Mill Brook near Northfield; Captain Lathrop, leading a provisional group of eighty men guarding the removal of the corn crop from Deerfield to Hadley, was ambushed and died with his whole command. Major Pynchon was relieved at his own request and replaced by Major Samuel Appleton. When the winter snows arrived and the Indians withdrew from the frontier towns, most of the Massachusetts forces were ordered back to Boston and dismissed.

The presence of strong garrisons in the western towns had not stopped the raids; in fact, the militia units themselves became prime targets for the Indians, who desperately needed muskets and powder to carry on the war. The garrisons would have to be strengthened again in the spring because the towns could not be left defenseless, but at the same time the United Colonies council realized that until the main body of Indians was destroyed the colony would never be safe from assault. Accordingly, in the last months of 1675 the council conceived a new plan of attack.

The Narragansetts under Chief Canonchet comprised the largest part of the fighting forces loosely organized under King Philip, and at this time they were in winter quarters in Rhode Island. The colonies decided to attack the Narragansetts as soon as possible, and they drew up quotas for the expedition: Massachusetts, 527 men; Plymouth, 158; and Connecticut, 325. The Massachusetts quota was filled by levy from the regiments.

The Massachusetts men left Boston on December 9, 1675, and, after uniting with the forces of the other two colonies, struck the Narragansetts in a swamp near West Kingston, Rhode Island, on Sunday the 19th. The Indians had constructed a strong fort in the center of the swamp, on a low island, but the now-frozen swamp offered little obstacle to the colonists. The bitter fight lasted three hours, with the colonists winning control of the interior of the fort at nightfall. Low on ammunition and faced with strong Indian counterattacks forming in the darkness, they decided to burn the fort and fall back on their supplies at Wickford, sixteen miles away. The night retreat, which took place in a severe snowstorm, was costly; some of the wounded died along the way, and the Indians managed to cut off and kill some of the stragglers. The total casualties for the expedition were 64 dead and 150 wounded, of which Massachusetts lost 31 dead and 67 wounded. About 300 Indians were killed and another 300 captured. The survivors of the Narragansett tribe retreated westward, pursued by the provincials in a march of forty miles from Wickford to Woodstock (later known as the Long March or the Hungry March) but the Indians melted away into the forests. The Massachusetts men returned to Boston and were mustered out on February 8, 1676.

The Narragansett fight was a serious blow to the major Indian tribe, but the war was far from over. The Indians regrouped under the leadership of King Philip and Canonchet and the towns of the Connecticut Valley again were chilled by Indian war cries. During February many towns were attacked, and Lancaster and Medfield were completely destroyed.

Back at Boston another army was raised under Major Thomas Savage. Three companies of foot and a troop of horse were levied from the regiments and these units again joined Connecticut companies in the frontier towns, placing themselves once again in locations where they could assemble rapidly if warning came of Indian attack.

At this time the minute man idea of mobile defense was challenged by a suggestion that a long defensive line be constructed connecting twenty of the outlying towns by a line of forest and a stockade eight feet high and twelve miles long. The forest and walls would close the gap from the Charles River north to the Merrimack in a long arc of palisades linking numerous lakes and rivers together and finally closing on the seacoast north of Boston. The possibility of a such a defensive belt was so intriguing and the situation for the colonists was so desperate that the towns were ordered to select commissioners to meet at Cambridge and discuss the wall, but after scrutiny of the plan several towns rejected it. It would cost too much in money, time, and effort, and, as the selectmen of Marblehead noted, it was "no sufficient security" because it could not be manned day and night. Another point, which the critics of the plan perhaps felt was too obvious to mention, was that it made no provision for protecting the towns that were in far deeper danger—those much farther westward, along the Connecticut Valley.

The council did, however, act to improve the system of alert forces and quick response. In addition to the troop garrisons, the council ordered "that there be appointed a select number of persons in each town of Middlesex, who are, upon any information of the distress of any town, forthwith to repair to the relief thereof; and that such information may be seasonable, the towns are to dispatch posts, each town to the next, till notices be conveyed over the whole country, if need be. . . . Also that they shall be in a readiness to succor any of these towns at any time when in distress; also shall be ready to join with others to follow the enemy upon a sudden after their appearing." This adaption of the old warning system was the beginning of the long history of the alarm riders.

Early in April the Narragansetts lost their chief when Canonchet was captured and executed by troops from Plymouth Colony; this marked the beginning of the end for King Philip. The Narragansetts were unable to hold together as a tribe and they split up, some following King Philip and others choosing new leaders. The final blow came when Captain Turner, now commanding the western garrisons, decided to take every available man and attack the Indians at their fishing area on the Connecticut River (at what is now Turner's Falls). In this fight Turner lost forty men, but the Indians lost two hundred. The Indians never recovered from this attack, especially because the Colonists' system of alarm riders and mutual support began to pay off. They tried to stand against Turner on July 2 and were again badly mauled in an attack that came close to wiping them out as a tribe. On August 12 King Philip himself, stripped of his power and his allies, was tracked down and shot near Mount Hope, his old home.

The death of King Philip brought to a close an era in which the military structure of the colonies was substantially changed. The war, and especially the new system of garrisons, alarm riders, and rapid counterattacks, caused neighboring towns to grow accustomed to helping each other, and a new fraternal spirit, fostered by cooperation in the face of a common danger, grew up among them. Arrangements to ship wagonloads of supplies to stricken communities, mutual assistance in harvesting and storing crops, coordination in planning the location of garrison houses, and combat assistance to towns under attack—all these collaborative efforts brought home to the towns the value of mutual support. The New England council and the individual colony leaders devised a variety of ways to put military forces in the field for this war. They began with the minute men, then called for volunteers to fill specific units or expeditions, then levied soldiers from the trainbands, and finally, as at the Turner's Falls fight, simply gathered everyone in sight, both soldiers and townsfolk.

The war served as a proving ground not only for the command system of the New England confederacy but also for the innovations comprising the minute man concept. The council of the United Colonies made intercolonial cooperation rapid and effective and allowed for the day-to-day planning and coordination that paid off handsomely. The minute man idea provided the initial rapid response that drove the Indians westward, but the plan faltered under the tactical reverses and heavy losses in the west, until the improved system of alarm riders, patrolling, and quick-response forces in widely spread garrisons made the defense much more mobile and effective.

Chapter 3

The Snow Shoe Men

With the close of King Philip's war, the Indians to the south and the southwest were eliminated as a major threat to the frontiers, but there was no bright promise of peace in Massachusetts or anywhere else in New England. The wars simply moved into a new phase—the opening of a long series of clashes between the British and French (each with Indian allies) in North America, a sporadic and drawn-out contest beginning about 1689 and dragging on for almost a hundred years. The French were expanding their holdings along the St. Lawrence and south as far as the Ohio Valley, and their drive southward cut across the territory being settled by the English moving westward from the coastal colonies. the antagonisms generated as both sides attempted to gain control of this rich area were reinforced from abroad by the rivalries that kept Europe an armed camp during the conflicts now called the War of the League of Augsburg (1689-1697), the War of the Spanish Succession (1702-1713), the War of the Austrian Succession (1744-1748), and the Seven Years' War (1756-1763). The colonists along the New England Coast named each of the first three wars after the British ruler who occupied the throne at the time—King William's War, Queen Anne's War, King George's War; the last one received a name appropriate for all the others, at least from the settlers' point of view: the French and Indian War. Whatever names it may be given, the sporadic violence which alternately flashed and sputtered over the years following King Philip's War kept the New Englanders almost constantly preoccupied with the search for ways to protect their towns, especially those along the western and northern frontiers, beyond the Connecticut and Kennebec Rivers.

French and Indian pressure built up slowly, but by 1690 many of the outlying towns, including Saco, Wells, and Dover, were under constant alarm, with so many men called out against the Indians that the farms were going untended. This threat caused a flurry of action in the Massachusetts council, which instructed the committees of militia in the towns to increase the readiness of their soldiers. In August, 600 horse and foot troops were sent "to the eastward," drafted from the regiments. The province decided to raise a force to attack the French settlements near the mouth of the St. Lawrence and, if possible, to proceed against Quebec itself. A call for troops from the regiments was sent out, and Sir William Phips was appointed as commander.

The force raised was the largest ever seen in the province up to that time: 2,300 men. The troops were called up first as volunteers, but when the quotas were not filled the voluntary response was supplemented by a levy for the remainder. Phips sailed northward and succeeded in capturing and sacking Port Royal, but in the following year another campaign ground to a stop in front of Quebec, forcing Phips to return home without taking the city.

Assisted by his new military reputation and some influential friends, Phips became governor of Massachusetts in 1692, and the many problems that he had encountered on his abortive attempt at Quebec made him turn a hard, incisive eye on the militia of the colony. Phips added nothing new—regulations were drafted which did not make any radical changes in the militia system but which buttressed the old plan with far better administration. Phips put teeth in the draft laws and made it very difficult for militia men to avoid being called up in times of emergency. He also made the scheduled militia musters a serious affair, with strong fines for truants, and added some much-needed flexibility to the old alarm-and-muster system with a law allowing commanders of units as small as companies to call their men together in the event of an emergency and to move against the enemy without waiting for orders from higher up. Phips was a gruff and salty character who as governor seemed to fight his way from one controversy to another, but under his guidance the day-to-day running of the Massachusetts militia was greatly improved.

These improvements were soon tested. The towns of Haverhill and Deerfield were raided by the French and Indians in 1702, and the New Englanders retaliated, raising a force of 700 men under Benjamin Church, who led an assault against the French settlements on the coast of Acadia (Nova Scotia) and sacked several towns. The new Massachusetts governor, Joseph Dudley, successfully raised several expeditions using the new levy laws, and these were sent out to the northeastern borders, where French and Indian marauders had kept the frontier in a continual state of fear and turmoil. But the raiders were hard to track down in the forest, and the expeditions came back empty handed.

It was at this time that the province of Massachusetts approved a grim plan that had been suggested several times in earlier years. The word went out that every Indian scalp would be paid for as follows: to regular troops, ten pounds; to volunteers, twenty pounds; to volunters without pay, fifty pounds. This new incentive was announced to all the towns, and the response was immediate. Several companies of volunteers made ready to scour the woods. The reward for scalps was more attractive than grisly to men of the western Massachusetts towns, hardened as they were by the ravages of the Indians, and there were many men anxious to take to the forest trails in this new occupation of scalp hunting.

The colonists had learned as long ago as the Narragansett fight that the Indians were most vulnerable in the wintertime, because they disliked traveling in the bad weather and because they could be tracked over the snow to their unguarded villages. With this in mind, the colonists decided to fight the Indians with small, well-armed patrols ranging through the winter forest on snow shoes. On March 11, 1703, the order went out that there be: "five hundred pairs of good snow shoes provided at the public charge, one hundred twenty five pairs thereof to be put into the hands of each Colonel or chief military officer of the regiments of militia within the county of Hampshire, the North Regiment of Middlesex, the North Regiment of Essex, and the regiment in the county of Yorke, lying frontier next the wilderness, to be in readiness for his Majesty's service."

Even before the snow shoes could be issued, a patrol under Captain William Southworth returned with the first four scalps and was duly paid, each man receiving a share of the money. The pay slip was signed by the speaker of the House of Representatives and the secretary of the Governor's council.

The new Indian hunters were looked on with approval and pride by the townsfolk, and the dangerous task of Indian warfare became a challenge to the young men of the outlying towns. The patrols grew in popularity and the "snow shoe men," as they came to be called, were the heroes of the day. In the years that followed, the militia regiments took responsibility for the snow shoe patrols which formerly had been pickup teams arranged by local leaders. Patrolling duties were rotated among the companies of the outlying regiments, and those companies not on patrol were expected to be ready to march to the aid of the snow shoe men if the Indian enemy proved too strong.

The long fight in North America dragged on in a constant string of plans and orders for the "reduction of Canada." Port Royal was attacked and captured by a combined fleet in 1710, and Quebec was once again attempted in a foolhardy and disastrous campaign the following year. Forces were enlisted for these expeditions by proclamations calling for volunteers, rather than by levy from the regiments.

In 1711, while the forces were off at Quebec, the people of Boston became worried about the defense of the port against French raiders. On July 30 the governor sent orders to Colonel Phillips of Charlestown and Major Spurr of Dorchester "to direct the commanding officer of each company in the nearest towns within their several regiments to muster to see their arms fixed and command them to be in readiness at a minute's warning to march to the castle [at Boston] for the reinforcement thereof upon the appearance of the enemy." In addition to this, he ordered the three regiments of the Essex county militia forthwith to review their companies and see to it that everyone was well supplied with arms and ammunition "and to draw half their foot and the whole troops of the horse entire, to be ready to march at an hour's warning to the place assaulted by the enemy." The French did not come, but the governor, employing once again a variation of the minute man concept, was ready.

Along the frontier the Indians and the settlers stalked each other through the forests and waited in ambush along the trails. The Abenaki tribe, under the leadership of French Jesuit Sebastian Rales, claimed the territory north of the Kennebec River and fought the settlers in that area until 1720, when expeditions from

The Snow Shoe Men

Boston killed Rales and forced the Indians back.

In addition to the regular militia, various irregular forces took to the woods around the Kennebec area in search of the valuable Indian scalps; the most famous leader of these groups was Captain John Lovewell, of Dunstable. After a successful long-range patrol which netted Lovewell and his men 1,000 pounds for ten scalps (in twenty years inflation had set in; the market price was now one hundred pounds per scalp), the captain found it quite easy to recruit a larger force for another raid on the Indians. With a company of seventy-seven men he entered the northeastern forests on April 16, 1725, and ranged upward past Ossipee to Saco Lake, where he ran into all the Indians he wanted and more: his column was ambushed, Lovewell and fifty of his men were killed, and the rest straggled back into various frontier towns in the weeks that followed.

Throughout this period the snow shoe men kept the northern and western borders relatively quiet. Year after year they continued their patrolling over an area of 150 miles, extending from Springfield and Westfield up the forested valley of the Connective River through Sunderland and Deerfield, across New Hampshire to the Merrimack Valley, and on to the Kennebec River. In 1725 the council ordered that every man who had provided himself with snow shoes and moccasins would be reimbursed ten shillings, provided he was a member of an organized company of snow shoe men, and during that year at least nine companies, averaging about thirty men each, were paid under this regulation.

In 1744 Governor Shirley convinced the Massachusetts House that Louisburg could be taken by a strong force from the combined provinces, and plans for an attack were soon under way. William Pepperrell, commander of the York county militia, was placed in charge of the expedition. He mustered 4,300 troops from the militia of Massachusetts (including Maine), of which more than 1,500 were from his own regiment, and with some help from New Hampshire, Rhode Island, and New York he sailed northward from Boston on March 24, 1745.

One of the reasons that the governor could deplete the militia and leave the province bare of troops was the shield that the snow shoe men provided. Thirteen companies of snow shoe men were ready in the outlying regiments of the counties of Worcester, Hampshire, Middlesex, and York, alerted, as usual, to "hold themselves ready to march on the shortest warning." The Massachusetts House of Representatives, late in 1743, had voted that:

His Excellency the Captain General be desired in such manner as to him shall seem best to Raise in the county of Hampshire Three companys of Fifty able bodyede Effective Men in Each, Three Companys in the countys of Middlesex and Worcester, and four Companys in the County of York of like number and quality with the first to situate and dispose as shall best serve the Defense of the whole Frontiers, that he be pleased to Order and Direct that Each officer and private Centinel in said Companys provide himself with a good pair of Snowshoes, one pair of moggisons and one Hatchett, and that during the Warr that may happen they hold themselves ready to March on the shortest Warning, and that the Commanding Officer of Each of said Companys shall Transmitt to the Captain General a List Containing the Number Names & place of aforesaid—with a Duplicate to be Lodged in the Secretarys Office and that on receipt thereof and in Consideration of their Charge and Duty in thus providing themselves and being always ready to March there be allowed & paid out of the Publick Treasure to Each such Officer & Centinel Ten Shillings and that a grant be & hereby is made for that purpose accordingly.

To provide patrol bases for the snow shoe men (and at the same time give greater protection to the outlying towns), a line of fortifications was built, including stockades at Fall Town, Blanford, Colrain, Sheffield, Stockbridge, and Upper Housatonnick. The general tactics were the same as those that had produced the successes of the last months of King Philip's War half a century earlier. The towns were fortified once again by adapting farm homes into the familiar "garrison houses," and the regiments kept companies constantly on the move among the towns, while the rest of the regiment waited to be called to action by alarm riders if the Indians should attack in strength.

One of the young captains commanding a snow shoe man company in Hampshire County at this time was Seth Pomeroy. Thirty years later, on the 19th of April 1775, Colonel Pomeroy was to force march his regiment all the way from Springfield in a vain attempt to hit the British column before it could get back to Boston.

Pepperrell laid siege to Louisburg, overcoming impossible obstacles created by lack of proper training and supply, and the garrison of 560 regular French troops and 1,400 militia, armed with 100 cannon, capitulated in June 1745, to provide the

Americans with the greatest military victory they had ever achieved. Pepperrell was made a baronet and allowed to recruit and command a regiment on the British regular establishment. Governor Shirley of Massachusetts, who raised and supplied the men led by Pepperrell, also was honored with a colonelcy in the regulars (both men did organize new regiments, the British 50th and 51st, which saw service later in the French and Indian War). The snow shoe men, who held the long open flank and rear while nearly the whole militia was pulled out of the colony, received their ten shillings each for providing themselves with equipment, and were soon forgotten by history.

But the minute man concept had been carried forward in this unit. Although the militia regiments around Boston were ordered to be ready "on a minute's warning," it was in Hampshire, Worcester, Middlesex, and York counties that hand-picked units were set aside from the militia in special companies, always ready to march at short notice. Originally only loosely organized marauders who fought fire with fire, bushwhacking the Indian bushwhackers, they evolved over a fifty-year period into a very significant part of the militia, a key to the northwestern flank of the colony's defense system, and an unseen agent in the successful strategy of Shirley and Pepperrell.

Chapter 4

The Picket Guards

At the conference table at Aix-la-Chapelle in 1748 the British traded the fortress at Louisburg back to France, to the disgust of every New Englander. In Massachusetts the council realized that this was a temporary truce—the French certainly would not relinquish their hold on the valleys of the St. Lawrence and Ohio unless forced to do so. This made the colonists anxious to keep the militia strong for the day that was sure to come—the re-opening of the war. That day was only six years off.

In June of 1754 the council ordered the purchase of 2,500 firearms, to be distributed to the towns in proportion to their respective province taxes, and in the summer of the following year, as it turned out, these muskets were put to work on three different expeditions. The general plan for the opening phase of the French and Indian War was to strike at four key places along the extended line of forest that served as the 1,000-mile-long backbone of the French trading system, from the mouth of the St. Lawrence southward to Fort Duquesne, where the Mononga-hela and Allegheny Rivers unite to form the Ohio. British Lieu-tenant Colonel Monckton and 2,000 New Englanders were to move on Fort Beausejour at the head of the Bay of Fundy to bring Nova Scotia under subjection; Governor Shirley of Massachusetts would lead a column from Oswego toward Niagara to cut the

27

French line along Lakes Erie and Ontario; Sir William Johnson of New York would take Crown Point at the south end of Lake Champlain; and General Braddock, the overall commander and also leader of the fourth column, would march on Fort Duquesne.

Massachusetts sent 1,000 men with Monckton and called up 1,000 more to fill the ranks of the 50th and 51st Regiments, the "regulars" of Shirley and Pepperrell assembling at Oswego. For Johnson, the province, along with Connecticut and New York, mustered 3,000 more men.

Monckton took Fort Beausejour in June with little trouble. In July, Braddock marched his doomed column of regulars and provincials into the wilderness and lost his life and half his command at the Monongahela. Shirley never got beyond Oswego, and ended the summer feeling lucky to be able to hold on to his own base of operations. Johnson assembled his troops at Albany during July and marched for Lake George in August. On the 26th he moved against Crown Point and met the French coming down on him through the woods—the same situation Braddock had encountered a few weeks earlier—but this time the New England and New York provincials fought Indian style, from tree to tree, in a wavering battle that finally broke French resistance and left Johnson, though wounded, in command of the field. Johnson, however, was content to fall back to Fort Edward, a few miles to the south, rather than pursue the French toward Crown Point.

A discouraging stalemate set in. The French went unchallenged in the south along the Ohio Valley; Colonel Monckton's seizure of Beausejour resulted in little more than the infamous forced movement of the Acadians, and General Loudoun, sent from England to take charge of the war, was content to let his disconsolate provincial troops sit idle at Fort William Henry while the French held the key waterways above him.

It was only the arrival of Robert Rogers and his Rangers in the fall of 1756, and their famous patrolling exploits during the following winter, that kept alive the spirit and initiative of the Americans. By the spring of 1757 Rogers and other Rangers, including Stark, had seven companies patrolling around Lake George, and the provincial soldiers, stagnating in their miserable encampments, applauded every move that Rogers made.

Little by little, perhaps because of Rogers, the provincial troops came out of their hut camps and began to patrol the forests and seek out their enemies. For the first time, units calling themselves "minute men" begin to appear in the records, with Abadiah Cooley's endorsement on the payroll of his Brookfield company, "Minute Men on the Crown Point Expedition, 1756."

In New England, fighting the French meant taking Louisburg again, and the eyes of the military leaders turned northward once more to the scene of their earlier great victory. Contributions to this effort, on top of the levies that had gone before, denuded Massachusetts of troops, creating a critical shortage of soldiers along the line of frontier towns. It was for this reason that on August 8, 1757, the new governor of Massachusetts, Thomas Pownal (in office less than a week), signed a draft of orders to be sent to the commanders of all militia regiments, requiring them "to cause the regiments under each of their command, and in particular the troop of horse belonging to such regiment to be completely furnished with arms and ammunition according to law, and to hold themselves in readiness to march at a minute's warning to such part of the Frontiers or elsewhere as he should direct or his Majesty's service require." Again the Massachusetts council fell back on the minute man idea to provide the province with some measure of security. Pownal was hoping to make up for the weakness of the depleted militia with a stand-by cavalry force, and this may have served the need; there was little trouble with Indians in the outlying towns from then until the end of the war. Outside the province, however, Pownals' orders had no effect. Minute man idea or not, Montcalm knew that the attack on Louisburg opened the door for him to move against the forces confronting him at Lake George, and he immediately pounced on Fort William Henry with a superior force of French and Indians, and captured and massacred its garrison.

Word of this disheartening defeat caused the council of Massachusetts to take a new look at the situation of the province, which had expended not only many of its soldiers but also a great deal of its resources—more than 287,000 pounds sterling in these first three years of the war, for which the British Parliament had reimbursed it only a little over 70,000 pounds. With the news of the fall of Fort William Henry came ominous rumors: the French and Indians were said to be moving down on Albany; their strength was exaggerated out of all proportion; some even guessed their destination as the city of New York. A feeling of impending disaster filled the colonies.

Then the losses in the west were compounded by Loudoun's failure to take the fort at Louisburg; after almost three months of relative inactivity, he became discouraged when a storm on September 24 caused heavy damage to his shipping, and he returned empty handed to New York. He was soon replaced by General Abercromby as Commander-in-Chief in North America— the position Abercromby had relinquished to Loudoun after holding it for one month in the summer of 1756.

This was the ebb of the tide in Massachusetts: spirits sank as low as they were ever to go in this war. The agonizing sacrifices on faraway battlefields had brought home no victories— the province had gambled and lost; in the pervasive atmosphere of defeat, it seemed the French and Indians were knocking at the gate. How could the remnants of the Massachusetts militia, its regiments depleted by the troop levies of the past three years, hold off the enemy? The council met in November 1757, and decided that although the militia had been extended to the utmost, there was no alternative: the regiments would have to be called on to produce another force. A new unit would be drawn from the Massachusetts militia, to be designated the Picket Guards.

The name was chosen from military terminology of the time; this was the guard that every garrison maintained on alert to reinforce its pickets, or outposts. Instances of these guards are recorded in the orderly books of the provincials at Fort Edward, where, for example, the general orders for May 31, 1757, require that "there be a piqt. guard raised consisting of one Capt. two subs. 2 sergts. 2 corpls. 1 Drums & 50 men to mount at 7 o'clock in the afternoon who are to lie on their arms all night and in case of any alarm be ready to turn out at a minute's warning."

The first words of the council's new plan recognized that in keeping an average of 5,000 men in the field over the previous three years the militia had been bled of its strength and was now depleted to the extent that it was not able to defend the province. Training was ragged, many leaders were already away on the western expeditions, and supplies and equipment were almost nonexistent. Attempts to alarm the militia and cause the companies to muster had produced only confusion and further loss of morale.

With this hard look at the state of the militia as a preamble, the council then embarked on a concept which was by this time quite familiar to New Englanders: it decided to select from the militia a hand-picked group comprising about one fourth of the best men in the companies and form them into a new unit, to be commanded by appointed officers. The men were to be permitted to volunteer, but if not enough did so to make up the quota, the officers could appoint the rest.

New regiments were to be drawn up, the whole not to total more than 8,000 men, and each soldier was to be provided with a complete outfit of the very best equipment that could be found, including a musket, bayonet, hatchet, cartridge box, twenty-four rounds, powder horn, a lead bag, knapsack, and twelve flints. He was further ordered to maintain these in good condition or pay a heavy fine.

The unit was to enlist no fishermen or others whose occupations took them out of the province, no Frenchmen unless they were landholders in Massachusetts, and no Catholics, whose sympathies were assumed to be allied with the aspirations (or machinations) of the French. In exchange for their services in the new elite unit (which was carefully distinguished from the "common militia") the men were to receive a number of privileges: service under "select and proper officers"; exemption from labor or taxes for highways (except bridges); excused from service in "burthensome" public offices such as constable, tythingman, collector of taxes; free from "impress" or the drafting of men from the militia; free to resign from the Picket Guards on provision of an acceptable replacement; excused from bearing arms in the common militia. All of these privileges were to be awarded not merely during their service with the Picket Guards, but for an equal amount of time after they retired from the unit.

If the Picket Guards were to be especially rewarded, they were also to be called on to give a good account of themselves. Each man would be required to take an oath of allegiance to King George, to his God, his country, his officers, and his fellow soldiers, in that order. He would be punished for failing to have all his equipment, or neglecting to perform the military exercise to the best of his ability, and especially for being absent from muster without a good excuse. If he did not answer when his unit was alarmed, he was to be court-martialed.

The council stressed that these men were not to be called on to leave the province. This was to be strictly a defensive unit, on standby alert, constantly ready to "take to the Field and act in Defence of the Province on such sudden & extraordinary occasions."

The parallel between the Picket Guards and minute men of earlier and later days is clear. This plan was approved in council and sent down to the House of Representatives for concurrence on December 2, 1757. At the last moment, the title Picket Guards was scratched out wherever it appeared in the plan and the name Province Guards was substituted, possibly to emphasize the fact that the new unit would not be sent out of the pro- vince.

The main reason that the Picket, or Province, Guards have been lost to history is that the House disapproved the plan. The voting took place on December 9, when "the Question was then put, Whether the House judged it convenient, that a certain Part of the Militia be selected, and on certain Occasions employed for the Defence of the Province, said forces to be put under New England Officers, and not carried out of the Province but with their own consent, or by Order of Government? And it Pass'd in the Negative."

It was a fairly close vote—forty-eight to thirty-three. Among those who voted in favor of the Picket Guards were John Tyng, Thomas Flucker, James Barrett, and a number of the military men of the province who were also representatives. There is no record, unfortunately, of the discussions that must have taken place. Were the leaders of Massachusetts afraid the new force would be taken from them and ordered to the west, leaving the province completely destitute of troops? Possibly; the House was always suspicious of the Crown-appointed governor and his council, after the high-handed regime of Sir Edmund Andros. Were the representatives simply convinced that the plan was too grandiose to be supported by the exhausted militia of the province? Probably not, since the House agreed to raise 7,000 men the following April for a new expedition to Ticonderoga. One good possibility is that the return of Loudoun from Louisburg meant that a large force of regulars and provincials was once more at home and in striking range of the French and Indians, and a majority in the House felt that this force could meet the immediate threat of Montcalm and his troops above Albany.

The decision, in the end, proved correct—the Picket Guards were not needed, because after the winter of 1757-1758 the tide finally turned in favor of the British and Americans. Although Abercromby failed again in front of Ticonderoga, Louisburg, Frontenac, and Duquesne fell to the British and Americans. By the end of another year Quebec had fallen, and the capitulation of Montreal in 1760 ended the fighting in America.

There were men from the Massachusetts militia in nearly every one of the battles of this war. Enlisted or impressed, they fought under Monckton, Shirley, Johnson, Loudoun, Abercromby, and Amherst, in the ranks of the 50th and 51st, with Gage's 80th Light Infantry, and with Rogers' Rangers.

With the troops in the Lake George area the minute man plan was a commonplace. Samuel Thompson, a lieutenant in a company of Massachusetts militia under Johnson, mentions in his journal entry for July 30, 1758: "Sunday, before day they did muster, and sent out seventy five men out of our Regiment, eleven out of our Company, who went a little after sunrise down the Lake, and what the News was, we could not tell; yet all sorts of camp news was *brief* [rife] about. But when our men were gone, they sent eleven more at one minute's warning, with 3 days provision, as those who were gone before, which did amount to 75 more out of our Regiment and the number of men already gone is gussed to be nigh 1,000 men, and ye same number to be at one minute's warning with 3 days provision. . . ."

At Boston it was the near-creation of the Picket Guards that most clearly showed the tendency of the province of Massachusetts to turn to the minute man concept when danger threatened.

Chapter 5

The Last Decade

The disappearance of a strong military threat from Canada left the province in a state of peace which was to be short lived. Within a dozen years the British attempt to tighten centralization of control over the North American colonies clashed seriously with a new American nationalism in the fields of trade and industry, but perhaps most of all in the field of American self-respect. In these new trying times the province of Massachusetts was to turn again to its soldiers and to the military creation that had proved so useful in the past: the minute man concept. To be sure, the minute men who fought the first hours of the revolution emerged from a long military tradition reaching back to the earliest days of the colony, but it was not tradition alone that called them once more into action. Within the towns there were other powerful forces that united to shape and mold and give direction to the discontent in the province—to reinforce and exploit the reaction of the provincials against the British attempts to strengthen their control over Massachusetts. The town meetings, the militia musters, the church services, and the newspapers all became part of a half-directed, half-spontaneous expression of a political philosophy which at first called only for restoration of old "charter rights" but rapidly grew into a demand for complete independence. The heat of this political

34

activity made the towns into incubators where the minute man developed, and where these forces of the pulpit, the town-house, the muster field, and the newspaper were concentrated.

The town meeting in the last decade before the revolution changed from a gathering for presentation of local problems, such as construction of roads and fences, to a political caucus where questions of worldwide importance were matters for discussion. To see the change in the nature of the local newspaper, especially the Whig publications, one has merely to look at the rapid increase in political editorials to the point where, by 1774, the *Massachusetts Spy*, for example, was printing a four-column front page editorial in every issue. The clergy of the province, long accustomed to giving temporal advice to the townsfolk, provided increasing support to the revolutionary movement—so much so that the governor in 1774 wrote to the secretary of state for North America to say that "sedition flows copiously from the pulpits."

The towns had come to control great political power. For the first fifty years after the founding of the colony under the Charter of 1629, Massachusetts Bay operated entirely free from control of England, restricted only by a requirement not to make laws contrary to existing British laws. This old charter was revoked in 1683 and control of the province was given to a governor appointed by the King, but the towns continued along as if nothing had changed, meeting and passing on anything and everything that they felt was of concern to them. The townsfolk considered themselves stockholders in a corporation, and their idea of how to run a town was not much affected by anything that happened after 1629. Provincial control of the towns, which had been strong and arbitrary in the beginning (when towns were reprimanded and fined for minor infractions), grew weak after the towns obtained representation in the General Court (the House). The governor had to have the cooperation of his council to get anything done, and the members of the council were picked from the General Court, which was elected from the towns. Although the governor had a veto power and exercised it often, he still was limited in his selection of a council to the men the towns wanted to provide. And he was always faced with the necessity to deal with the assembly of the General Court. The towns felt that they sustained the law of the province, and this was true. When the resistance to the realization of British aims in America began to grow after the French and Indian War, the towns became the centers of political activity.

The main instrument of control was the town meeting, where every man who owned an estate worth twenty pounds or more was a "freeholder" and had the right to speak and vote. Normally these meetings concerned run-of-the-mill town problems— road repair, boundary disputes, help for the poor—but since the towns were in effect the controllers of the militia companies (most of the town leaders were also militia officers, and the town was responsible for equipping and supplying its men) the town meetings were potential forums for discussion of military and political subjects.

James Otis and Samuel Adams, among other leaders of the early revolutionary activities, recognized the crucial importance of the town governments and wisely moved to split the strength of the towns away from the structure of Crown control. The first step in this break-away process was to gain influence in the town meetings, which were dominated by Loyalists (although the number of Whig sympathizers was at this time increasing rapidly). Otis and Adams began in their own town, Boston, and their first tangible success came with the meeting of November 3, 1772, when they were able to muster enough support to vote in a resolution establishing a Committee of Correspondence. This committee was immediately ordered to "Prepare a statement of the rights of the colonists as men, as Christians, and as subjects; Prepare a declaration of the infringement of those rights; and Prepare a letter to be sent to all the towns of the province and to the world, giving the sense of the town." The completed papers were read and approved at the November 20 meeting, at which Otis presided for the last time.

This Committee of Correspondence and the men who brought it into being well understood the psychology of the provincial town meeting. The first communication sent out to the towns was no more than a list of grievances with a request that the towns endorse the view of their Boston neighbors. It is apparent that the effort was well calculated; it is easy to imagine the effect of this letter when it was read aloud to the freeholders at all the town meetings, contrasting the matter-of-fact monotony of normal business. The massed evidence of Crown interference and injustice, enumerated statement by statement, was an attempt to overwhelm any Loyalist apologists and to bend the sympathies of the towns in the direction of revolution. The list contained these major points:

1. British Parliament has assumed power of legislation for the colonists without their consent.
2. Parliament has raised illegal revenues.
3. Tax collectors have been appointed by the Crown, a right reserved to the province.
4. Tax collectors are entrusted with power too absolute and arbitrary. Private premises are exposed to search.
5. "Fleets and Armies" are quartered on the townsfolk in time of peace without their consent.
6. Tax revenue has been used by King to pay provincial government officers, making them dependent on him, in violation of the charter.
7. General assemblies are forced to meet in inconvenient places. Activities of the council have been limited.
8. Colonists accused of crimes are to be tried in admiralty courts.
9. Restraints are placed against iron mills, hat manufacture, and transport; wool cannot be carried over a ferry; many other businesses are curtailed.
10. Colonists accused of destroying any British naval property are to be transported to England for trial.
11. Parliament is attempting to establish an American Episcopate.
12. Parliament is making frequent alteration of the bounds of the colonies, not according to charter.

The request accompanying the list asked for "a free communication of your sentiments to this town, of our common danger." The towns were not expected to take any action—merely to agree that the grievances were legitimate. The paper was well suited to be discussed in public assembly and the content would make it difficult for the Loyalist faction to ignore or suppress it. Even the use of a Committee of Correspondence, rather than a single secretary, was fortunate in its effect, since the word *committee* does not carry the authoritative ring that a request from a single representative or even a single town might have. Boston was asking for moral support, and the old traditional awareness of inter-town responsibility and cooperation was put to use again by Adams as he searched out and measured the sentiment of the province.

Most of the towns immediately formed their own branch committees to correspond with Boston, thus taking the first concerted step in opposition to British rule.   The influence of the Boston committee is easy to see in many of the replies which came in from the countryside.   A letter from the town of Fitchburg on December 1, 1773, makes record of a resolve that stands out from the commonplace notes of normal town business: "Chose Isaac Gibson Capt Ruben Gibson Phineas Hartwell Ebenezer Woods Kindall Bontall Ebenezer Bridg Solomon Steward to be a Committee to Draw up and report to the town of Fitchburg a Draft of our Rights & Privilgs as free members of Society: in order to make return to the Town of Boston or to the Committee of Correspondence at Boston."

The Committee of Correspondence was changing the town meeting from a dry discussion of local matters to a far-reaching political forum; the town was becoming the action level for the revolutionary movement in the province, and the townsmen were growing more and more concerned with the great questions which the revolutionaries were asking.

And the Whigs kept busy.   The second big step came in June 1774, when the Committee of Correspondence, after a hard fight at a Boston town meeting, pushed through a resolution calling for the Solemn League and Covenant, an agreement to boycott all British goods.   This was the first request which committed the towns to resistance, although even in this case the resistance was passive.   The rapid compliance of most of the towns soon suspended all commerce between England and the province of Massachusetts, and the league spread rapidly down the Atlantic coast.   This unity of the towns in the province later facilitated the creation of the Provincial Congress in the fall of 1774.

What the minute man missed at town meetings he could pick up in the newspaper.   Local news gave way to reports of town meetings, county congress resolves, and scores of "letters to the editor" from avid Whigs and Loyalists writing under pseudonyms. Rivington's *Gazette* (New York) and other Tory papers were outnumbered more than four to one by Whig publications, but they kept up a running fight until the opening of the war.

The enthusiastic Whig editors and the forceful Whig town meeting moderators and faction leaders were assisted by a no less able group: the clergy.   The great majority of the pastors of the province were condemning the actions of Parliament, if not actually advocating rebellion.   The pastor was always one of the best-educated men of the community, and usually he took an active part in town affairs. In many towns he was the moderator or one of the officials at town meetings; he served in the militia; he often wrote all the official correspondence of the town. Reverend Samuel Cooke of Menotomy, for example, was a constant attacker of the British. His sermon, preached to the minute men of his town on April 6, 1775, is an indication of his attitude:

> We cannot indeed expect to be saved, but in the way of duty, and in a prudent, manly resolute defense of our rights, dearer to us than our lives dragged along in cruel slavery! Does the courage of anyone among us under fresh alarms begin to fail? Recall to remembrance the wonders God hath wrought for our fathers, and in our days. How was the yoke of barbarous oppression suddenly broken under the rule of that despotic *monster*, Sir Edmund Andros! How have we seen Louisburg, that Thorn in our sides, brought to the dust, to the astonishment of the world, by New England troops. . . . How was the detested Stamp Act and other cruel impositions, prevented having their baneful effect, by our own spirited and united opposition! Our leading enemies are now the same; and God, with the same ease, can again turn their counsels into foolishness. The union of the Colonies is great and marvellous in our eyes! But as Ministerial Vengeance is pointed at this devoted Province, it will be expected that we take the lead in every prudent and constitutional measure for a general defence.

This advice to the flock is not an isolated example. In 1772, 250 Massachusetts ministers—nearly every clergyman in the province—had refused to read from the pulpits the governor's customary Thanksgiving address, on the grounds that the words therein were not appropriate in view of the late actions of the home government.

The Provincial congress when it was formed in October of 1774 was quick to recognize the clergy as a potential line of communication to the countryside, and within two months the congress was in contact with all the ministers in the province. The first letter to the clergy was in effect a call to duty, reminding them of their historical position as *temporal and spiritual* advisors to the townsmen of Massachusetts, and requesting them to "assist" by "advising the people of their several congregations, as they wish their prosperity, to abide by, and strictly adhere to, the resolutions of the Continental Congress."

The clergy responded almost to a man with sermons supporting the revolutionary activities. An extract from Reverend John Marrett's interleaved almanac shows that the preachers were not limiting their work to the Sunday services; on Tuesday, April 4, 1775, he writes: "Rode to Wilmington and Reading P.M. Heard Mr. Stone preach a sermon to the minute-men."

The Provincial Congress soon found that setting aside a special day of prayer throughout the province would allow the ministers an opportunity to stress the aims of the movement. The multiple impact of a day of fasting and prayer called attention to the specific reason for the day (to mourn the fate of the citizens killed by the British in the 1770 "Boston Massacre," for instance) and also put the ministers in a position to support the Provincial Congress.

The new Intolerable Acts closing up the port of Boston were a weapon in the hands of the Whigs, who used the force of angry reaction to bring pressure on the Tories in every town. The Tories did not collapse all at once, however; they had been fighting Whig ideas for more than a hundred years and they were not ready to stop in 1774. Worcester was a Whig stronghold, yet in July a letter was published there signed by fifty-two "free men," denouncing rebellious ideas. It read in part: ". . . the committees of correspondence in the several towns of this province, being creatures of modern invention, and constituted as they be, are a public grievance; having no legal foundation; contrived by a junto, to serve particular designs and purposes of their own; and that they, as they have been, and now are managed in this town, are a nuisance."

In some towns the Loyalists were able to block, temporarily, the attempts to join the revolutionary movement led by Boston. The first Liberty Pole brought into Deerfield was found cut down the following morning. In Weston, the first motion at a town meeting "to correspond with the neighboring towns, and to consider what is best to be done, that our injured rights and privileges may be restored and secured" was defeated by a large majority after "full debate." The tide was moving against the Tories, however; regardless of a few scattered victories, they were forced to give ground. In the fall conventions of 1774 they made their last strong bid for control, but the rally failed and they were forced out of power in the province. Some Loyalists were able to accept the revolutionary spirit of the times, but those who could not soon left their homes and moved to Boston where they could be protected by the British garrison. In the end, when the British evacuated the town, 1,100 Loyalists embarked with them (of this group, it is interesting to note that while over one hundred were political officials, only eighteen were clergymen). Some went to Canada, others to England; very few ever returned to their old homes.

The minute man was not isolated on his farm or in the village; on the contrary, he was in communication with all the sources of revolutionary theory. In the parish church he heard the pastor urge support of the resolutions of the Provincial Congress; at the town meetings he kept in touch with the situation in Boston and the other towns through his Committee of Correspondence; at the militia drill meetings he saw the Whigs taking over as the Loyalists were forced out; in the newspapers he read long front-page editorials condemning the activities of Parliament and supporting Whig attitudes. Such were the men who stood in the ranks as Major General Gage, the newly arrived governor of the province, reviewed the militia on Long Wharf in Boston on May 13, 1774.

Chapter **6**

The Showdown at Worcester

On August 27, 1774, the new Governor of Massachusetts sat at his desk in the Hooper house in Danvers and penned a furious report to his superior, Lord Dartmouth, Secretary of State for the Colonies. Gage usually wrote his letters to Dartmouth in a clipped, reserved hand but in this one his anger boils behind every line: "In Worcester they keep no terms; openly threatening resistance by arms; have been purchasing arms; preparing them; casting balls; and providing powder; and threaten to attack any troops who dare to oppose them. Mr. Ruggles, of the new council, is afraid to take his seat as judge of the inferior court, which sits at Worcester on the 6th of next month; and, I apprehend, that I shall soon be obliged to march a body of troops into that township, and perhaps into others, as occasions happen, to preserve the peace." After three frustrating months of attempting to restore peaceful Crown government to a confused and violent province swept by disorders, Gage was on the point of giving up the idea of a settlement without resort to arms. He had seven regiments of regulars in Boston now, and he was preparing himself to take a fateful step: to pit his 2,500 troops against the unknown power of the Massachusetts countryside.

As Governor of Massachusetts and Commander of His Majesty's Forces in North America, Thomas Gage was a good man for

42

the job, perhaps the best that could have been found in the British service at the time (Sir Jeffrey Amherst, beloved by Americans, may possibly have been better—but, asked to return at this time by King George III, he declined). Politically, Gage certainly was qualified; he had been Governor of Montreal from 1760 to 1763, and his many years of service in America had brought him into contact with many men of political prominence, among them George Washington, Robert Hunter Morris, William Allen, and Benjamin Franklin. Militarily, he knew both the formal, parade-ground style of battle and the informal Indian warfare.

Married into the well-known American Kemble family, Gage was quite acceptable socially. He was a handsome and moderate man, well liked by both sexes. Psychologically, his even temper and his sympathetic understanding of the provincial mind moderated his rejection of the American rebel view. But even the best of royal governors was not good enough for Massachusetts now, and Gage, as well as everyone else, could see that under the barrage of punishing "acts" arriving from across the Atlantic the situation was fast becoming hopeless.

When he arrived in Boston in May, burdened though he was with the King's orders to close the port, Gage was still able to achieve a few of his immediate goals. He shut down the port, moved the seat of government to Salem, and quartered five new regiments in Boston without a major incident. For a few brief weeks Gage allowed himself to think he might be able to subdue the radical faction and bring the province back into the fold, but it was the King himself, in London, who destroyed this illusion. Boston was prostrated by the Port Bill and the arrival of troops, and the city and the whole province smoldered with resentment, lacking only a focal point—a flag under which to ignite the fire of rebellion. King George, anxious to increase the punishment of this insolent colony and make it an example to the rest, soon gave the rebel leaders just the kind of rallying cry they were seeking.

In May the British Parliament passed "An Act for the better regulating the Government of the Province of Massachusetts-Bay" and "An Act for the more impartial administration of justice in said Province." These new laws removed from Massachusetts the right to name the Governor's Council, to elect judges, sheriffs, and justices of the peace, to summon juries, and to hold town meetings (with certain exceptions). In addition, colonists accused of crimes could be carried out of Massachusetts to Admiralty Courts in Halifax, Nova Scotia, for trial. Few acts could have done more to destroy hope for a peaceful settlement of differences; these new acts virtually wiped out all old allegiances to the Crown. It was a massive attack on the old charter—and it was, of all the moves and countermoves leading to the revolution, the point of no return.

Needless to say, this made Samuel Adams a very happy man. Adams had many irons in the fire, and one of these concerned the militia of Massachusetts. For many years he had been trying to improve the militia, knowing that in any emergency it would side with the province, since only the ranking officers (and a dwindling number, at that) could be considered strong Loyalists. In 1770 he had risen in the court to ask for a strengthening of the militia regiments. He described in detail the poor state of training, the lack of junior officers, and the deficiencies in arms and ammunition. The militia was being neglected, said Adams, and the governor ought to do something about it right away. Three years later he was still agitating, getting a committee appointed to draft a bill for improving the militia, and Governor Hutchinson, being nobody's fool, was still ignoring Adams. But now, in the fall of 1774, things were different. Adam's plan for a series of county conventions, which was an outgrowth of his Committees of Correspondence and which he hoped would lead to some kind of provincial convention, had been stumbling along slowly and cautiously until word of these new repressive acts reached the province in late June. Fast schooners outstripped the government frigate and, as usual, embarrassed the authorities, who in this case did not get the official word until early August. Now the quiet Committees of Correspondence exploded with the news and in a matter of days there were conventions scheduled in the counties of Berkshire, Middlesex, Essex, Suffolk, Hampshire, Plymouth, Bristol, and Worcester. The whole province was now making ready to challenge Gage with mobilized power, and Gage knew he had to answer the challenge or lose what control remained to the Crown in Massachusetts.

On August 9, three days after the official publication of the act forbidding town meetings, Adams called for a Boston town meeting at Faneuil Hall. Gage reacted quickly. Calling the Boston selectmen on the carpet, he had the new act (which they well understood) read to them; he then informed them that they would be held responsible for any violation of the act. But the selectmen were ready for Gage. This meeting, they said, had not been *called*; it was a continuation of a previous meeting which instead of being closed had been adjourned until now. Gage knew he had been outmaneuvered. There was only one thing to do: take action—backed up, of course, by the new council which he had just appointed under the new acts. He gathered as many of the council as he could find—twenty-four of the thirty-six—and told them of the selectmen's position.

But the council, already intimidated by Adams and the belligerent townsfolk, were not anxious to support Gage. After conferring with them, Gage said he "found some of opinion that the clause was thereby clearly evaded and nearly the whole unwilling to debate upon it, terming it a point of law which ought to be referred to the Crown lawyers, whose opinion is to be taken on it, and by which I must govern myself."

Adams held the town meeting as scheduled, and the encouraging correspondence went out to the towns: *resist the Intolerable Acts!* On the same day as the Boston meeting, the first convention of Worcester County Committees of Correspondence gathered at a Worcester inn. Fifty-two delegates attended—not enough to be really meaningful as a representation of the county; so after passing resolves which vehemently denied the right of Parliament to cast aside older laws without the consent of the colony, the delegates drafted a circular letter to the absent towns, calling upon them to meet on August 30 at the same place to "adopt some wise, prudent, and spirited measures, in order to prevent the execution of those most alarming acts of parliament, respecting our constitution." The Worcester assembly of Committees of Correspondence was not the first (Berkshire county committees had met on July 6 to pass some mild resolves), but it soon became the most belligerent of all.

At the next Worcester meeting 130 delegates were present, representing nearly every town in the county. They chose a committee to "take into consideration the state of public affairs," and the next day, August 31, after listening to the report of this committee, the convention voted to refuse to allow the Court of General Sessions to sit at Worcester because the judges had been appointed by the governor rather than by the province. Gage, as governor, already had announced that this court would open at Worcester on September 6; the resolution of the convention was in direct opposition to the orders of the Crown. The delegates felt that if Gage ever intended to march

against them, it would be now. But by this time Worcester
County was in an uproar, and only a few days earlier, on August
26, over 2,000 provincial soldiers had marched into Worcester and
paraded on the common—some of them in companies and led by
their militia officers—in a gesture of defiance aimed at intimidating the new judges. The delegates were confident that they
could muster a force to meet any troops Gage could send, and
they were determined to do it. Before they adjourned the convention there was a motion "whereas, it is generally expected,
that the governor will send one or more regiments to enforce the
execution of the acts of parliament, on the 6ᵗʰ of September,
that it be recommended to the inhabitants of this county, if
there is intelligence, that troops are on their march to Worcester, to attend, properly armed, in order to repel any hostile force
which may be employed for that purpose." This motion, it
seems, made the delegates look too aggressive and outside the
law, so they reworded it, and the final motion, substantially the
same as the earlier one, talked of the "danger of invasion" and
their determination to "all come properly armed and accoutred to
protect and defend the place invaded." The Middlesex Convention, meeting at Concord on the same day, passed resolves which
were much milder, but the news of the Worcester Convention
spread posthaste, and the whole province waited for September 6.

Gage, however, seized the initiative once again on the first
day of September, moving quickly to catch the provincials completely by surprise with a march of the British regulars out of
the town of Boston. It was a perfectly executed operation. The
towns around Boston had been quietly withdrawing town-owned
gunpowder from the powder house on Quarry Hill in Charlestown,
and the provincials had their eye on the "King's powder," the
government-owned powder not specifically intended for the
militia, over 200 half-barrels of it. Gage was informed by
General Brattle, the Loyalist commander of the Massachusetts
militia, that "the King's powder only" remained in the
magazine—the town of Medford had just taken away the last of
the supply belonging to the province. When Gage heard this, he
decided it was time to clean out the powderhouse.

Two hundred and sixty men were "draughted from the several
regiments," given a day's provisions, and ordered to be ready to
march in the morning under Colonel Maddison of the 4th (King's
Own) Regiment. At dawn on September 1 the regulars marched
down to the foot of the common, embarked in thirteen boats be-

longing to the men-of-war and the transports, and rowed up the Mystic River to Temple's Farm in Charlestown. They landed and marched across country to the knoll on which the powderhouse stood, where Loyalist Sheriff Phips handed over the keys. The removal of the powder, which was rowed out to the transports and taken to Castle William in the harbor, was carried out without resistance, and the troops were back in quarters in Boston almost before anyone knew what had happened. A detachment from the main force of regulars also marched to Cambridge, where Brattle turned over to them two brass cannon that he feared the rebels were planning to steal. This, too, was accomplished without a hitch. Gage had a right to be pleased; his first march on the provincials, limited though it may have been, was a complete success.

The reaction of the province, however, was astounding. News of the "raid" traveled rapidly from town to town, distorted by messengers into a tale of aggression and carnage: the British ships had fired on Boston; the troops were killing citizens; at Shrewsbury, eight miles from Boston, news arrived that night, "the doleful story that the powder was taken, six men killed, and all the people between there & Boston arming and marching down to the Relief of their Brethren at Boston; and within a Qr. or half an hour . . . fifty men were collected at the Tavern tho' now deep in night, equipping themselves & sending off Posts every Way to the neighboring towns." A traveler coming into Boston from the Worcester area reported later that "For about fifty miles each way round there was an almost universal Ferment, Rising, seizing Arms & Actual march into Cambridge."

By noon the next day, over 4,000 men from the surrounding towns had gathered on the common in Cambridge. As the companies of armed men arrived they discovered that the reports had been exaggerated, that although the powder was gone, no provincial had been killed or even molested. Confronted with this *fait accompli*, the loss of the powder and of the two field pieces, they were not sure what to do next. It was generally agreed, however, that something had to be done.

At this point some of the members of the Boston Committee of Correspondence took over the leadership of the group, convincing the men that they should take the occasion of this gathering to demonstrate their disapproval of those Crown-appointed judges who had not resigned their commissions. Under the direction of the Boston committee the provincials sent word to Judges

Lee and Danforth, requesting them to appear before the crowd on the common and state whether or not they would resign. Both men were property owners, and evidently both understood well the temper of the times. They came and spoke to the assemblage, agreeing to step down.

Lieutenant Governor Thomas Oliver, another of the new judges, observed the arrival of company after company of provincial minute men and militia, and got off a hasty note to General Gage, begging him *not* to send any regular troops to the town. Oliver was not sure he could survive if an incident were to occur between the Crown soldiers and the provincials. After obtaining the resignations of Danforth and Lee, the provincials surrounded the home of Oliver and sent word to him that he, too, would have to make a public withdrawal from the office tendered him by the King, and that he must put his resignation in writing. He did so, saying, "My house at Cambridge being surrounded by about four thousand people, in compliance with their command I sign my name."

The provincials, at last satisfied that nothing more could be accomplished for the time being, started back for their homes. Messengers were sent out on the roads to stop the companies still arriving from distant towns. Ezra Stiles noted that "30,000, or near perhaps more than one third the effective men in all New England took arms & were on actual march for Boston. But posts were dispatched every way and stopt them." Joseph Warren was elated. He had gone out to Cambridge on the day of the alarm, and, as he wrote to Samuel Adams three days later, the size of the muster convinced him that "had the troops marched only five miles out of Boston, I doubt whether a man would have been saved of their whole number." Gage, who described the assembly as "a vast concourse of people," was quite surprised—enough so that he reconsidered his plan to send troops to Worcester.

The new Governor's council also was against the idea of the march. On the day before, while Colonel Maddison and the regulars were planning and preparing for the seizure of the powder, Gage had called a meeting of the council to ask "what they thought it expedient and proper to do in this exigency of affairs, and whether they would advise to the sending of any troops into the county of Worcester, or any other county in the Province, for the protection of the judges and other officers of the courts of justice." The councilors answered: No. The opposition to the recent acts of Parliament was so widespread and so strong, they feared, that the troops might have their hands full simply defending Boston.   This reply, coupled with the provincial response to his seizure of the powder on the following day, was enough for Gage. He resolved not to attempt the expedition to Worcester.

Dawn of September 6 found 6,000 provincials assembled under arms in the town of Worcester, determined to refuse to allow the seating of the court, and ostensibly ready to fight Gage's regulars if necessary. Most of the Worcester County towns sent men in organized companies under the command of elected officers, prepared, as far as possible, to stop the King's troops.

But there were no King's troops; they were not sent. Gage later wrote home to England that he had intended "to send a body of troops to Worcester, to protect the court there; and if wanted, to send parties to the houses of the councillors who dwell in the county; but finding, from undoubted authority, that the flames of sedition had spread universally throughout the country, beyond conception; the councillors already driven away; and that no court would proceed on business; I waited the event of the sitting of the superior court here. . . ."

As far as the men of Worcester County (and for that matter, all the rest of the province) were concerned, they had called Gage's bluff and he had not dared to act against them. It would be impossible to say what might have happened if Gage had sent a brigade to Worcester. Perhaps the war would have begun at that point, before the province had time to create an army; or perhaps, if Gage had been successful, it might never have begun at all, at least at that time. What might have been can only be conjectured; what did happen is that the move toward a provincial army was given its greatest push forward, the morale of the Whig opposition soared, and for the first time many provincials began to believe that a revolution was indeed possible.

The Showdown at Worcester

Chapter 7

The Birth of the Minute Men

Without support from Gage the Crown-appointed court at Worcester was powerless. The judges were forced to parade in front of dozens of provincial militia companies drawn up on the green and to declare their submission to the rule of the county assembly. For the provincials it was a turning point and a proof of their own rising power. Heartened by Gage's failure to take action, they dispersed peacefully, and on the following day the convention passed strong new resolves for improving the military organization of Worcester County. The new militia plan, modified and accepted at the following meeting on September 21, was later to serve as the pilot model for the minute men and the basis for the creation of the new militia system throughout the province. The convention first required that all field officers of the militia resign immediately and publish their resignations in the Boston newspapers. They then voted

> that it be recommended to the several towns in this county, to choose proper military officers, and a sufficient number for each town, and that the captains, lieutenants, and ensigns, who are chosen by the people in each regiment, do convene, on or before the tenth day of October next, at some convenient place in each regiment, and choose their

field officers to command the militia until they be constitu-
tionally appointed, and that it be recommended to the officers in each town of the county, to enlist one third of the
men of their respective towns, between sixteen and sixty
years of age, to be ready to act at a minute's warning; and
that it be recommended to each town in the county, to
choose a sufficient number of men as a committee to supply
and support those troops that shall move on any emergency.

The officers of the minute men were ordered to meet on October
17 to "proportion their own regiments and choose as many field
officers as they shall think necessary." Once again, as in earlier
days, the minute man concept was superimposed on the existing
military organization. This action paved the way for the complete reorganization of the provincial militia.

The success of the Worcester convention was echoed in the
next few weeks by the assemblies in Suffolk, Essex, and
Middlesex counties and in the attitude of the provincials in
general. Only two weeks after the Worcester convention, John
Andrews wrote from Boston: "This day a deputation of twelve
came to town with a *very* spirited remonstrance from the *body* of
Worcester county, which consists of five and forty towns; where
they have incorporated *seven regiments* consisting of 1,000 men
each, chose their officers, and turn out twice a week to perfect
themselves in the military art—*which* are call'd *minute men*, i.e.,
to be ready at a minute's warning with a fortnight's provision,
and ammunition and arms."

The move toward a provincial congress now became inevitable,
but its organization was a masterpiece of opportunism on the
part of Samuel Adams and the Whigs. In September Gage had
announced that October 4 would be the date for convening the
General Court at Salem. In a matter of a few days he realized
that the General Court would be worse than useless; there was
no hope that the delegates in any way would assist him to restore order and carry out the edicts of the Crown. In fact, Gage
knew that many of the towns were holding extra-legal meetings
in order to give instructions to their delegates to the court and
these instructions in all cases were very clear: *do not accept
any of the recent rulings of the King, including the mandamus
councilors. If the Governor dissolves the assembly, unite with
the other delegates and form a new one of our own.* Gage saw
that the assembly of the court would be a farce, and on Septem-

ber 28 he canceled his request for the convening at Salem. The towns, however, insisted on holding the meeting in order to form their own congress, under the excuse that Gage had failed to honor the court which he himself had ordered to convene and which, by law, was supposed to meet every year. Gage refused to preside over the court, which was exactly what the delegates wanted. They then proceeded to organize themselves as the First Provincial Congress, and when this was completed they adjourned to meet at Concord on the following day.

The congress, like any other congress, was not free from time-wasting digressions, especially in the first days. Its members composed a letter of complaint to the governor, discussed the appointment of agents for establishing liaison with Canada, sent for and examined, with proper outrage, Loyalist newspapers, and fought the tea tax once again with a resolution against consumption of this "baneful vehicle of a corrupt and venal administration." But in addition, in the middle of all the digressions, they appointed a committee "to consider what is necessary to be now done for the defense and safety of the province." The new committee was loaded with key figures of the revolutionary movement, including Artemus Ward, William Heath, Samuel Dexter, and Azor Orne. Together these men worked out and submitted the drafts of resolutions to form the provincial army, sparking the first of the long and profitable discussions of the congress.

The committees knew that widespread militia regiments would be difficult to control and would be too slow in forming to meet an attack by the regulars. At the same time the creation of a standing army in the province would be certain to precipitate a British countermove. The other New England colonies and many of those to the south were considering plans to oppose the Crown, but no one was ready at this time. Until they were, a provincial force in Massachusetts would present the kind of target Gage was prepared to attack. Some kind of military force had to be created to meet the needs of the moment, to oppose the British until a stronger army could be built, and this force would have to be composed of well-trained, lightly armed infantry, capable of rapid assembly and rapid movement to any point in the province.

This interim unit was, of course, the minute men. As at Worcester, the committee employed the basic principles of the minute man concept, and within twenty-four hours a plan for the organization of the minute men and militia was laid before the Congress.

The report touched off a hammer-and-tongs debate that lasted from October 21 to 26, during which time the plan was read and amended six times before it was finally accepted. The first resolve created the Committee of Safety, consisting of three delegates from Boston and six from the rest of the province, empowered to "alarm, muster, and cause to be assembled" as much of the provincial militia as needed at any time. All officers and soldiers of the militia were "earnestly recommended" to carry out the orders of this committee. The second resolve established the Committee of Supplies to provide logistical support for any muster of the militia. Other resolves covered the appointment and pay of the officers and men of the new army.

The final point approved by the congress was the organization of the army itself. The new army was created from the old militia. All militia companies were to elect new officers. These officers were to assemble and elect battalion and regimental commanders and staffs. Once the regiments were formed, the commanders were to enlist one quarter of the men into new companies of fifty privates "who shall equip and hold themselves in readiness, on the shortest notice from the said committee of safety, to march to the place of rendezvous; and that each and every company so formed choose a captain and two lieutenants to command them on any such emergent and necessary service as they may be called to. . . ." The men were to form themselves into battalions of nine companies each, and the company officers were to elect officers from their own group to command the battalions. All men were directed to supply themselves with weapons and to become proficient in military training. Selectmen of all the towns were told to insure an adequate supply of ammunition for their own minute man and militia companies.

The formation of a provincial army from the King's loyal militia was now well under way. The congress, of course, was completely dependent on the individual towns to carry out the resolves, to reelect officers, to form battalions, to supply arms and ammunition, and, especially, to put their minute men under the immediate command of the Committee of Saftey—which meant that men could be taken away from any towns and used wherever necessary.

It is significant that the appeal was sent directly to the individual towns rather than to the counties. No attempt was

made to strengthen the county conventions, which had been almost entirely responsible for the creation of the Provincial
Congress. This was a tacit recognition of the power that, since
the early settlements, the towns had been able to exercise. (A
good indication of the strength of the towns at this time was
their ability to absorb the responsibility for law and order in the
province from the time the Regulating Acts dissolved the old
judgeships in August 1774, until courts of law were opened almost
a year later.)

The Provincial Congress printed extracts of its resolves and
sent copies to every town in the province. The congress then
adjourned until November 23, and in the meantime the new Provincial Army committees got down to work—and there was plenty
of work to be done. The job of the Committee of Supplies was
easy enough to state but hard to accomplish: to get hold of all
the arms, ammunition, and equipment it could beg, borrow, or
steal, and to deposit everything in safe supply points in towns
scattered throughout the province.

The Committee of Safety was faced with problems no less difficult. Some of the powers given to this committee were later to
prove a harassment to it; it was empowered, as an example, to
"carefully and diligently inspect and observe all and every person
or persons as shall, at any time, attempt or enterprise the destruction, invasion, detriment or annoyance of this province," and
the members soon found that "suspicious persons" were being
sent in for inspection from town committees all over Massachusetts. But what gave the Committee of Safety its real strength
was the clause that placed the new army directly under its control. With the help of the Committee of Supplies (which it later
absorbed) the Committee of Safety functioned as an army commander and staff, responsible only to the Provincial Congress,
controlling a military organization which was able to put 14,000
men into the field against Gage on April 19.

The reaction in the towns and in the old militia to the
resolves of the Provincial Congress was immediate and hearty.
New elections took place at once in most of the towns, and the
die-hard Loyalists who were reluctant to leave their commands
were forced out. Tory Major Thomas Bourne reported to General
Gage that he was made to resign "after being obliged to ride six
miles in the night to sign under their liberty pole." Colonel
Isaac Williams of Hatfield was seized at his home and taken to
the town of Hadley, where he was locked in a room and forced

to endure the smoke of a stopped-up chimney until he promised to discontinue his correspondence with Gage. Major General Brattle, trying to please his Whig friends and hold his Loyalist position as militia commander at the same time, informed Gage of the convulsions taking place in the lower levels of command of the militia. His letter, discovered and printed in the Whig news-papers, was an obsequious account which ruined Brattle in the eyes of the officers in the regiments. Brattle tried to redeem himself with a letter of explanation to the press, in which he said, in effect, that he was a friend and supporter of both sides. Brattle, too, was "elected" out of the militia.

The response to the call for minute men was remarkable. This was a touchy point, since it meant that the regimental commanders, in allowing the minute men to organize themselves and elect their own officers, would actually be giving away not only one-quarter of their strength but also many of their best fighters. In view of this, the active support that the regimental commanders gave to the reorganization is one of the best indica-tions of the strength of the minute man concept. Colonel Samuel Johnson, commanding the 4th Regiment of Foot, Essex Militia, is a good example. He went to Boxford, Haverhill, Methuen, and Bradford, speaking to the men in his companies and urging them to volunteer for the minute man units. At Boxford "he addressed himself with great zeal to the two foot-companies of the Fourth Regiment, recommending to them the necessity of enlisting them-selves into the service of the province, and in a short space of time fifty-three able-bodied and effective men offered themselves to serve their province in defence of their liberties."

The *esprit* of the minute men was high from the very begin-ning. Town after town called meetings to act on the new re-solves and no town seems to have had any trouble finding men willing to fill the ranks. In Dudley a committee was formed to "assist in settling and establishing of the minnit men," thus providing the company with its own military staff. In Harvard, the town voted to pay their minute men, but the members of the newly organized company sent their captain, Jonathan Davis, to say that "as they had inlisted Voluntears so they do & will Remain Voluntears, nither acceptin nor Dispising what the town has voted for them." In Framingham an artillery battery was being formed, but the promised cannon did not appear. The men decided to enlist as privates in a minute man company then in the process of organizing; the interchange between militia and minute men offered no barrier. The town of Roxbury voted "To encourage one quarter part of the Militia Minutemen, so cal'd . . . that they hold themselves in Readiness at a Minute's Warning, compleat in Armes and Ammunition. . . ."

The Provincial Congress, after publicizing the resolves that formed the minute men, sent a steady succession of notes to the towns, encouraging the rapid organization and training of the units. In December 1774 the congress sent a letter to all the towns, saying,

> We now think that particular care should be taken by the towns and districts in this colony, that each of the minute men, not already provided therewith, should be immediately equipped with an effective fire arm, bayonet, pouch, knapsack, thirty rounds of cartridges and balls, and that they be disciplined three times a week, and oftener, as opportunity may offer. To encourage these, our worthy countrymen, to obtain the skill of complete soldiers, we recommend it to the towns and districts forthwith to pay their own minute men a reasonable consideration for their services: and in case of a general muster, their further services must be recompensed by the province. An attention to discipline in the militia in general, is, however, by no means to be neglected.

This was followed by another letter containing a resolve of February 15, 1775, "holding up to the people the imminent danger they are in" and recommending that "neither time, pains, nor expense" be spared in putting the minute men and militia in a state of readiness.

A few of the more independent towns were not easily convinced that the minute man concept was the best solution, nor were they anxious to transfer control of their men to the Committee of Safety. These towns did not follow to the letter the recommendations of the Provincial Congress, but adapted them to suit themselves. A few decided to train the soldiers but not to place them under the Committee of Safety. Some did not allow election of the new officers, but rather appointed officers and let the officers select the men, a procedure opposite from that intended. Other towns allowed elections of the officers by the rank and file, but took other measures of control. In general, however, the revival of the minute man concept caught the imagination of the whole province. In a short time the minute men were the pride of their towns, and the cost-conscious citizens of Massachusetts did not overlook the fact that here was an ideal army to fit the situation in the province—an army that had to be supported only when it was actually fighting.

The acceptance of the minute man concept by the towns and by the old militia itself was a great encouragement to the Provincial Congress, which had moved from Concord to the meeting house at Cambridge. In its short existence it had thus far abolished the old militia, created a new military organization, collected a respectable amount of supplies and equipment, and provided a planning staff for the rapid employment of the new force.

At Boston, Gage was ordering additional reinforcements to join him: during the month of October, the 10th and 52nd Regiments arrived from Quebec, along with the 18th and 47th from New York and the two detached companies of the 65th from Newfoundland, bringing that regiment up to strength. Gage had said that four regiments in Massachusetts would be quite sufficient to intimidate the province. Now, with nearly triple that number, he was aware that his control did not extend beyond the port of Boston; the General Court had been dissolved, the Crown-appointed judges had been unable to act, the militia—stripped of reliable Loyalist officers—was now turned against him, and the Provincial Congress governed the colony.

Chapter 8

Winter Preparations

The new spirit in the ranks of the militia was immediately evident. Younger men were elected to replace the old Loyalist colonels and majors; veteran company commanders with experience in the French and Indian War took the places of the high-ranking officers whose loyalty to the Crown had been primary among their military qualifications. With the clean sweep of the militia and the company elections to provide the new officers, there was a spontaneous burst of self-confidence and determination that had been missing in the lackadaisical militia so criticized by Pickering, Samuel Adams, and others in the previous decade. The meetings to choose leaders by open vote provided the men with a sense of involvement and responsibility, and the expansion that occurred with the organization of the minute men created a need for more leaders than ever before.

Many provincial soldiers were drawn by the challenge of building an elite fighting force. The attractiveness of such a force to the provincials was rooted in their feeling of military inferiority to the regular troops—and the Massachusetts men were deeply concerned about this. As part-time soldiers they had long been the butt of jokes among the regular troops, and they knew that they were considered second rate by Gage's men in Boston.

The provincial troops had been looked down on by the regulars since they first operated together. When the Massachusetts men went to the West Indies to serve under Admiral Vernon in the 1740s, they found that in promotions, pay, and military status they were given something less than equal treatment. In the French and Indian War, complaints of this sort punctuate the journals of the provincial troops fighting alongside the regulars, and these injustices created a distaste for service with the armies of the Crown and a general recognition of the disdain they could expect from the regulars.

It is also evident that the militia units went downhill after the end of the fighting in 1758 and that training days became more or less farcical. The men who had suffered through the earlier campaigns could not seem to find the interest or the will to make the home town militias into effective units, and company musters on the common deteriorated into social get-togethers where military training was second to ceremony or entertainment. The influence of the French and Indian War had a strong effect on these training days. After Braddock's defeat and after the success of Rogers and the Rangers (perhaps the two most publicized episodes of that war) it was difficult to make the provincials see the need for parade-ground maneuvers.

But even when the level of training reached its lowest ebb, late in the 1760s, the militia troops still practiced their marksmanship, and handling of weapons remained important. There developed an easy-going familiarity with weapons, something that can be best described as the Rogers influence: care of the weapon and marksmanship received attention, and sham battles (Rogers' favorite training) took place at every muster, but orthodox drill was made a burlesque: one of the common ways to salute an officer, especially the company commander, was to fire a blank charge into the ground near his feet, and if a soldier could catch him by surprise, the salute was that much more effective. This kind of good-humored disregard for parade-ground discipline made the militia look a bit worse than it was, and because they would not drill in the European style it was assumed that they could not amount to much against any well-drilled regular force.

In the fall of 1774 the picnic atmosphere disappeared from troop exercises and the men began to train in earnest. Prefacing a muster roll of sixty-six men of a newly formed company in the town of Methuen is a scrawled note, "Whare Milartray Exercise hath ben much Nelicked We the Subscribers being the first Comptney in Methuen Do Covenent and Engage to from our Sevels in to a Bodey in order To Larn the manual Exercise to be Subegat to Such Officers as Comptney Shall Chuse by Boat in all Constutenel manner accorden To our Chattaers." In this and in dozens of other similar resolutions there is a sense of urgency and determination which was not evident before the upheaval in the militia. These men knew they might soon be facing the regulars on the battlefield, and they did not intend to be scoffed at this time. Would there be time enough to form the militia and minute men under new officers and prepare them to stand against the regulars?

Luckily, the provincials were not starting from scratch. They possessed two important assets which were to be of immeasurable help in the coming months: the minute man concept, which was well understood by all the soldiers, and—what is more important —by the townsfolk throughout the province; and a heavy distribution of combat veterans from the French and Indian War. The province was to make maximum use of both advantages.

In the process of the elections and the establishment of the minute men, the natural leaders tended to move into command positions. There were veterans of the campaigns of Louisburg, Fort Ticonderoga, Lake George, Quebec, Half Moon, and the "Reduction of Canada," men who had served with Shirley and Johnson and Amherst, and soldiers who scouted with Rogers' Rangers. Four company commanders in Sudbury and Framingham, Captains Nixon, Gleason, Eames, and Edgett, had served in the same unit in several campaigns of the past war. Commanding the Groton minute man company was another veteran of Crown Point, Captain Abijah Childs; his brother Abraham, the lieutenant of the company, had served under Amherst in 1759 at Ticonderoga and Crown Point and also later at Montreal and Quebec.

Captain John Wood of Woburn had enlisted at sixteen for the French and Indian War. The enlisting officer at Concord thought him a little young, but he replied, ". . . I think I can fire a bullet into an oak stump as far as any other man." During the expedition, on a midwinter outpost patrol through a snowy wilderness, Wood volunteered to stay behind with a wounded man who had to be left on the trail. When hostile Indians tracked him down, he gave the Indians his supply of rum and somehow got them to aid the wounded man enough so that he could travel.

Men with that kind of experience were scattered through the

ranks of the new army; possibly more than one-third of the provincials had seen extended service before, and these men were drawn to the minute man companies.

There were training problems to overcome in 1774, but the minute men and militia were in many ways at least as well off as Gage's troops. Quite a few provincial soldiers had fired more rounds in the service of the Crown than had the supposedly well-drilled and battle-experienced regulars in Boston. The total time that the provincial junior leaders had spent as soldiers was short —only two or three years—but it was all served in active campaigns.

On the other hand many of the regular regiments under Gage, though they possessed past records of distinguished service, had not seen action for years prior to 1775. Most of the soldiers and a number of the officers had never been in combat. The 4th Regiment (King's Own) was in garrison in the West Indies during the French and Indian War, and in England and Scotland until 1774, when it was sent to America. The 5th Regiment (Northumberland Fusiliers) had an excellent combat record in France and Germany from 1758 to 1763, but then spent ten years in Ireland before coming to North America. The 10th Regiment was stationed in Ireland during the Seven Years' War and had garrisoned Gibraltar for nineteen years before that. It had not been in action since 1730. The 18th Regiment (Royal Irish) was in England from 1755 to 1767 and did not participate in the Seven Years' War; in fact, it was "not engaged in any particularly important operations" from 1715 until April 19, 1775. The 23rd Regiment (Royal Welch Fusiliers) were the heroes of Minden, where they hurled back "the line of French cavaliers, gay in splendid uniforms," but that was fifteen years before Lexington. The 38th had served an unprecedented sixty years in the same place—the West Indies—before going to Boston by way of England. The 52nd had just been formed, as had the 59th, and this was their first service. The 64th had been in the West Indies (as had the 65th) and in Ireland. Only the 43rd had fought at Louisburg, Quebec, and Montreal in the French and Indian War. Ezra Stiles quoted in his diary a Bostonian who remarked, about the time of the Powder Alarm, that "General Gage dare not venture his troops, the most of which are newly raised and never in action."

In addition to their marches into the countryside and their guard duty and work on the fortifications, the regulars tried to do some firing to improve marksmanship. Musket practice was sporadic during the early fall but as the months wore on the regulars fired much more frequently at their "marks," which often were targets about the size of a man, set up on floats in the Charles River at the foot of the common. The soldiers formed in a file and stepped forward, one by one, to fire a single round at the mark. Each man would then reload and await his turn. A normal day's firing would allow for six rounds per man, and two soldiers were detailed daily from each regiment to make musket cartridges (a paper or cloth wrapping containing the powder and ball) to replace those fired by the regiment. One of the regulations in effect at the time required "no recruit to be dismissed from the drill, till he is so expert with his firelock, as to load and fire fifteen times in three minutes and three quarters." Since the soldiers were required to carry only thirty-six rounds, this rate of fire seems quite high. Volley fire was practiced in a number of different exercises, but normally with unloaded weapons.

It is a little-known fact that Gage, with his experience of earlier years, was also making sure that his light infantry companies (units, one from each regiment, used to protect the flanks on the march) were trained in Indian-style bush fighting. In this training the companies would disperse as skirmishers along the line of march of the regiment and fire blank powder loads at a simulated enemy closing in on the column. The regulars would then reload their weapons, Indian style, "while lying on their bellies." Some of the light infantry soldiers, according to at least one source, were equipped with powder horns, probably to keep their powder dry while the soldiers moved cross country on the flanks. Such training was in progress at least a month before the April 19 battle, indicating once again Gage's long-standing interest in light infantry bush fighting and his recognition of the need for such tactics in North America.

The regulars were armed with the famous old Brown Bess musket, as were the provincials wherever and whenever they could get their hands on one—which was often. At that time the Bess had already been in the service of the Crown for over fifty years, and hundreds of them had drifted into the colony during the earlier wars, to say nothing of those that were bought or stolen from the regulars just prior to the start of the war. There were other weapons in the provincial companies, muskets made by local gunsmiths. These, however, were modeled on the

Bess, and though sometimes of slightly smaller caliber, were very much the same musket.

The Brown Bess was a smoothbore flintlock of .75 caliber, muzzle-loaded and firing a round ball. It was rugged and dependable but not accurate even by the standards of that day. A British officer, Major George Hanger, who served in the Revolution and was an authority on marksmanship, said of the weapon, "A soldier's musket, if not exceedingly ill-bored (as many of them are), will strike the figure of a man at 80 yards; it may even at 100, but a soldier must be very unfortunate who shall be wounded by a common musket at 150 yards, provided his antagonist aims at him; and as to firing at a man at 200 yards with a common musket, you may just as well fire at the moon and have the same hopes of hitting your object. I do maintain and will prove, whenever called on, that no man was ever killed at 200 yards, by a common soldier's musket, by the person who aimed at him."

A contemporary gun expert field-tested a Brown Bess of the Revolutionary period, attempting to duplicate as closely as possible the conditions of 1775, and commented as follows:

> Aiming as carefully as I could, I fired 10 shots—and only two hit the cardboard. To give the gun at least a fighting chance, I closed the range to 50 yards and fired 10 more rounds. Again, only two struck the silhouette. A friend, spotting my shots with binoculars, said that the other balls had kicked up mud in the backstop, close to the target.

> In accounting for this poor showing, it is only fair to mention that the fault was as much the ammunition's as the gun's. I had duplicated the ammo that was used in the 1770's, and this meant that the balls were undersized and wobbled from side to side in the bore. Under the combat conditions of the times, a well-handled Brown Bess probably would have hit a man-sized target with only one shot out of 10 at 100 yards, though it was more effective against advancing battle ranks.

The Brown Bess weighs about ten pounds, has a good balance, and compares roughly in range and general handling to a twelve-gauge shotgun. It has a front but no rear sight, and aiming is uncomplicated, if inaccurate. The barrel is normally from thirty-nine to forty-six inches, and with its black powder charge the recoil is light. The musket makes plenty of smoke, of course, and the flintlock action, in which the spark from the flint ignites the powder in the pan which sets off the main charge, thus providing two explosions in rapid succession for each round fired, is no real help to proper aiming. There was no adjusting of sights; "Kentucky windage" was the rule. It goes almost without saying that the strike of a caliber .75 soft lead ball is a very solid impact, and this characteristic, combined with the rapid-fire potential of the Brown Bess and the durability of this musket, made it an excellent general purpose weapon for both sides.

It is often said that the British had an advantage, possessing bayonets while the provincials had none. This was not the case. Returns for the militia and minute men on April 14 show a total of 21,549 muskets and 10,108 bayonets, or a bayonet for every two soldiers. Many of the minute man companies received bayonets that had been taken from the militia to make sure that every minute man was equipped with one (the Acton, Lincoln, and Andover companies are examples). Many of the Massachusetts soldiers also carried hatchets, a weapon they copied from their old enemies and one they had used in the French and Indian War.

While the British troops were quite heavily committed to work details involved with constructing housing and shops for the regiments and fortifying key places within the city, the provincials were finding time on evenings and weekends to practice military drill and marksmanship; in many cases provincial companies received throughout the winter nearly as much individual training as did their counterparts in Boston. A minute man from Framingham wrote, "I have spent many an evening, with a number of my near neighbors, going through the exercise on the barn floor, with my mittens on." Many of the towns required their minute men to train twice a week at the "place of parade" (usually the common, in the center of town). At Marblehead by October the companies turned out "three or four times a week, where Col. Lee as well as the clergymen there are not ashamed to be taught the manual exercise, in particular." In Reading, Captain Bancroft's men met to practice even in the worst weather, sometimes going through the manual of arms in their commander's kitchen.

As with the weapons, the training on both sides was very much the same. The regulars drilled under the guidance of the Crown manual of 1764, which was also adopted as the source of tactics by the Provincial Congress in October, replacing the somewhat simpler Norfolk Exercise, or Draper's Plan, which had been in use in the loyal militia (though not much attention was paid to it). The "exercise" most often mentioned is a drill for platoon-size units, executed in fifty consecutive movements, each with a separate order, done either with loaded weapons or, more often, with simulated firing. In this exercise the platoon forms three ranks, one behind the other, the front rank kneeling and the other two standing. Firing is in volleys by rank, each rank reloading rapidly and again firing in turn until ordered to cease. Like all close order drill in all armies, it saw little use in actual combat; but again as in all armies it served a good purpose: it taught precision, discipline, teamwork, and mutual confidence— and perhaps most important of all, it allowed the junior leaders to accustom themselves to giving orders. Neither side used the firing movements on the 19th of April, although the regulars executed a number of "drill" maneuvers in the course of the march, some poorly and some well. But during the winter such exercises were the core of training.

While the provincials trained, they continued to build up their stockpiles of military supplies. Worcester and Concord were key towns in the effort to bring together supplies for the minute men and militia. Wagons from all over the province rolled toward these depots with food, powder, lead, cannon, and other supplies, but the stockpiling was not completed before the threat of a British march stopped the operation. In all the towns, the minute men tried to provide for themselves as much as possible. Framingham required its minute men to have a musket, bayonet, cartridge box, and thirty-six rounds. Lincoln voted to "Provide for those persons, who have enlisted as minute-men, each one a bayonet, belt, cartridge-box, steel rammer, gun-stock, and knapsack; and that they attend military exercises 4 hours in a day twice a week." Watertown voted to "mount & equip two pieces of cannon now lodged in the town," and on the day the money was allotted for the gun carriages, the town meeting resolved to "draw out one quarter of the militia company as minute men," and later allowed one shilling for each meeting "to pay for fifing." The units made up in spirit for what they lacked in equipment—the Acton, Bedford, Concord, Lexington and Lincoln companies had fifers, as did many of the others.

As the winter wore on, the new strength of the minute men met with mixed reactions in the province. The Tory element was still powerful enough to voice a loud protest, but the complaints against this new military force provoked a strong reply from the expanding Whig faction. *Rivington's Gazette* (January 26, 1775) noted with approval that "in some counties the minute men are dismissed," but continued, "yet the madmen of Marblehead are preparing for an early campaign against his Majesty's troops, without waiting for the result of the Congress's measure in England." This comment touched off a fiery reply from the all-Whig *Massachusetts Spy* (February 16, 1775), which quoted the *Gazette* and called it "as gross a slander as it is a falshood. The minute men in every county are indeed diligently preparing and qualifying themselves to defend their lives and properties when attacked. But they are to annoy no body, if no body annoys them. . . ."

The Committee of Safety hoped to be able to train the minute men in regimental-size maneuvers, but exercises on a large scale were difficult to arrange, and pay for the troops was a problem. A few field days were held (on Sunday, March 13, the militia and the minute man regiment from the Concord area both mustered on Punkatasset Hill in that town) but the fighting began before most units were well enough prepared for such musters.

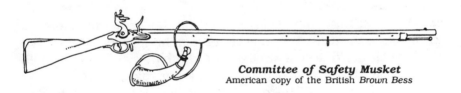

Committee of Safety Musket
American copy of the British *Brown Bess*

Chapter 9

Marches

After dark on Thursday, the 8th of September, 1774, a detachment of Gage's troops marched down to the foot of Boston common and quietly embarked in the longboats that had been lowered from the men-of-war and transports. The regulars, fully armed and equipped and ready for a fight, sat silent in the boats, their eyes fixed on the dark shoreline of Charlestown as the sailors rowed them across the narrow strip of water. When the boats nosed up against the wharves on the far side, the soldiers scrambled out, formed up quickly in marching order, and moved off through the deserted streets toward a battery of cannon sited at water level and aimed down the harbor, part of the defense system of the town of Boston. These guns were intended to provide a cross-fire at the mouth of the Charles, operating in coordination with a similar battery on the Boston side.

Only a few hours earlier Gage had received intelligence that the guns positioned there were in danger of being stolen away by the provincials, who up to this time were still theoretically responsible for manning the battery. He sent an officer across to investigate, and in the meantime ordered a regiment to prepare to march, and sent word to have the longboats brought around. From the start, the expedition proceeded right on schedule and without a hitch. The cooperation of the fleet was excellent, and the fast-marching troops were at the gun positions of the Charlestown battery in a remarkably short time. The ferrying operation was the second use of the longboats of the fleet in this manner; a raid on the powderhouse at Cambridge a week earlier had been the first.

When the troops arrived at the battery they broke off into squads as planned, with orders to take possession of guns, powder, and shot. At the embrasures, however, they discovered that the cannon and ammunition had disappeared without a trace. Everything except the fort itself was gone.

The provincials, alerted by the presence of an officer inspecting the works, had sent out an emergency call to all the neighboring towns asking for every available heavy wagon to carry away the guns and supplies. Scores of log-hauling wagons rolled down the dark roads into Charlestown and labored back out toward Salem and Concord weighted down with the dismantled cannon and with shot, and in a matter of hours there was nothing left in the battery but the silent walls to greet the British column. According to a letter written at the time, the people of Boston felt "a foot higher on the occasion." The provincials had been caught by surprise when the column of regulars moved out to seize the powder at Quarry Hill, but never after that would Gage be able to steal a march on them. The system of communicating the alarm through riders and signals was now working with amazing efficiency, and it was augmented by scores of self-appointed observers tagging on the heels of the regulars at every move they made. With the port closed, its population idle, and its commercial life at a standstill, every roll of British drums commanded not only a military response but also a whirlwind of activity among the townsfolk.

The events of late August had their effect on Gage, and he worked rapidly to turn Boston into a fortress town that he could use as his base of operation. On the 3rd of September he had moved four large field pieces from the common to the entrance to the town over "the Neck" on the Roxbury side, the only land approach to Boston. After the loss of the cannon of the Charlestown battery he moved the twenty-gun frigate *Lively* into the ferry-way between Boston and Charlestown. On the 15th of September he ordered all cannon in the North Battery spiked, fearing they might be stolen also. As additional reinforcement he ordered to Boston a company of Royal Artillery stationed at New York (it arrived on the 23rd of October). When *Somerset*, *Asia*, and *Boyne*, the three big men-of-war of the North American Squadron under Admiral Graves, arrived a few weeks later with a combined firepower of 196 guns, he placed them at anchor "within musket shot" of the town.

A few days later, even though Gage had doubled the guard, it was discovered that four cannon were missing from their place of storage in a gun house near the common. They, too, had been spirited away by the provincials. And these were not the old guns of the sea forts, but brass cannon especially made for field use.

It is not hard to understand Gage's feelings at the loss of these cannon. His second-in-command, General Haldimand, had been keeping a notebook of facts and figures, and among his entries was the estimate that New England could at that moment furnish 30,000 men for field duty without making a harmful dent in the work force needed for the farms. With such statistics in mind, Gage was convinced that his primary duty, at least for that moment, was to keep the provincial town militias from organizing into an army. The specific point his attention fastened on was the rebel capability to employ artillery. He felt that he would have to prevent the organization of the provincial army by making a series of bold and rapid sallies from the fortified town into the countryside whenever a target presented itself. And these targets, it will be seen, tended to be rebel cannon.

There were other reasons, Gage knew, for marching the troops out of Boston as often as possible, even when there was no target to strike. The men were stagnating in their makeshift billets on the common and in requisitioned old warehouses down along the docks. They needed the training, the exercise, and above all the relief from the destructive boredom which was all that a hostile town offered them. Also, the marching columns would be a show of force to intimidate the provincials and keep them off balance and on the defensive. The officers and men would gain an acquaintance with the roads and terrain of the neighboring towns that was certain to be valuable later. And perhaps most important, the practice marches would accustom the provincials to the routine of seeing large bodies of troops in the countryside and would relax their system of alerts and warnings, thus making it easier to mount surprise attacks against them.

A false alarm that took place on Sunday, September 18, ten days after the abortive Charlestown raid, is a good indication of the state of tension existing in the colony. The British soldiers and even the officers, to their later regret, looked on the alarm of that day as evidence of the buffoonery characteristic of provincial military operations; the citizens themselves saw the whole day quite differently.

It all began early Sunday morning when the men of the 38th Regiment, in full equipment and carrying their weapons, marched down the common toward the embarkation area, causing immediate consternation in the ever-watchful town. The provincial dispatch riders dashed off in every direction to warn the neighboring towns, and these towns in turn carried the alarm farther on, breaking up morning religious services and causing minute man companies to form and march in the direction of Boston.

The 38th Regiment actually intended no march at all; its normal weekly inspection day was Monday, but because the men of the regiment had been scheduled to work on the fortifications that day, they marched on Sunday to the inspection site at the edge of the common, meanwhile observing the panic of the townspeople with not a little humor.

Out in the countryside the distorted reports carried the word that the rapid mobilization of the minute men had caused the British to cancel their intended march and settle for an inspection. Ezra Stiles recorded the event in his diary as a victory for the province: "On Lordsday before last," he wrote, "a body of the troops were in motion equipt on the common for embarkation on several boats to go up to Watertown to take some brass and iron cannon which the people had removed thither from Boston— but dispatches were sent out & the alarm convened a body at Watertown—the Governor desisted & the troops did not march— & the Tories say they had no such intention. The General is afraid that we shall come down to Dorchester neck & thence bombard the Fort or Castle on Castle Isld. half a mile offshore." To many of the provincials, this incident proved that a determined stand by the minute men would dissuade the regulars from raiding the countryside, and the concept of rapid assembly along the line of march of the regulars became more and more important.

Now Gage's battle-equipped troops began to make short marches out of Boston on a more or less regular schedule, over routes which crossed the Muddy River into Brookline and ran on to Newton, Dedham, or Milton. The columns nearly always returned by a different road.

During October regiments arrived from Quebec, Halifax, and

New York, bringing Gage's strength in Boston up to three brigades—nearly 3,000 men—supported at sea by the North American Squadron. The troops were by no means well received in the town. The Boston Massacre was still a fresh memory, and placing the port out of bounds to all shipping had caused an oppressive unemployment. For many citizens the red uniform was a symbol of the weight of unsympathetic and coercive rule, and the troops were greeted with epithets of which some of the more mild were Lobster Scoundrel, Red Herring, and Bloody Back. Gage himself came under attack from the Whig press, where editorials and open letters made no attempt at cordiality. A letter by "Junius Americanus" republished in the *Massachusetts Spy* of October 13 speaks directly to Gage: "You are so far from possessing any extraordinary merit, that you have defeated the designs of your friends, who attempted to supply your want of the qualities of a governor, and a general, by ascribing to you the simple virtues of a good man. You have not been condemned by a transitory faction, but by the permanent unbiassed suffrages of every freeman in America. By assuming to your self therefore, these credentials of merit, which justice and wisdom derive from calumny, you commit a more criminal act of forgery, than ever was expiated at Tyburn."

Gage's continued sympathetic and mild-mannered rule of the city in the face of such insults was disheartening to his men, including the officers. He became more and more unpopular with his troops, who felt that he was allowing them to be harassed and oppressed by the people of Boston. The soldiers were convinced that the high death rate (over 100 troops and dependents during the winter of '74-'75) resulted from the poor quarters in which they were forced to live, and they found dozens of other complaints for which they blamed their commander. Several officers were put under arrest that winter: Lieutenant Colonel Walcott, Captain Gore, Lieutenant Hawkshaw, and Ensigns Patrick, Murray, Butler, Raymond, and Balaguire. Four of the eight were directly involved in affrays with townspeople; the others fought among themselves, probably exasperated by the difficulties of garrison life in Boston. A number of officers were responsible for acts of indiscipline—slashing John Hancock's fence, breaking windows in the Providence Stage, disturbing citizens, "rioting" in taverns. A local man caught trying to buy weapons from the soldiers was tarred and feathered, apparently with the approval of the officers of the 47th Regiment, much to

Gage's vexation. The general's response to minor delinquencies by the troops was to order more and more marches, and to some extent these sallies into the open air of the countryside probably were helpful in keeping things from getting worse. The weather all that winter remained extremely mild, so much so that it was the subject of comment in many of the diaries kept at that time. Gage often sent two or three regiments out of town on the same day. They visited the towns of Cambridge, Dedham, Roxbury, Dorchester, and others farther out, with marches averaging about fifteen miles, round trip. Major Pitcairn, commanding the battalion of marines assigned to Admiral Grave's squadron, was glad to get his troops out for some much-needed exercise. The marines had been held aboard ship for weeks after their arrival in Boston, apparently because the admiral was not anxious to give them over to land duty and thus risk losing control of them; after a direct order from Gage, they were finally landed. According to his letters, Pitcairn marched them hard and often, and this toughening-up helped save them from destruction on the return from Concord and Lexington, where as rear guard they received the heaviest casualties of the day. On these practice marches Pitcairn was rarely out of sight of Breed's Hill, on whose slope he was soon to receive a fatal wound.

In December Gage lost more artillery when the Rhode Island assembly removed the guns from Fort George at Newport, and New Hampshire seized the cannon at Fort William and Mary in Portsmouth Harbor. The Rhode Islanders also formed a committee along the lines of the Massachusetts Committee of Safety, distributed arms to all the militia, and ordered them to be ready to march at a minute's warning. The loss of cannon was substantial—the list at Fort George alone included forty-four guns ranging from twenty-four-pounders down to six-pounders.

Late in January 1775, Gage received a letter from the town of Marshfield, on the coast a few miles south of Boston, requesting him to send troops to the town to protect the peace. This was a pleasant surprise, to say the least, and Gage responded immediately with a provisional company of 110 men, commanded by Captain Nigel Balfour of the 4th Regiment. Balfour put his men aboard two armed schooners, *Diana* and *Britannia*, and sailed down to occupy the town.

When he arrived off Marshfield the local minute men made a feeble attempt to rally against him, but to the amusement of the troops and the Loyalists, only twelve men responded to the alarm, and these quickly dispersed when the regulars marched into the town square. There was no firing, and Captain Balfour quartered his men in the town and placed himself at the disposal of the local authorities, ready to quell any disturbance.

The troops remained in Marshfield and were well treated there, although an attack against them immediately on the outbreak of hostilities perhaps shows more accurately the feeling of the provincials in and around Marshfield. Until that time the provincials confined themselves to venting their frustration in the newspapers; a letter to the editor of the *Massachusetts Spy*, printed on March 2, complains that "Of all the numberless farces, that have been acted by the British troops . . . the removal of a few soldiers from Boston to Marshfield is the most completely ridiculous. . . . We are not, however, to be diverted, by such flimsy devices, from our determined purpose of acting *only* on the defensive: should a wanton attack make it necessary for us to change this mode of action, we are resolved not to sit still, and be butchered without resistance; at least, this is the resolution of one Minute Man."

As the marches out into the countryside grew longer and longer, Gage now began to think of a new show of force, the march of a brigade in the direction of Worcester, forty-eight miles away. (No doubt he was still bothered by the results of his failure to march there at the time of the county conventions.) He therefore sent two officers, Captain John Brown and Ensign John DeBerniere, to survey the route of march. "You will go through the counties of Suffolk and Worcester," he wrote, "taking a sketch of the country as you pass; it is not expected you should make out regular plans and surveys, but mark out the roads and distances from town to town, as also the situation and nature of the country; all passes must be particularly laid down, noticing the length and breadth of them, the entrance in and going out of them, and whether to be avoided by taking other routes." The orders also required a careful reconnaissance of river crossings, commanding hills, roads parallel to the route of march, camp sites, and defensible positions (especially in towns), and the capability of the land to supply forage and provisions.

Brown and DeBerniere were successful, at least to the extent of proving that the march of a brigade to Worcester might well be a disaster. The route was full of good ambush sites, resentment in the countryside boiled against the British, and the people assembled rapidly; only good luck and a heavy, blustery snowstorm saved these two astoundingly naive officers from capture by various groups of provincials. DeBerniere's simple-minded, almost slapstick account of the trip is one of the truly amusing stories of the period.

During the last weeks before the opening of the war Gage's regiments continued to march out into the countryside. The first time that a complete brigade left Boston was March 30, 1775, when Percy took his command, about 1,200 strong, to Jamaica Plain, four or five miles south of Boston. They marched at six in the morning out across Boston Neck in full battle gear with colors flying: 315 men of the 4th (King's Own), 314 of the 23rd (Royal Welch), 296 of the 47th, and 336 Marines.

The size of the column spread consternation through the neighboring towns as alarm riders carried the news on all roads leading away from Boston; at first it was assumed that the march would be in the direction of Concord, where the Provincial Congress was in session, and the minute men tore up the bridge over the Charles at Cambridge to block this route. On nearing the bridge, however, Percy continued along the south side of the river and did not attempt to cross. There was a bridge three miles farther upriver, at Watertown, and when the column came near it the regulars could see that it was manned by a group of provincials with two cannon. Lieutenant Barker, who was along on the march, was disdainful. "At Watertown, about nine miles off," he wrote, "they got 2 pieces of cannon to the bridge and loaded 'em but nobody would stay to fire them."

Percy marched around to Jamaica Plain and turned back toward Boston. At no point was he opposed by the provincials, although at several places along his route they assembled to observe him from a distance, and he made no attempt to molest any of them. They interpreted Percy's turning away from both the Cambridge and Watertown bridges as a sign that the British could be deterred if the minute men and militia were resolute enough to make a defensive stand. Dr. Warren wrote, "Great numbers, completely armed, collected in the neighboring towns; and it is the opinion of many, that had they marched eight or ten miles, and attempted to destroy any magazines, or abuse the people, not a man of them would have returned to Boston." At possible ambush sites along the route Percy had his men knock down the stone walls to keep them from being used as cover for snipers. This accomplished little beyond exercising the troops and enraging the local farmers, who complained loudly of the "wanton destruction of private property." Percy's outing was the last march before the opening of the war.

A winter of marching had some good results for Gage. He exercised his troops and probably cut down the number of incidents between them and the people of the city; his officers became more familiar with the lay of the land; his show of force influenced the people of at least one town, Marshfield. But there was much that he did not accomplish.

Although he felt that the marches proved he could move at will through the countryside, he also knew that he dared not stray as far as Worcester; moreover, he did not understand that the provincials had an entirely opposite interpretation of these marches: they believed that their own quick responses often had foiled Gage, as at Charlestown, or had forced him to curtail his marches, as in the case of the Sunday inspection on Boston common. The minute men, even though they were called out several times, did not become tired of the game; on the contrary, their self-confidence climbed when they saw the regulars, time after time, appear to start for Cambridge or some other town, only to turn back after a few miles. It gave them the illusion that they had intimidated the King's troops or that Gage would not pit his soldiers against them. With all the alarms, marches, and countermarches, it might be said that Gage trained the minute men almost as well as he trained his own troops throughout that last winter.

Chapter **10**

The Salem Affair

Near the end of February, 1775, General Gage's attention was drawn once again to the port of Salem, fifteen miles up the North Shore from Boston. This town had been a thorn in Gage's side from the time of his arrival. When Gage closed Boston to all shipping, Salem gave free dock space to Boston merchants and was one of the first towns to respond with food and other aid for the bottled-up Boston citizens. As soon as Gage published the edict forbidding town meetings except by permission of the governor, Salem went ahead and held a town meeting, and when Gage responded by sending the 23rd Regiment (Royal Welch Fusiliers) to break up the gathering, the troops were summarily locked out of the town hall by the delegates, who sat inside and carried on with their extra-legal proceedings. About the only event occasioned by the sending of the regulars was a message from nearby Marblehead announcing that the soldiers of that town were "ready to come in at a minute's warning, sufficiently provided to lend assistance." When Gage pulled the regiment back to Boston a few days later, the provincials counted it another victory, stressed the growing power of the towns, and were themselves convinced that when facing the regulars, a little stubbornness would go a long way. At the meeting, incidentally, Salem went ahead to elect representatives to the Provincial Congress.

That was in August 1774. Six months later, Gage was faced
with the unsavory prospect of sending a regiment back into
Salem again, and this time the situation was more serious. The
British commander received word that the rebels had gathered
about twenty cannon at a Salem forge, where they were building
carriages for these guns (Gage's informer may have been Benjamin Church, or possibly the Salem Tory Colonel Sargent—
several persons have been accused of passing the word on to the
general). Gage's reaction, as might be predicted, was immediate.
Since there was a good possibility that these were the guns
recently spirited away from the artillery train of the old Boston
militia, Gage felt he could not leave such weapons in the hands
of the provincials. He sent for Lieutenant Colonel Alexander
Leslie, commander of the 64th Regiment (North Staffordshire)
stationed at Castle William in Boston Harbor.

Colonel Leslie knew Salem well. His regiment had been in
Boston for two and a half years, and two of his companies had
spent most of the past year guarding the Hooper House at Danvers, just a few miles from Salem Harbor, while Governor Gage
lived there during a sojourn out of Boston (a gesture that was
supposed to show the King's dissatisfaction with the Bostonians).

Gage ordered Leslie to sail his men by night up to a landing
point close to Salem, then disembark and march to seize the
cannon. The point chosen to land the troops was Homan's Cove,
near the North River bridge. Troops landed at this cove could
skirt the edge of the town of Marblehead and move quickly into
Salem. Gage hoped also that a landing at that spot would confuse the provincials as to the intentions of the regulars.

It was not difficult for the 64th to file out of Castle William
and slip away unnoticed from their garrison. After dark on
Saturday, February 25, one of the transports eased up to the
wharf and took on company after company, 240 men in all, until
only a small detachment remained to look after the fort. At
midnight the transport stood out of the harbor and turned north
to Marblehead, arriving at nine o'clock Sunday morning. In
addition to their regular equipment the troops were carrying
lanterns, hatchets, pickaxes, spades, hand-spikes, and several
coils of rope.

Leslie kept the men hidden below deck and ordered the captain to lay off the cove until two o'clock, when he was sure that
most of the people of Marblehead would be back from their noon
meal and once again in church, participating in the usual day-

long Sunday services. He hoped to march past Marblehead and out on the road to Salem without attracting attention, and (with a little luck) to arrive at the forge and seize the weapons before the rebels figured out what he was up to.

But Leslie did not have that much luck. He thought that the appearance of a transport off Marblehead Neck would arouse little attention. While this might have been true of Boston, now crowded with more than twenty ships of the North American Squadron, Marblehead was a small place, and Leslie actually caused as much of a stir as he would if he happened to sail in there today. Everyone in town, it seems, kept his eye on the transport riding at anchor off the cove, and when Leslie put in to dock, he did not lack an audience. As his soldiers assembled on the road leading out of the neck, his troops were carefully counted by the Marblehead residents. But Leslie moved quickly and was on the road to Salem, his fifers playing *Yankee Doodle*, before anyone could get a message off to that town. He put out no scouts and no flankers—he just marched as fast as he could for the forge, along the shortest route.

The people at Marblehead recovered quickly, and dispatched several messengers to warn Salem. One of these was a local landowner, John Pederick, formerly a major in the 5th Regiment of the old loyal Essex militia, who had known Leslie at military meetings in Boston. Pederick had recently decided that the rebel cause was his own. Now he saddled his horse and galloped toward Salem—down the same road Leslie had taken. He caught sight of the redcoat column in a bad spot. There was no way to get around the troops except to beat through the fields and woods on the shoreward side of the road, and that would eat up precious time. He decided to gamble that his recent ouster from the 5th Regiment would make him a friend of Government in Leslie's eyes; he reined his horse to a nonchalant walk and slowly overtook the marching column.

It worked. The soldiers were suspicious of him, but after he stopped to chat for a moment with Leslie they stepped aside and let him pass on ahead. He nodded cordially and thanked them, and as soon as he was out of sight of the column he spurred on to Salem, to the house of Captain David Mason.

Mason lived near the forge, which was just over the bridge at North River. He was a self-taught armorer, a man of good mechanical ability who had served as a lieutenant of artillery on the Canada campaign of 1756 and as a battery commander at Fort

William Henry in 1757, where it was said he fired the last ball at the oncoming French and Indians in the fall of that fort. He was later to be a major of artillery in Washington's army. At this time he had arranged to purchase seventeen cannon from the shipowner, Colonel Derby, old iron twelve-pounders captured from the French at Nova Scotia and later used by Derby to arm his merchant ships in the West Indies trade. The guns were being fitted with carriages, and Mason's wife and daughters were busy sewing hundreds of flannel powder bags for use with them.

Mason ran into the meetinghouse next door and startled the congregation with the news that the British were on the way. His words sent men running in all directions, some to the forge, others for teams to haul the cannon, still others to spread the alert to the rest of the town and on to Danvers, Lynn, and Beverly. Half a dozen men set out for the South Mills bridge, between the town and the oncoming British column, and tore up some of the planking to stall the regulars for a few minutes.

The ranking militia leader in Salem, Colonel Timothy Pickering, heard the news of the approach of the troops and tried to muster the Salem companies of his regiment, but there was too little time. He gathered the men at hand—about twenty or thirty, and headed for the bridge over the North River, the single approach to the town from the direction of Marblehead.

Pickering was one of the few officers who had managed to keep his place during the reorganization of September, 1774. He was commissioned a Lieutenant in Salem's 4th Company, 1st Regiment, Essex militia, by Governor Barnard in 1766, and became captain of the same company three years later. A Harvard man, Pickering was intelligent and ambitious, and he had become well known for his articles in the local press, usually criticisms of poor training in the militia (although he was careful to praise his own company). Pickering acquired a reputation as a tactician and was looked to for advice by local military men. Just two weeks before Leslie's march Pickering had been elected colonel of the new 1st Regiment, replacing his old commander, Loyalist Colonel William Brown.

Pickering was a moderate Whig who felt that there was no need to break with England. "It is my firm belief," he said, "that the king has not, in any part of his dominions, subjects more loyal than the inhabitants of the British Colonies." He thought the letter circulated by the Boston Committee of Correspondence "inflammatory" and the non-consumption agreements both illegal and unprofitable. He wanted to get rid of the Tory elements in government but not the government itself, and he felt that a war would plunge the colonies into "irretrievable ruin." Pickering also knew Leslie through his military connections, and admired him as a conscientious soldier. Even after this affair, Pickering when writing his account said he regretted that an officer of Leslie's character and ability had been forced into such an awkward situation by Gage's orders.

When Pickering arrived at the North River bridge he found about twenty men hard at work. At that time light shipping passed up and down the river on the tides, and the bridge could be drawn up to let ships by. The mechanism for raising and lowering the bridge was on the north side, the far side for Leslie, and the forge was only about a hundred yards or so beyond the bridge. A dozen men were there at the forge, working feverishly to get the heavy guns out of sight. Men struggled to back teams of horses and load the timber-hauling wagons with the old cannon; others rolled the new gun-carriages down the road toward Danvers. With the British drawing close it became obvious that there would not be enough time to carry away all the cannon, so the men rolled the remaining ones into a field and covered them with hay and leaves. This did not provide much in the way of concealment; a thorough search certainly would turn up the guns. The only thing left to do was prevent the British from making the search.

The men ran down to the drawbridge and raised it, cutting off Leslie on the opposite side.

Leslie had been slowed down at the South Mills bridge where he had to replace some planks to file his men across; nevertheless he marched quickly into town, sent a company in the direction of Long Wharf, and marched on toward the forge. Along the short distance from the town square to the bridge, Leslie managed to pick up several advisors with various points of view, all anxious to explain to him what he should do next. Apparently by previous arrangement, the Salem Loyalist John Sargent joined Leslie as a guide at this point and led him in the direction of the forge. Captain John Felt, a local shipowner who was interested in keeping the peace, got in step with Leslie and remained at his side up to the bridge.

There the troops halted, since the provincials had drawn the bridge up and there was no way to pass. Leslie walked to the head of the column where he was confronted by an angry group

of Salem men, now about forty or fifty of them, who were determined that he should not cross.   Some men climbed up and
perched on top of the upraised bridge on the opposite side and
shouted such insults as, "Soldiers, red jackets, lobster coats,
cowards—damnation to your government!"   It was a cold day,
and apparently some of the regulars, standing around in the wind
after their fast five-mile march, began to shiver.   One provincial
yelled across, "I should think you were all fiddlers, you shake
so!"

From this point on, the story of Leslie's march really becomes
two very different tales.   First, there is the version related by
Colonel Leslie to General Gage in his report, publicized by the
Tory press and believed by those sympathetic to the Crown.   In
this arrangement of the details, Leslie warned the rebels that
their taunts might provoke reprisals, but the rebels merely became louder, insulting the troops and daring them to fire.   There
were only twenty or thirty provincials at the bridge, all unarmed,
and Leslie had no intention of firing on them.   In the first place,
there was no assurance that killing some few of them would
materially assist him in getting across the river.   But he was
determined to assert his right to cross the bridge, and he had
orders to search the forge.   He continued to discuss this matter
with the local provincial leaders until at length he convinced
them of the error of their obstinacy and they lowered the bridge
to let him pass.   On the opposite side he found no cannon.   General Gage later wrote in his report home to London that the mission went entirely according to plan.   "The circumstances of the
eight field pieces at Salem," wrote Gage, "led us into a mistake,
for supposing them to be brass guns brought in from Holland or
some of the foreign islands, which report had also given to sus-
pect; a detachment of 200 men under Lt. Colonel Leslie was sent
privately off by water to seize them; the places they were said
to be concealed in were strictly searched, but no Artillery could
be found.   And we have since discovered that there had been
only some old ship guns which had been carried away from Salem
some time ago.   The people assembled in great numbers with
threats and abuse, but the Colonel pursued his orders, and returned to Marblehead where he had first disembarked."

Other British writers were equally convinced that all had gone
according to plan at Salem, and that the rebels had been dealt
another blow.   One of the most interesting comments is found in
a letter written by Major John Pitcairn, the officer who later

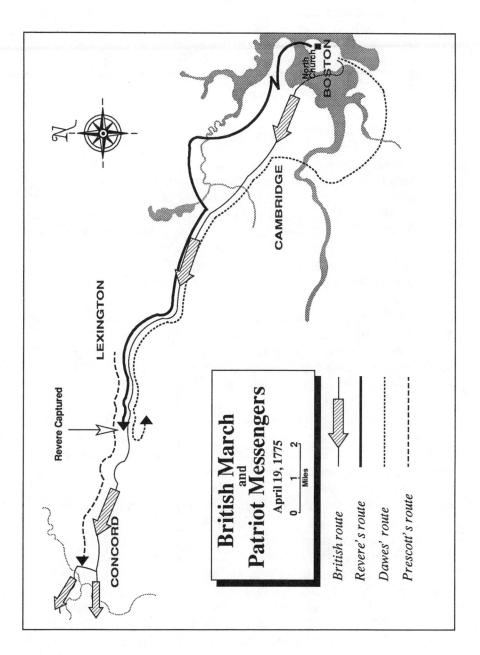

British March
and
Patriot Messengers
April 19, 1775

0   1   2
Miles

British route
Revere's route
Dawes' route
Prescott's route

was to lead the regular light infantry in the march to Lexington and Concord:

> The General had intelligence that there was at Salem some brass field pieces.   He sent Colonel Leslie with four companies of the 64th in a transport to Marblehead.   The Colonel landed, and marched with great expedition to Salem: the people beat their drums, rung their alarm bells; but the Colonel saw none in arms but five, and those took care to get out of the way as fast as they could.   The people behaved as I suppose they will ever do, made a great noise when there is nobody to oppose them, but the moment they see us in arms and in earnest they will talk very differently.   The Colonel found no guns—it is supposed a false information. He marched back to Marblehead and embarked for this place.   The moment he left Salem I am told the people got arms and paraded about, and swore if he had stayed half an hour longer they would have cut him to pieces.   If he had continued there till now, none of them would have dared to have appeared in arms.

Hutchinson, the former royal governor of Massachusetts, later noted in London that he heard that the cannon "were a parcel of old guns belonging to a ship, which they removed, probably to make a noise, and increase appearances of preparation."   The Loyalist press reported the event as an enlightened tactical move by Gage.

It seems clear that the British were convinced they had achieved a minor victory, and this is important, because it increased Gage's reliance on these short marches as a way to control the province, make a show of force, encourage the Loyalists, and punish the rebels.   Of more immediate importance is not whether or not the British version is correct, but rather what was the version that the provincials believed.

The provincial story, which was of course quite at variance with Leslie's report, received a far broader publication and immediately became the talk of the province. A long account of the action in the *Essex Gazette* on February 28, 1775, and another in the *Massachusetts Spy* on March 2 were attacked by the Tory *Massachusetts Gazette*, and a Whig rebuttal followed in the *Essex Gazette* of March 7. The provincial account maintained that Leslie's march had been a complete failure, mainly because the righteous determination of the assembled provincials had overawed him.

In this view of the incident, the provincials at the bridge had remained calm and resolute in their attempt to convince the blustering colonel that he had no right to cross the bridge, which was built not on a public way but on private property. Leslie retorted that he was determined to cross, private property or not —the King's troops were not to be obstructed in carrying out their orders. Calm reasoning failed. A further refusal angered Leslie to the point that "turning about, he ordered an officer to face his company to a body of men standing on a wharf on the other side of the draw-bridge, and fire." John Felt, who was still at Leslie's side, told the Colonel that he had no right to fire on the people without orders, and added, "You had better be damned than fire—if you fire you'll all be dead men!" Others on the far side took up the cry, shouting to Leslie that he'd better be careful—the alarm was out and companies of minute men would soon be on the scene.

Leslie's determination faltered, but just then he noticed two or three boats which, though they lay nearby, apparently had escaped his eye until that moment. He ordered some of the soldiers to seize the boats and effect a crossing, but the provincials, anticipating his order, ran quickly to the boats and with an axe knocked the bottoms out in a trice and rendered them useless. (The boats appear to have been rather weak-bottomed.) In the scuffle around the boats, one Salem man, Whichener, was wounded by a bayonet.

At this point, Leslie, in a quandary as to what to do next, told some of the nearby townsmen that he had been ordered to come for the cannon. This announcement, coupled with the ever-present danger that the regulars might fire, prompted the Reverend Barnard, the local minister, to suggest that perhaps there was a way in which Leslie could extricate himself from this dilemma without disobeying his orders; if the provincials agreed to lower the bridge, would the colonel consent to the face-saving gesture of merely marching across the bridge and a few yards beyond, and then return to Marblehead and his ship, leaving the provincials with their cannon? Leslie jumped at the chance to comply with the letter of his orders. The drawbridge was lowered, the regulars marched across and fifty yards beyond the bridge, then the regiment faced about and marched off in the direction of Marblehead. Colonel Pickering later wrote: "Various reports were spread abroad respecting the troops. The country was alarmed; and one company arrived in arms from Danvers just as the troops left the town. We immediately dispatched messengers to the neighboring towns, to save them the trouble of coming in; but the alarm flew like lightning (and fame doubtless magnified the first simple reports) so that great numbers were in arms, and some on the march, before our messengers arrived."

The *Essex Gazette* for March 9th reported "Col Leslie's ridiculous expedition, on the 26th ult. occasioned such an alarm, that all the people of all the neighboring towns, as well as those at thirty or forty miles distance were mustering, and great numbers actually on their march for this place, so that it is thought not less than 12 or 15,000 men would have been assembled in this town within twenty-four hours after the alarm, had not the precipitate retreat of the troops from the Draw-Bridge prevented it." In this issue also was the information that "last Friday night twenty-seven pieces of cannon were removed out of this town in order to be out of the way of robbers."

Ezra Stiles, later president of Yale, wrote in his diary a long account of the happenings at Salem, concluding, ". . . thus was Gage shamefully out-generalled,—he sent out a regiment to surprise and seize the Salem ordnance; but they not only returned without it but with the circumstance of repulse derogatory to the honor of soldiers, besides hazarding a trial in which they might have been swallowed up by the thousands which would have appeared in arms." Once more the alarm system had been thrown into action, and as at Temple's Hill, at Charlestown, and at Worcester, the provincials felt they had won the day.

A number of minute man companies actually did march toward Salem. Besides Danvers, Beverly, and Marblehead, the Reading company was called out when "the drums beat to arms, the bell was rung, and alarm guns were fired in the parish," and the word was spread of the British march. "The report was that a regiment of the Cambridge troops had landed at Marblehead and marched to Salem to take some cannon there, and that the people were defending the cannon, and wanted assistance." The Reading company formed up and had marched about five miles when they met the company from Lynn End returning with the news "that the Regulars were retreated without the cannon, embarked and set sail." The Reading company turned about and marched home again in high spirits. On the way back they met the town's west parish company and the Stoneham company, which also had marched, "all which joined together, returned in order to this parish, and went through the military exercise. The whole were more than two hundred."

The impact of the Salem affair on the minds of the provincials cannot be underestimated. To them, Leslie's march and his "retreat" strengthened the conviction that the regulars could be faced down by determined action, and that the minute man system was the answer to British belligerence. On the following day the town of Beverly voted to raise two companies of minute men.

What really happened at Salem? There is little hope that anyone ever will be able to answer that question now, and perhaps even the day after the event the details had already become hopelessly distorted. Many contradictions obstruct the search for the facts. Would Colonel Leslie, in front of his regiment, disobey the orders he had been given, then lie in his official report to Gage and expect not to be discovered? Did Gage cover up for Leslie with the explanation about old ship cannon? It would seem that twenty cannon, whatever their condition, would be dangerous weapons to leave in the hands of the provincials; and Gage, who by this time was resolved not to allow the provincials to build artillery units, would not be inclined to let these guns slip by him.

What was the part Colonel Pickering played in this? Even at Medford on the day after the battles at Concord and Lexington, Pickering was still anxious to restore a good relationship between the province and the King. Concerning a meeting on that day with Dr. Warren and other leaders Pickering later wrote, "They were consulting on the formation of an army. To me the idea was new and unexpected. I expressed the opinion which at the moment occurred to me—that the hostilities of the preceding day did not render a civil war inevitable: That a negotiation with Genl Gage might probably effect a present compromise and therefore that the immediate formation of an army did not appear to me to be necessary." Possibly this spirit of conciliation also prevailed at the North Bridge, where the two opposing colonels were old acquaintances.

Possibly. But such conjecture was of little importance in comparison to the powerful impact of the distorted versions of the story on the British and on the Americans in Massachusetts. In the actions of both sides a stereotype was beginning to develop: the provincials gathered cannon or supplies, the regulars marched, the provincials assembled, and the confrontation *without resort to arms* was judged by both sides to be a victory. It does not matter whether or not John Felt actually said to Colonel Leslie, "You've no right to fire without further orders." The newspapers, in attributing this to him, were expressing a provincial conviction that the troops might menace the Massachusetts men, but they probably carried orders (as even in the case of the Boston Massacre) not to fire except in self-defense. And whatever the correct version of this story may be, it led both sides one step closer to Lexington.

Chapter 11

Gage

On March 28 Gage wrote to Barrington, the British Secretary of War, ". . . it appears to me that you are now making your final efforts respecting America; If you yield, I conceive that you have not a spark of authority remaining over this country. If you determine on the contrary to support your measures, it should be done with as little delay as possible, and as powerfully as you are able, for its easier to crush evils in their infancy than when grown to maturity."

Strike hard or don't strike at all. This seems to be strong and sound advice to the politicians at home from their commander in the field; in view of comments such as this from Gage, one might wonder at first why the authorities in London were so hesitant and vague both on the means to be taken and on the military support to be sent to the commander.

The correspondence from London to Gage over the months says very little about specific orders from the King with reference to Massachusetts; in fact, some of the letter orders are masterpieces of careful side-stepping. One of the early letters tells Gage:

> His Majesty trusts that no opposition will, or can, with any effect, be made to the carrying of the law into execution;

nor any violence or insult offered to those to whom the execution of it is entrusted. Should it happen otherwise, your authority as the first magistrate, combined with the command over the King's troops, will, it is hoped, enable you to meet every opposition, and fully to preserve the public peace, by employing those troops with effect, should the madness of the people, on the one had, or the timidity or want of strength of the peace officers on the other hand, make it necessary to have recourse to their assistance. The King trusts, however, that such necessity will not occur, and commands me to say that it will be your duty to use every endeavor to avoid it; to quiet the minds of the people; to remove their prejudices, and, by mild and gentle persuasion, to induce such a submission on their part, to this law, and such a proper compliance with the just requisitions it contains, as may give full scope to his Majesty's clemency, and enable his Majesty to exercise the discretionary power given him by the act, of again restoring the town of Boston those commercial privileges and advantages which it hath so long enjoyed, and which have raised it to its present state of opulence and importance.

At the same time the sovereignty of the King, in this parliament, over the colonies, requires full and absolute submission. . . .

And so forth. The details, of course, would be left up to the general's discretion.

Later the King wants to know why Gage has not disarmed the rebels. Surely that would render them ineffective as a threat to order in the province. Gage tells him, again and again. In his letter to Dartmouth on December 15 he puts it as succinctly as he can: "Your Lordship's idea of disarming certain provinces would doubtless be consistent with prudence and safety, but it neither is nor has been practicable without having recourse to force, and being masters of the country."

Gage himself is to blame for at least part of this misunderstanding. There is an inconsistency in his letters, revealing that up to the beginning of armed hostilities he was not himself able to see clearly what was going on in the province. His letters over the months from May 1774 to April 1775 show reversals of his evaluation of the political realities in Massachusetts.

In his first few months as governor he thought he saw oppo-

sition building to the small Whig faction, but by late July he was
ready to admit that this element was much stronger than he previously had supposed. Then, in September, just after the belligerent assemblies at Worcester and Cambridge, he was very pessi-
mistic, noting in one letter that the persons taking up arms
against the King were "not a Boston rabble but the freeholders
and farmers of the country" and in another that Connecticut and
Rhode Island also were arming.

By October, however, the storm seemed to have blown over,
and in his reports he was happy to see that there was confusion
and hesitation in the Provincial Congress (though he writes they
are attempting to create an army "to be ready at a moment's
warning"). A month later he found the people of the province
"cooler than they were" about their rebellious ideas, and in
December he continued to ask for strong reinforcements but
added that "numbers will declare themselves" in favor of the
crown if he were to make a strong show of force.

The letters reached a second peak of optimism in the first
two months of 1775. "Friends of the government have shown
themselves in many places," he said, and he was beginning to see
that his hopes "were not without foundation." Repeating his
earlier phrase, he found cooler heads among the people and said,
"its the opinion of most people, if a respectable force is seen in
the field, the most obnoxious of the leaders seized, and a pardon
proclaimed for all the others, that Government will come off vic-
torious, and with less opposition than was expected a few months
ago." He thought a general moderation was evident, and he now
spoke more patronizingly of the provincial militia. "They have
been training men in several townships," he wrote, "as they
could get them in the humor to assemble."

Gage at this time had become caught up in the optimism of
the men surrounding him—the Tories who were by now flocking
to Boston. After their overwhelming defeat in the county conventions of September and October, the Tories were informed,
often rudely, that they could either change their political attitude
or leave town. Many, thinking of their responsibilities to home
and family, accepted the new situation, but for others the change
of view was quite impossible. Their political convictions represented a way of life too deeply ingrained to be forgotten, and
the humiliating public recantations demanded by the Whigs were
not calculated to ease the burden. Hundreds of Loyalists gave up
their homes and moved into Boston to live under the protection

of the British soldiers (and later to accompany the troops in their withdrawal).

Once in Boston, many of these men had access to Gage's office, where their advice and conversation did nothing to help him understand the true condition of the province. Most of them saw the Whig leaders as mere rabble, and felt that the outlaw Provincial Congress did not represent the majority of the people.

Among these Loyalists a good example was Brigadier General Timothy Ruggles, an ardent servant of the King and a tough old veteran of the French and Indian War. He had fought tooth and nail against the changes in the militia, especially the dismissing of the old officer corps, and as a result he was among the first swept out. When he continued to object, his cattle were poisoned, his horse was painted garishly, and he was driven from his home town of Hardwick and forced to take refuge in Boston. Ruggles was not easily defeated, however. From Boston the old soldier printed and distributed a covenant calling for opposition to the activities of the committees of correspondence. Ruggles remained convinced that the Loyalists were still in the majority and he was disgusted by their passive acceptance of Whig control; he reasoned that they had only to make a forceful stand in the name of the Crown and they would be able to reestablish their former positions. His covenant called for an association against "the dissolution of all government, whereby our lives, liberties, and properties are rendered precarious" and emphasized the duty of all persons to protect themselves against lawlessness, then went on to list six rules by which the Loyalists could "recover and secure the advantages which we are entitled to have from the good and wholesome laws of the government." These in general called for armed mutual assistance, rejection of the economic boycott of English goods, repudiation of the recent county conventions and the Provincial Congress, and obedience to the King.

The letter was sent to all the towns of the province, where Ruggles hoped that he could obtain long lists of signatories and thus exhibit the continuing power of the Loyalists. And although the letter was ignored or suppressed in most of the towns, there were just enough pro-Loyalist replies to give the Tory refugees in Boston some justification for their assertion that the unrest was caused by a few political opportunists and was not a general uprising. And these men were at this time Gage's only advisors among the natives of the province.

What the Tories told Gage was reinforced by the Marshfield affair. For three months the troops had occupied this town out in the Massachusetts countryside, and contrary to the predictions of violence there had been no trouble. The regulars at Marshfield were one of the distractions that continually emphasized the possibility of calming the province through judicious use of military force. Gage was encouraged more than he should have been by delusions such as this; he sometimes mentioned Marshfield as a "turn of events" and he spoke of the "good effect" of the troops on the town and the surrounding countryside.

In the early weeks of 1775 Gage changed his mind again as he watched the growing power of the revolutionary leaders, and by February, if not before, he was finally prepared to act.

Gage's letters to Secretary of War Barrington usually were written in stronger terms than his letters through Dartmouth to the King, and in one of his last to Barrington before the march of April 19, his attitude was clear: "I have hitherto observed a conduct, the most salutary, by which the prejudices of the people are in a great measure removed, and the hot headed leaders baffled in their projects." He then added, "Your next dispatches will probably require a different conduct, and I shall wait for them impatiently, as I conclude they will require me to make many preparations to act offensively; for to keep quiet in the town of Boston only will not terminate affairs; the troops must march into the country."

Since Gage was the only official link between the Crown authorities and the province, his interpretation of events in Massachusetts was crucial in determining British policy. Any analysis of the steps that resulted in the march to Concord would have to include a look at Gage himself, as an administrator and as a military leader.

He was from the beginning very much a man of the establishment; that is, he counted his success in his advancement within the structure of the army rather than in the results of his specific duties at any given time. He saw his assignments as stepping stones to higher positions, and he lived in anticipation of the next promotion. His letters show him always quite conscious of the tangible rewards of achievement: pay, rank, extra allowances, privileges. This in itself is no great fault, but it tended to make him far more concerned with the inner politics of the army than with overall British strategy.

As a young aide-de-camp Gage saw action in 1745 at Fontenoy

on the Continent, then in the defeat of the Scots on Culloden Moor and in the Low Countries campaigns of 1747-1748. He rose to the rank of lieutenant colonel in the 44th Regiment and served in America under Braddock in the march against Fort Duquesne, where he commanded the advance guard at the Monongahela River and was the first to be struck by the attacking French and Indians. As the unseen enemy poured a relentless fire into his ranks, Gage displayed the cool courage which was to become one of his trademarks, and though twice wounded he formed and re-formed his men, vainly slamming volley after volley into the deadly green forests. Such fire was ineffective, and his own unit and many of those reinforcing it were completely cut to pieces. When the remnants fell back to the river, Gage managed to build up a rear guard of eighty stragglers to cover the retreat of the mortally wounded Braddock and the rest of the command. Gage has not been held responsible for the fiasco at the Monongahela, nor has he been credited with any overabundance of imagination in his deployment of the advance guard or in his tactics during the fight.

Shortly after the Monongahela, Gage convinced General Loudoun to create the first regiment of light infantry raised by the Crown in America. This was the 80th Regiment, a unit composed of provincial soldiers, led by regular officers, and trained to fight in the wilderness. Gage saw to it that he was chosen to command the 80th, which meant a promotion to colonel, and he led it into battle in Abercromby's ill-advised frontal attack against Montcalm at Ticonderoga, where he was again wounded. Gage's connection with the light infantry reveals a great deal about him as a soldier. He was intelligent enough to recognize the need for a unit of wilderness fighters who abandoned formal fighting ranks in favor of guerrilla tactics and he was brave enough to lead it well. But his rigid orthodoxy made him dislike the whole idea. If there was one man he could not stand, it was Robert Rogers, who he felt lacked the qualities of an officer and a gentleman, regardless of his success in the field.

Gage was promoted to brigadier general in the fall of 1758 and sent out to Niagara by General Amherst with orders to move on the French fort at La Galette and seize it, to assist operations taking place in other sectors. On arrival at Niagara Gage decided that taking La Galette would not materially benefit the over-all campaign and was not worth risking his small command. He stayed at Niagara while Amherst fumed, but managed to convince Amherst later that the move would have come to nothing. Since Wolfe pushed on to success at Quebec even without help on the flank from Gage, Amherst was content to let the whole affair drop, and by 1760 all Canada had fallen, and Gage was military governor of Montreal; his "muddle-through" approach had succeeded.

After three years at Montreal Gage was called to New York to take the post of commander-in-chief in North America when Amherst decided to go home in 1760, and for the next ten years, until he returned to England for a short visit, he controlled all the military forces from Canada down the Atlantic coast to the West Indies, and from New York and Philadelphia deep into the Indian country of the Ohio Valley. In the administration of this far-flung enterprise Gage spent his ten most successful years, keeping the French and Spanish from encroaching on the southern boundaries, pacifying Pontiac and quieting scores of small Indian tribes up and down the western boundaries of the thirteen colonies, and holding on to the recent gains in Canada, as well as maintaining order in the colonies. The job, beyond the administrative details, was basically one of preserving the status quo, and on this he received, as always, much advice but little support from London.

The crisis that came about in New York City after passage of the Stamp Act in 1765 is an indication of the kind of problem Gage had to deal with, and it is especially interesting as a preview of his actions at Boston nearly ten years later. When the new stamps arrived in New York Harbor there was great public unrest and a bit of high comedy as everyone—the acting governor, his council, the navy, and the army—tried to avoid any responsibility in the matter. Mobs ruled the streets and the situation looked grim, but Gage in this case rode out the storm by doing nothing: he ordered his troops to man the fort, but with orders not to fire except in self-defense, and advised the acting governor to stay out of the way. The mobs might demonstrate, he felt, but soon they would be buying the stamps. In the end, he was right, proving to his own satisfaction once more that in North America he who hesitates is probably better off.

Gage also was ordered to protect the rights of the Indians by enforcing the decree that kept settlers out of Indian lands west of the Alleghenies, and he attempted to do so by ordering squatters out of the area; but when he saw that they returned faster than he could push them out, he simply gave up and looked the

other way. Although he was very much in favor of withdrawing
the regular troops from Indian country and leaving that problem
up to the colonies (it would save troop strength and also give
the colonists something to think about besides stamps and taxes),
he would never come out strongly for this. It was, he felt, a
decision that London would have to make. He was also in favor
of strong measures against recalcitrant colonies, especially Massachusetts, so long as these measures clearly originated in England; and in his audience with King George III on a visit home in
1772, he recommended stern treatment for Massachusetts and
ended up with the assignment as the province's new governor.

Boston in 1775 was far different from Montreal in 1763, but
Gage felt up to the challenge, and if fair treatment and excellent
administration could have won over the townspeople, Gage would
have succeeded. The people liked him as well as Bostonians had
ever liked Shute, Burnet, Hutchinson, and the others who preced-
ed Gage, but on the surface they resented him as the chief local
symbol of the oppression which the mother country had chosen to
visit upon them. Massachusetts was a headache for any governor, but for Gage the province made a special effort in that
direction.

The pressure on Gage built up rapidly in the last weeks before
the opening of the war. On April 4 local newspapers published
the word, just in from London by fast ship, ahead of any official
news, that reinforcements were on their way to Boston, and that
the province had been declared by Parliament to be in a state of
rebellion. On the 5th, Gage, after studying the report of Brown
and DeBerniere, requested Admiral Graves to reconnoiter a good
place to land small boats in the vicinity of Lechmere Point, and
later concluded that the Phips farm was the best site. On the
7th Gage was informed of the proceedings of the Provincial Congress: they had drawn up their Rules and Regulations for the
Establishment of the Army. He learned this from a man who was
a member not only of the congress but also of the Committee of
Safety—and at the same time in Gage's employ as a spy.

The entry for Dr. Benjamin Church in the *Dictionary of American Biography* begins "physician, traitor, poet, and author . . ."
It may be assumed that this does not represent the order of
importance of Church's interests, for it was through Church, an
influential delegate from Boston respected by his contemporaries
as an outstanding patriot, that Gage was receiving almost day-to-
day information on the doings of the congress, their possible fu-

ture actions, and the general atmosphere surrounding their meetings, arguments, and decisions.

On April 3 Church informed Gage that the congress was resolved, in the event the British marched out of Boston with their artillery and baggage, "to oppose their March, to the last extremity." Another note, a few days later, told Gage of the consternation in the Provincial Congress at the news of the coming of reinforcements and contained an interesting query for the general: a recess, Church stated, "could be easily brought about." Would the General be in favor of such a move? "It would prevent their taking any hasty steps till he received his dispatches." Obviously, Church knew that Gage did not want to be drawn into any clash with the provincials until he had his final confirmation from London that such a course of action was approved. Church added another suggestion: "A sudden blow struck now or immediately on the arrival of the reinforcements from England should they come within a fortnight would overset all their plans."

Gage may have answered "Yes—get an adjournment if you can," because four days later, on the 15th, the Provincial Congress did adjourn for two weeks, after declaring a day of fasting and prayer. How instrumental Church was in effecting this, or how much was simply his opportunistic use of an event he knew was soon to happen will probably never be known.

The letter of that day contained other important information: the congress definitely would raise an army immediately, and it had sent delegates to Connecticut, New Hampshire, and Rhode Island to enlist the aid of those provinces; the size of the army was to be about 30,000 men, of which Massachusetts would provide half; notification was being sent to all the towns in the province to send the collected tax money to the Provincial Congress rather than to Boston. One last item was sure to make Gage move, if nothing else did. The congress had voted to raise and equip six thirty-man companies of artillery "to attend said army when they take to the field." The cannon stolen from Boston and collected from other places were now to be put to use.

"A sudden blow . . ."—why did Gage not wait for the arrival of reinforcements? First, they might not arrive "within a fortnight" (in fact, they did not arrive in strength until May 25). Second, they would not be in shape to make a hard march without the kind of training Gage had been providing the Boston regulars. Third, Gage no doubt felt that he had enough troops to accomplish the limited mission, a short surprise raid, that he contemplated at this time.

It was a counsel of Lord Dartmouth that finally decided Gage; this was the letter he had been waiting for, and it arrived on April 14. Dated January 27, it was sent out to Gage early in March. Gage received a copy of this letter on April 14, when the *Nautilus* docked at Boston, and the original on the 16th with the arrival of the *Falcon*. It was more specific than earlier letters, telling Gage that the reassembling of the Provincial Congress (which had occurred by the time this letter arrived) should be considered an aggressive act, that the ringleaders of the rebels should be seized, and that forceful action should be taken immediately, before the rebellion grew into a "riper state."

Dartmouth's letter told Gage, in effect, that the King wanted a showdown with the provincials in Massachusetts, and he wanted it as soon as possible. Over and over again Dartmouth insists that Gage must move against the rebels before they become organized. The provincials, he writes, are "a rude rabble without plan, without concert, and without conduct," and if confronted with a regular military force they are sure to melt away.

Gage now had his orders; the Provincial Congress was to adjourn on the following day, thus spreading the rebel leadership out to the four corners of the province. The stores only a few miles away at Concord presented an excellent target, if he moved quickly enough to strike it before the rebels—now working frantically to disperse these goods—could get them away from the town.

Immediately after his receipt of the first copy of this letter Gage issued orders for the two special companies of each regiment, the company of light infantry and the grenadiers, to be relieved of all duties and brought together to train "in new evolutions." He had made his decision: the regulars would march to Concord to destroy the stores there, and strike the first heavy blow against the embryo provincial army.

Chapter 12

The Order

For the march to Concord, Gage decided that a regiment (about 400 men) would not be enough, but that a brigade (three regiments) would be too much. He therefore fell back on a practice that had been used in the Seven Year's War in France: he took two companies from each of his infantry regiments and one from his Marine regiment, forming a provisional expeditionary force totalling twenty-one companies, or about 700 men. Each of the regiments had ten companies, of which eight were ordinary infantry, one was a grenadier company, and one was a light infantry company of agile and aggressive men who normally protected the flanks of the regiment. These companies of grenadiers and light infantry were the ones selected to form the provisional unit.

To lead the expedition to Concord Gage selected Lieutenant Colonel Francis Smith, of the 10th Regiment, senior officer among the regimental commanders. Smith was not a young man, and he had grown quite fat, but he had his good points. One of these was his imperturbability, something which, beyond the point of rank and precedence, may have led Gage to select him. Smith, unfortunately, could match this steadiness with an equal slowness and lack of imagination, a fact that has received more than enough attention over the years, perhaps obscuring his coolness and courage.

The second-in-command was to be Major John Pitcairn, commander of the marines and ranking major in Gage's Boston command.   Pitcairn, like most of the regular officers at the time, felt that the troops had allowed the provincials to go entirely too far, and that a firm step was the only thing necessary to stop all the disorders and restore the prestige of the Crown. He was a good, brave man, and personally well liked by many people in Boston who were not especially fond of the King's troops in general, but he was quick tempered and antagonistic at a time when a calmer approach might have been better.

The order Gage gave to Smith, along with a very interesting rough draft, has been preserved. The order itself, which is fairly well known, is addressed to "Lieut. Coll. Smith, 10th Regiment Foot," and runs as follows:

Having received Intelligence, that a Quantity of Ammunition, Provision, Artillery, Tents and small Arms, have been collected at Concord, for the Avowed Purpose of raising and supporting a Rebellion against His Majesty, you will March with the Corps of Grenadiers and Light Infantry, put under your Command, with the utmost expedition and Secrecy to Concord, where you will seize and destroy all Artillery, Ammunition, Provisions, Tents, Small Arms, and all Military Stores whatever. But you will take care that the Soldiers do not plunder the Inhabitants, or hurt private property.

You have a Draught of Concord, on which is marked, the Houses, Barns, &c., which contain the above military Stores. You will order a Trunion to be knocked off each Gun, but if it is found impracticable on any, they must be spiked, and the carriages destroyed. The Powder and flower, must be shook out of the Barrells into the River, the Tents burnt, Pork or Beef destroyed in the best way you can devise, and the Men may put Balls or lead in their pockets, throwing them by degrees into Ponds, Ditches &c., but no Quantity together, so that they may be recovered afterwards.

If you meet with any Brass Artillery, you will order their muzzles to be beat in so as to render them useless.

You will observe by the Draught that it will be necessary to secure the two bridges as soon as possible, you will therefore Order a party of the best Marchers, to go on with the expedition for that purpose.

A small party on Horseback is ordered out to stop all advice of your March getting to Concord before you, and a small number of Artillery go out in Chaises to wait for you on the road, with Sledge Hammers, Spikes, &c.

You will open your business and return with the troops, as soon as possible, which I must leave you to your own Judgment and Discretion.

The order is strangely incomplete, even though Gage has gone into great detail on matters such as the supplies and cannon and what to do about them, which the colonel and his men could be expected to know without having instructions so carefully spelled out. It is immediately evident that he has made no provision for a much more important eventuality—the strong possibility of contact with armed rebels. The order does not even bring up the subject.

It is here that the rough draft of the order becomes important. This draft contains much more detailed information on the location of arms and equipment, and it also mentions the actions Smith should take on meeting any resistance. This part of the draft states, "If any body ['of men' inserted above the line] dares ['attack' written, then crossed out] oppose you with arms, you will warn them to disperse ['and' written, then crossed out] or attack them." Obviously, Gage had some trouble finding exactly what he wanted to put on record about the conflict that both he and the King were convinced was inevitable and necessary.

In the end, it appears that he resolved this by telling Smith in private what actions were expected of him, and covering only administrative details in the written order. This brings up another question: why did Gage write the order at all? It is possible that the detailed directions in reference to the destruction of military stores were written more with an eye to justifying the march than to telling Smith what to do. No private property will be touched, no inhabitants plundered—only the military stores will be destroyed. The order is careful to note that these supplies are for "the avowed purpose of raising and supporting a rebellion. . . ."

Gage wanted the march to be a kind of spoiling attack; it was meant to set back preparations for organizing and supplying the Provincial Army and to put the rebels off balance. It was also calculated to be a show of force to intimidate the Provincial

Congress and to attract support for the King.

The march, however, was primarily an answer to the orders Gage had received. Dartmouth's letter made it clear that people in England were wondering why Gage was calling for reinforcements when he had made no attempt to use the forces at his disposal. More regiments were on the way, Dartmouth wrote, and three major generals (Howe, Burgoyne, and Clinton) were being sent to assist him. Gage was enough of a politician to realize that he needed a military success *before* the arrival of his new "assistants." If he waited, they would share his success, or —more likely—replace him.

The main flaw in the plan for the march on Concord was the failure to take into account the reaction of the provincials. Gage underestimated them, to say the least.

Given that the whole idea was feasible, the tactical planning was not very good. In a way that seems to be characteristic of him; Gage was not able to bring his excellent general knowledge of light infantry tactics to bear on the immediate situation confronting him.

Experience should have taught him more than it did in this case. He knew how quickly the provincials had gathered to meet his other moves, at Worcester and Cambridge in September, at Salem in February, and on every practice march all winter long. Anything that was not reported to him by his own officers and by Loyalists was broadcast in the Whig press, where if anything the numbers of provincials involved in the alarms was overstated. In retrospect it is difficult to understand why Gage and the other officers did not foresee the rapid assembly of the provincials. Gage's comment in his letter to Dartmouth after the battle was, "the whole country was assembled with surprising expedition. . . ."

Nothing that the provincials did on April 19 should have surprised Gage. Not only had he fought with Braddock and Amherst against irregulars employing Indian warfare tactics, and commanded the first regular light infantry regiment, but he knew personally such men as Rogers, Bouquet, Washington, and other bush fighters. His own prediction of the tactical style of a provincial uprising is as accurate as any that was made: "The most natural and most eligible mode of attack on the part of the people is that of detached parties of Bushmen who from their adroitness in the habitual use of the Firelock suppose themselves sure of their mark at a distance of 200 rods. Should hostilities unhappily commence, the first opposition would be irregular, impetuous and incessant from the numerous Bodys that would swarm to the place of action, and all actuated by an enthusiasm wild and ungovernable. . . ."

How can it be that with this knowledge he was unable to bridge the gap between general planning and specific implementation? He wanted to catch the countryside with a rapid sally that would strike a hard blow before the provincials could react in force; if small groups resisted, so much the better—in sweeping them aside and destroying their supplies he could present a stern example to the rest of the province and to all of the Crown colonies in North America.

To do this he sent a provisional unit composed of companies from eleven different battalions—men who had not operated together before, and who were not informed of their mission until they were on the way to Concord. Although the companies were relieved from all duties three days before the march, there is no record that this allowed them to make any specific preparations for the expedition.

Major Donkin, a member of Gage's command at Boston, later wrote the rambling little book *Military Collections and Remarks*, which was first published in 1777. In reference to Smith's column of grenadier and light infantry companies drawn from all the regiments, Donkin says, "The famous partizan St. Croix, did very extraordinary things with his free company, consisting of between three and four hundred men; but he never could perform the like with the same number of volunteers taken from the several corps of the army. . . ."

As to whether or not the advantage of an elite fighting group outweighs the disadvantages resulting from the assembly of a provisional unit composed of men from various commands—this problem has been argued pro and con many times in the history of the British army.

The overriding disadvantage of the motley mixture of units— the one which caused poor coordination in Smith's column that night and all the next day—was a loose command structure. The company commanders, taken away from their regimental command chain, were forced to operate with new procedures under unfamiliar leaders.

If all the men had come from the same brigade (if, for example, Percy's First Brigade had been sent initially instead of as a later reinforcement), this would have provided not only unity of command and experience in working together, but an organic staff of officers ready to deal with problems such as the crossing of Boston's Back Bay. As it was, the assembly, embarkation, and marching of the column were characterized by mixups and delays, and when the fighting began the senior officers had difficulty maintaining control.

There is some question, also, as to whether or not the plan was realistic in terms of the job Smith was assigned to do. Smith has been criticized for his slowness on this march, but it would have been quite difficult to accomplish the mission in less time. To march eighteen miles out and the same distance back even without opposition would take twelve hours, with an additional four hours to shuttle his troops across Back Bay (he lacked the proper number of boats). To complete the destruction of all the arms and stores would certainly take time. Twenty hours does not seem to be a high figure for the over-all operation as planned. In actuality, the troops were back in Charlestown twenty hours after they left the common at Boston.

Gage thought that a night crossing of the Charles followed by a rapid march through Menotomy and Lexington could be achieved with surprise, but to execute this operation he had to take men off duty, prepare provisions, and arrange for the longboats to be assembled—all under the eyes of watchful provincials in Boston and Charlestown. Needless to say, Gage failed to surprise anyone.

One of Gage's junior officers, Lieutenant Frederick Mackenzie (of whom more later), in his diary on the day after the battle gave an excellent analysis of Gage's attempt at surprise, the results, and the ways it might have been done. He writes:

It is conceived by many that the expedition to Concord for the destruction of the Military Stores, which it was said were deposited there in considerable quantities, might have been conducted with greater secrecy, and been effected without the loss which ensued and the consequences which must now inevitably follow. It had been usual for some of the troops, whenever the weather was favorable, to march several miles into the Country, and return in the Afternoon. The 38th and 52nd Regiments marched once to Watertown, which indeed occasioned some alarm, and Cannon were fired, bells rung, and expresses sent off, to give the alarm; but as they returned again the same Evening after refreshing their men, the people were eased of their fears, and there was no assemblage of any consequence. This mode might have been continued, still increasing the number of troops, and going different roads, until the time intended for putting the design in execution; when the troops destined for that service, might have marched as far as Watertown, which is near 11 Miles on one of the roads to Concord, whence, after remaining 'till towards Evening to rest the men, instead of returning to Boston, they might have pursued their march to Concord, where they would have arrived & effected their purpose before the Country could possibly have been sufficiently alarmed to have assembled in any numbers, either to prevent them, or molest them in their return to Boston. For greater security a brigade might have marched by different roads from Boston at daybreak, which would have prevented the Rebels assembling in one point, and have secured the return of the troops without any material loss. But as it was, it was known early in the day, the 18th, that provisions were dressing on board the transports for a body of troops, that the boats were ordered to be on the beach near the Common at night, and that several Officers had gone out towards Concord in the afternoon. As the people in Boston were constantly on the watch, these indications of some enterprize, were sufficient; accordingly expresses were sent out early in the Evening, and the whole Country was soon alarmed. It was not until 10 at night that orders were sent to The Lines to prevent any person from going out there. There is no doubt but the Country had information of the movement of the troops, as a Company was found under arms at Lexington at daybreak.

Gage's actual plan, which included sending a handful of mounted men out into the country to stop all traffic on the roads and keep the word from spreading, shows once again that he had the right idea in general, but his specific execution was so lacking in imagination that it was bound to fail. That he underestimated the organization, strength, and readiness of the provincials is obvious: he was sending 700 men twenty miles out into the countryside without artillery, without supplies, and with only thirty-six rounds of ammunition apiece.

Chapter **13**

The March to Lexington

T he moon, nearly full, broke into view over the Atlantic horizon at 9:45 P.M. on Tuesday, April 18. The night was starry, cool, and windy. The tide was high and the east wind carried a briny smell through Boston and Charlestown and into the dark countryside.

In Boston's crooked streets the redcoats of the light infantry and grenadier companies were moving in small columns on their way to the common. Some had to come from the Neck on the south side of town, others from Fort Hill on the west side and from the warehouse barracks near Long Wharf on King Street. The companies belonging to the 4th, 23rd, and 42nd Regiments, all in Percy's brigade, were encamped on a hill next to the common and thus were closest to the embarkation point. This was one reason the men of the 23rd Regiment were the first to arrive on the beach "near the magazine guard," about at the corner of the present Charles and Mount Vernon Streets. The other reason was Frederick Mackenzie.

As adjutant of the 23rd Regiment, Welch Fusiliers, the briskly efficient Mackenzie had an eye for detail and a disdain for poor administration, and he was not happy when he found that there was no one in charge at the embarkation point. The longboats, about twenty of them, were drawn up with their bows resting on the "beach," a flat place on the river bank. Offshore the sailors waited on their oars, prepared to lash on to the boats and tow them across the river.

What Mackenzie saw was not a pleasing sight for an adjutant. There were not enough boats to take all of the column across at once. (In the two earlier amphibious sorties, to Quarry Hill and to Charlestown, there were more than enough boats for the regiment, but the force under Smith was double the size of the previous expeditions.) As the light infantry and grenadier companies of the other regiments arrived they climbed into whatever boats were available, until all were full. Mackenzie was appalled at the haphazard manner of loading the troops; he knew they would arrive on the opposite shore all out of order, and would have to be straightened out over there before they could march. He saw his own men into the boats, then went back to his regiment.

Colonel Smith arrived some time after ten o'clock, and when Major Pitcairn came along with his marines, Smith sent him off in the boats with the first shuttle across the Charles. The sailors hitched the longboats in groups of three or four, one behind the other, and bent to their oars, heading for Lechmere Point, a little downstream, about a mile away across the river basin. Smith watched each string of boats move out on the moonlit river, then he settled back to await their return. The trip would take an hour and a half, possibly two hours.

As he waited he noticed Ensign Jeremy Lister of his own 10th Regiment preparing to go along with the light infantry company. Smith knew Lister did not belong to that unit, and he called him over to ask what he was doing there. It turned out that Lister had volunteered to take the place of a lieutenant who failed to answer the call to march.

Smith didn't like the idea of Lister's going out to Concord. First of all, it wasn't according to established procedure, and Smith lived by the book of regulations. Second, Lister didn't know what he was getting into. But Lister replied that "it would be rather a disgrace for the company to march on an expedition, more especially it being the first, without its complement of officers." The colonel, who never dreamed that an intense battle was only a few hours away, and that the job Lister was asking for was far more dangerous than either of them anticipated, decided to let him go.

The boats carrying the first half of the column were lost in the darkness now, and the remaining companies could only wait for their return. This was the first of several delays that dragged out the march. There had been much fumbling up to this point, and there was much more to come; the regulars, it seems, were the only people in the province of Massachusetts who were caught by surprise when Gage issued marching orders. Even though the light infantry and grenadier companies had been relieved from all duties since the 15th, they were not given any orders until the last minute because Gage did not want to tip his hand.

But everyone in Boston saw the boats being prepared and the companies off duty, and for three days messengers had been riding to the neighboring towns arranging for signals to warn of the march of the regulars. Not only were the alarm riders ready to go, but every townsman for miles around kept a wary eye on the road to Boston—and everyone knew that Concord was one of the obvious goals of any British foray. On April 15 the Provincial Congress had adjourned, planning to meet again at Concord May 10, but the delegates from Boston and the surrounding towns sensed that something was in the wind. They were no sooner home than they formed a committee of the representatives from Cambridge, Charlestown, Brookline, Roxbury, and Dorchester, and sent urgent messages to all the other members of the congress requesting that they return to Concord immediately to discuss "the industrious preparations making in Boston for a speedy march into the country." This message went out to all parts of the province on the morning of the 18th.

A month earlier, on March 14, the Committee of Safety ordered that all provincial powder magazines be guarded day and night, and requested members of the town committees of Charlestown, Cambridge, and Roxbury (the towns straddling the main routes of march out of Boston) "at the province expense, to procure at least two men for a watch every night, to be placed in each of those towns, and that said members be in readiness to send couriers forward to the towns where the magazines are placed, when sallies are made from the army by night." Paul Revere and the other members of the Sons of Liberty had been called on to supplement this alarm system by riding as special messengers, and Revere, of course, was at this moment preparing to make his ride.

The bright moon that helped the regulars in assembling and getting into their boats was not so much help to Revere, who also had to leave Boston "by sea." He had made arrangements to be rowed across to Charlestown where other members of the Sons of Liberty were to meet him and provide him with a fast horse. But down along the ferry way the moonlight sparkled on 500 yards of water separating Boston from Charlestown, and halfway across, astride the ferry route, the man-of-war *Somerset* rode at her mooring. With a crew of 520 and mounting 68 guns, she was the largest ship in the harbor.

Somehow, Revere had to get by that ship. Dr. Warren, only a few minutes earlier, had given him orders to get word out to Adams and Hancock that the British were on the move. Dawes would try to slip past the guard at Boston Neck and go by the land route, crossing the Charles at Cambridge. John Pullen would place signal lanterns in the Old North Church to inform members of the Sons of Liberty on the Charlestown side: one lantern if the British marched out over the neck; two lanterns together if they took to the boats again and crossed over Back Bay.

While Smith waited for his boats to return and Revere worried about getting past the *Somerset* without being seen, the patrol of officers and sergeants sent out earlier by Gage was passing through Lexington. This small group and especially its commander, the excitable Major Edward Mitchell of the 5th Regiment, was to have far more influence on the events of the next day than was ever intended by Gage when he gave them the mission of stopping the spread of information about the march of the regulars.

The mounted patrol had left Boston in the afternoon with about ten officers and ten sergeants. As it passed through Roxbury, several of the riders stayed behind to watch the exits from Boston toward the south and west. Later, at Cambridge, more horsemen left the patrol and rode northeast to Charlestown Neck, to cover routes leading north and west. The remainder, including Captains Charles Cochrane of the 4th Regiment and Charles Lumm of the 38th, and Lieutenants Peregrine Thorne of the 4th and Thomas Baker of the 5th, continued on with Major Mitchell to block the road directly before Concord.

In the past months it had been the habit of many of the regular officers to ride out in the countryside for exercise and a bit of fresh air, and Mitchell felt that the patrol could pose as just another party out for recreation. They rode along at a leisurely pace, stopping at an inn north of Cambridge for supper. A member of the Lexington minute men, Solomon Brown, as he was returning from the market in Boston, saw the riders. It was rather a large number of redcoats to be out that far at sundown, he thought, and all of them heavily armed. Brown rode homeward, but stopped at Munroe Tavern in Lexington center to tell his sergeant, William Munroe, what he had seen.

Munroe was John Parker's first sergeant, and a good one. To him, this news could only mean that the British were out after John Hancock and Sam Adams. He got together a squad of nine men right away and sent them up the road to the Clarke house, where Hancock and Adams were lodged, with orders to guard it and let no one get close to it without proper authority. He also sent someone for Captain Parker, who lived on the outskirts of town.

The patrol of regulars lingered over dinner at Cambridge, as confident as Brown and DeBerniere had been that their mission was undiscovered, and as unsuspecting as Gage and Smith of the power of the countryside. They finally set out once again toward Lexington after dark. The patrol passed right through Lexington, to the frustration of Sergeant Munroe, who watched from the shadows as they continued on toward Concord. What could they be up to? Did they miss their turn in the dark, or had they something else in mind to do? Since Captain Parker had not arrived yet, Munroe decided to send out a patrol of his own—three men, Jonathan Loring, Elijah Sanderson, and the same Solomon Brown who had first sighted the British. Munroe told them to catch up with the redcoat patrol, follow it, and find out what it was up to.

From this time on, the village green at Lexington became the scene of increasing activity. Munroe sent messengers out warning the militia that something might be up, and more and more of them gathered on the green to discuss the patrol and the possibility that the regulars were preparing to march out.

About two miles out of town, Major Mitchell and his officers were riding along looking for a good spot to set their trap and block the road to Concord. They passed the home of Josiah Nelson, a Lincoln minute man who lived near the road to Bedford and who had been appointed to warn the Bedford minute men if the British marched toward Concord. Nelson, hearing them and mistaking them for alarm riders, rushed out and asked, "Have you heard anything about when the regulars are coming out?" He may have stumbled on their preparations for an ambush, for one of the exasperated officers, reacting angrily, swung his saber at Nelson, cutting him on the head. "We'll let you know when the regulars are coming out." That was a very clumsy move. Nelson, stunned, managed to get back into his house, where his wife bandaged the wound; in a few minutes he was off to Bedford with the alarm, and because of the bleeding saber cut, unmistakable evidence that the British meant business, dozens of provincial companies were spurred on their way to intercept the redcoats. The saber-swinging officer was probably Mitchell; his subordinates would have been hesitant about striking a provincial.

A few hundred yards further down toward Concord, at a place where a patch of woods grew close to the road, the British set up their trap, and waited.

Back at Boston the first crossing of the Charles was completed about eleven o'clock and the boats returned for the rest of the column. The landing site was a swampy piece of ground at Lechmere Point. Major Pitcairn and the men with him waded ashore through shallow marshes and found a dirt road, where they, too, sat down to wait.

Revere and two companions set out to seaward of the *Somerset*, managed to row past it without being noticed, and slipped safely into the shadows of the docks at Charlestown, where Richard Devens and several others waited to give Revere a fast horse, a powerful mare belonging to Deacon Larkin, saddled and ready to go. Devens had just come from Menotomy, and he told Revere of the patrol of riders on the road ahead.

Amid whispered warnings and words of encouragement, Revere set out through Charlestown toward the Neck. At the same time, William Dawes, also commissioned by Dr. Warren to get news of the march to Adams and Hancock at Concord, eased past a friendly British guard at Boston Neck and set out through Roxbury and Brookline along the other good route to Concord. The two lanterns had flashed only for a moment or two in the steeple window of the Old North Church, but that was enough to set riders off along the many roads that radiated away from Boston like the spokes of a wheel.

When Revere crossed the narrow piece of land at Charlestown Neck, he came to the fork where the road split left to Cambridge and right to Medford. Either way could lead eventually to Concord, but it was shorter to go through Cambridge, and Revere turned that way, riding at a canter and trying to look like a man not in too much of a hurry. He had not ridden far when he saw horsemen waiting in the dark: time to put the deacon's horse to the test! He pulled around and headed for a short cut to the

Paul Revere's Ride

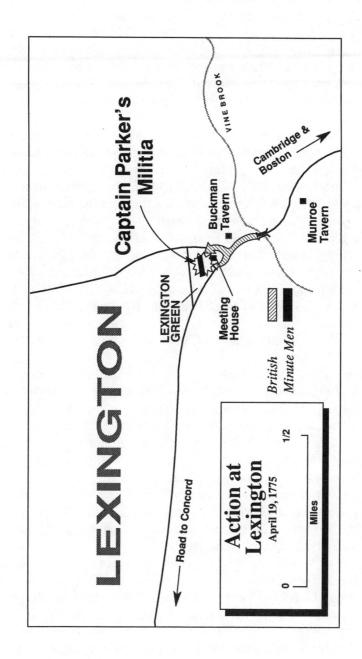

LEXINGTON

Captain Parker's Militia

VINE BROOK

Cambridge & Boston

Buckman Tavern

Munroe Tavern

LEXINGTON GREEN

Meeting House

British
Minute Men

Road to Concord

Action at Lexington
April 19, 1775

0   1/2
Miles

Medford Road with two blue-caped officers riding hard on his heels. The deacon's mare lived up to her reputation, and left the British floundering in a clay pit as Revere broke free and galloped toward Medford and on to Lexington.

Revere triggered the alarm system with his arrangement for the lanterns and with his own ride, and he deserves recognition for that. He also figures more closely in the events on Lexington Green than has been generally recognized, as will be seen.

There were many other riders out that night, too—men who were not part of the alert plan but who heard the news and carried it on. As Revere came into Medford Square, he met Martin Herrick, a young medical student from Lynn End, who studied under Dr. Tufts. Herrick, who was also mounted, carried the word northward from Medford to Stoneham, then turned eastward toward his own home, warning the minute man leaders in South Reading as he passed through there. On arrival at Lynn End he alerted the minute company and accompanied it, later in the morning, on its march. Another rider started from Charlestown and warned townsfolk in West Medford, Winchester, Woburn, Wilmington, and Tewksbury. The men alerted by William Dawes in turn warned Watertown, Newton, Needham, Dedham, and Framingham. The large number of alarm riders made it impossible for a handful of regular officers and sergeants to stop them all.

After midnight the boats of the second shuttle touched the shore at Lechmere Point. The soldiers of the first echelon had been waiting for about two hours and they were anxious to move off, but the whole column had to be reshuffled to place all the companies of light infantry up front so that they could march out ahead and secure the bridges when Smith gave the word. The order of march was finally settled with the light company of Smith's 10th Regiment leading off and the rest following in numerical order, and with the same arrangement for the grenadiers in the rear half of the column. Each company marched three abreast and about twelve deep.

The 10th Regiment light infantry was commanded by Captain Lawrence Parsons, with Lieutenant Waldron Kelly and the substitute Ensign Lister. This company led the march all the way to Concord and was one of the three companies at the North Bridge. It was to return to Boston next day with all officers wounded and only eleven men, led by a sergeant, remaining for duty; all the rest were casualties. For many soldiers in the column who turned to look once more across the Charles before they marched away, it was the last time they would ever see Boston.

Smith gave the orders to march, and the word passed down the column. The regulars moved off down the dirt road and soon found themselves waist deep in salt water: the Phips farm area was low and swampy and laced by many small tidal inlets up to three feet deep, and the old road, such as it was, wound through these for the first quarter mile until it reached the bridge over Willis Creek. Another few hundred yards and the regulars were on a good road that led, after some windings, into the present Union Square near Prospect Hill.

Out in front of the column was a motley group of scouts: Lieutenant Sutherland of the Infantry, Lieutenant Grant of the artillery, Lieutenant Adair of the marines, and Surgeon's Mate Sims of the 43rd Regiment. How this volunteer group came to lead the column is of interest, because their actions became quite significant later on.

The most energetic man of the group was not supposed to be there at all: this was Lieutenant William Sutherland of the 38th Regiment. Sutherland saw the detachment preparing to leave and "resolved to go with them." He followed some of the fully equipped men he saw marching down the street toward the common and when the troops embarked, he jumped aboard one of the longboats. As far as is known, he asked permission of no one, and reported to Major Pitcairn only after he arrived on the Cambridge side. His own regiment, the 38th, part of Pigott's 3rd Brigade, remained in garrison in Boston and did not take part in the battle, except for its light infantry and grenadier companies. Sutherland had been a lieutenant for fourteen years, nine of them in this regiment. Lieutenant Adair of the marines was a very aggressive officer, always spoiling for a fight. Later, at the battle of Bunker Hill, he distinguished himself leading one of the bloodiest assaults on the redoubt, although he had not been assigned to any of the units taking part in the action. The artillery officer was Lieutenant Grant, who had come through Roxbury, Brookline, and Cambridge with the light wagons loaded with shovels, picks, ropes, and other gear the troops would need to destroy the stores at Concord. He had seen the temper of the countryside and he informed the others that there would probably be trouble ahead, and soon. The surgeon's mate, Mr. Simms of the 43rd Regiment, seems also to have had no justifiable reason for scouting ahead of the column, but there he was.

In addition to these officers Pitcairn also had the services of Captain Brown and Ensign DeBerniere, the two men who made the reconnaissance to Concord a few weeks before, and Daniel Murray, a Tory who volunteered to go along as a guide. Murray, a 1772 Harvard graduate, was the son of Colonel John Murray, ex-commander of a Worcester County militia regiment, and one of four fighting brothers. He was taken prisoner before this battle was over, and he languished in a Worcester jail while his three brothers served as officers in the King's American Dragoons, a Loyalist battalion, throughout the war. On this night he was more than a guide—in fact, he captured one of the first two prisoners taken by the column.

The expedition marched on in the bright moonlight, past Prospect Hill to the road to Menotomy. They were about three miles inland from their debarkation site when Adair, out ahead, called, "Here are two fellows galloping express to alarm the country!" Sutherland and Murray managed somehow to catch the reins of the heavy farm horses, and the column had its first two prisoners, Thomas Robins and David Harrington of Lexington. These two were taking a wagon load of milk to Boston, and on seeing the British they pulled off the road, unhitched the team, and tried to ride the horses back to warn the town; but Murray was too quick, and they spent the rest of the night as prisoners of the column. They were released when the shooting began at Lexington.

The redcoats crossed the Menotomy River, the town line between Cambridge and Menotomy. It was then after three o'clock, and the advance party could hear scattered musket shots ringing out ahead—warning signals. Sutherland and his companions pushed rapidly through the center of Menotomy and up a long hill toward the Lexington line. They were now about a half mile ahead of the main column.

A mile or so away and riding toward them at the gallop was Major Mitchell's patrol, carrying exaggerated news of the dangers ahead. About an hour earlier, Mitchell's trap on the Concord road had captured its most important prisoner: Paul Revere. Revere had ridden from Medford down through Menotomy and was in Lexington to warn Hancock and Adams before the column began its march into Cambridge. Dawes rode into Lexington a half hour later, having met no trouble along his route. Seeing that all was ready in Lexington, Dawes and Revere together decided to move on to warn Concord. They were told about the

British patrol that had passed through ahead of them, but were informed also that the Lexington minute men were dogging the patrol to observe its activities.

Revere and Dawes set out, accompanied by Dr. Prescott, who lived in Concord but who had spent the evening in Lexington visiting at the home of his girl friend. They traveled along slowly, warning the houses on the way: Ebenezer Fiske, Jacob Whittemore, Josiah Mansfield. The trap was sprung by Revere, who had ridden ahead of his companions when they stopped to warn a household. Two officers blocked his way and others came out of the woods along the road on both sides. Before he could warn Prescott and Dawes, they too were captured.

As the officers tried to force them into a meadow, Prescott signaled the others to make a break, and all three spurred their horses. Dawes regained the road and headed toward Lexington with two regulars in close pursuit, and knowing his horse was too tired to outdistance them he tried a desperate trick: pulling into the front yard of a house he reined up hard, yelling, "I've got two of them—surround them!" The trick worked, even though Dawes in his excitement lost his balance and fell from the horse.

Prescott turned the opposite way—toward Concord, through fields and a creek bed which he knew well—and soon lost the men who chased him. Revere never had a chance. He headed straight north into the field, trying to get to the woodline, but his tired horse could not get far enough ahead. Revere slowed down to dismount at the woods and was recaptured.

Prescott, once he was sure he had made good his escape, headed through fields and an orchard to the rear of Samuel Hartwell's house. Hartwell was a sergeant in Captain Smith's Lincoln minute men, as was his cousin John, next door. They took the news to Lincoln while Prescott continued on to Concord, where he got word to Colonel James Barrett, commander of the militia regiment in that area.

It was in the questioning of Revere that Major Mitchell first came to understand the extent of the alarm throughout the countryside. Revere told him quite frankly and belligerently that he had warned the towns all the way from Boston that 500 men were assembling at the moment, and just for effect he added that the British longboats had run aground. These words set Major Mitchell thinking. He knew that in letting the other two messengers escape he had failed in his mission of keeping the news of the march from getting to Concord; perhaps now the best thing to do was to warn the oncoming column that the provincials were mustering. He started back toward Boston with his patrol and his prisoners.

Nearing Lexington the group heard a ragged volley from the green. It may have been an alarm signal or, more likely, men firing to clear their loaded muskets when their commander dismissed them. It was now 1:30 A.M. It would not be a good idea, Mitchell thought, to try to take prisoners past Lexington Green. He released Revere, and the patrol threaded its way around the outskirts of Lexington, regained the main road, and headed back toward Boston at full gallop. In Menotomy they ran into Sutherland with Pitcairn's advance party.

Mitchell was not the most level-headed officer of the Boston command, and his influence on the column there was important. He told the lieutenants of the point squad that his patrol had barely escaped with their lives, that the whole country was alarmed, and that 500 men in arms had gathered at Lexington to block the way. He then passed on toward the main column and repeated this distorted report to Lieutenant Colonel Smith.

Smith had already noticed the state of alarm in the surrounding countryside, and he had detached six of his ten light infantry companies and ordered them to march rapidly on ahead to secure the bridges at Concord. Pitcairn, who was to command this detachment, was still with Smith when Mitchell arrived. On hearing Mitchell's news he mounted and rode to the head of the six companies.

Here, a short time later, Mitchell's unintentional distortion was reinforced by what was apparently a deliberate lie: Sutherland stopped a carriage whose well-dressed occupant informed him that there were 600 men waiting at Lexington and ready to fight. The lieutenant waited for Pitcairn to come up, then had the man repeat his statement.

It was past first light of day by this time. Sutherland had commandeered a horse and Adair a carriage, and these two rode out ahead once more. Since the column now stopped to put out flank guards and a point squad, the two lieutenants got some distance ahead by themselves. Here they met another provincial, this one driving a wagon loaded with wood, who told them that there were "a thousand" men at Concord, ready to defend the town.

By this time Sutherland began seeing "vast numbers" of armed provincials crossing the ridge lines and heading for Lexington, and for the remainder of the march his estimates of the strength of the provincial troops tended to be at least double the actual number.

Why Revere and the other Americans felt it necessary to overrate the size of the forces ready at that moment to oppose the British is a matter of conjecture. It may have been pride, or the exhilaration of that night, or perhaps a hope that the British might turn back. Whatever it was, this exaggeration had a telling effect on the British officers in the column approaching Lexington.

Pitcairn now was prepared more for a fight than for a quick march to Concord. With flankers out, the six light companies, which had moved out a little ahead, now slowed down so much that the main body began to catch up again, and the gap between the two groups grew shorter and shorter as they neared Lexington. The excitable Major Mitchell and his patrol were riding with Pitcairn, a fact which was not going to help matters when the column reached the town.

Lieutenant Colonel Smith, on hearing from Mitchell, halted the main column, and while the soldiers checked their weapons and equipment he sent a messenger back to Gage, apprising him of the situation and requesting reinforcements.

The sun was up now, on a clear, breezy day. Pitcairn, riding at the head of the six light companies, was now just outside the town of Lexington, where the road ran along the north slope of Munroe Hill. Lieutenant Sutherland rode up to him with an interesting new piece of information, the last he got before he entered the town: a provincial off in a field on the right had aimed his weapon at Sutherland and pulled the trigger. The piece misfired. It was not difficult to judge Major Pitcairn's frame of mind at this point. Of the others, Sutherland had been fired at, Adair had witnessed the incident, Mitchell was convinced that only hard riding had saved his life and those of the men in his patrol, and all had been told by two different provincials that a large force was in Lexington waiting for a fight.

Chapter 14

Lexington

In the center of the town of Lexington the meetinghouse, a bulky building two and a half stories high, blocked a view of the village green behind it. In front of the building, the road coming in to town from Boston split off to either side; one branch ran past the right side of the building and on to Bedford, four miles away, while the other angled to the left at the meetinghouse and went on a distance of six miles to Concord. The green was bounded for about 200 yards on each side by these two roads, from the fork to the point where a connecting road completed the triangle. Around the sides of the green were houses and yards, and on the east side sat another large building, the Buckman Tavern. Because of the warm winter and the early spring, the grass was taller than usual and the green was covered with dandelions.

In the first light of that morning, Captain John Parker stood on the side of the green near the Buckman Tavern, where he could look past the meetinghouse and down the road toward Boston. Parker had been elected the commander of the Lexington militia company at its organization. He was a tall, heavy-set, ruggedly handsome man, a veteran of the past war, and a stern commander who took no back talk once he had given an order. The men liked him, and he could inspire them to remarkable efforts, as he was to prove more than once that day. At the time of the battle he was forty-five years old, the father of seven young children. Strong as he looked, he was to die of tuberculosis six months later, while serving with Washington's Continental Army.

Parker had not arrived at the green until after midnight. Dawes and Revere had passed through already with their warning for Hancock and Adams, and about half the men in Parker's company were formed in their regular mustering place on the green, waiting for orders.

But Parker had no orders to pass on to them. The Provincial Congress had announced its intention to use the militia and minute men to defend the province, and two months earlier had empowered the Committee of Safety to "alarm, muster, and cause to be assembled with the utmost expedition, and completely armed, accoutred and supplied with provisions sufficient for their support in their march to the place of rendezvous, such and so many of the militia of this province, as they shall judge necessary. . . ." Beyond the order to be ready to march, however, the regiments had no specific assignments. Nothing was said about what to do if the town happened to be directly in the path of the oncoming regulars.

This made matters difficult for the militia and minute man companies of the towns close to Boston and those along the line of march to the supply depots at Worcester and Concord. The companies could not be expected to stand against brigades of regulars, but at the same time the defense of the home town always had been the first mission of the militia.

With the many British marches through the countryside and with the obvious threat of a raid on Concord, the Lexington soldiers could hardly have avoided discussing what the company would do in the event a large British force marched on the town. This must have been especially true in the last few days before the battle, when the impending march was a subject of wide discussion in the Boston area.

Parker had known all the men in his company for years, and he would have been well aware of their viewpoints on the actions that the company should take; in the face of this threat, nevertheless, he followed the old militia custom of calling all the men together in conference to consider the latest news and decide on a course of action. In this case, the consultation was probably a renewal of an earlier general agreement "not to meddle or make with said regular troops," but to let them pass on through the town (as long as they did not cause any damage) and to wait for orders from the regimental commander or the Committee of Safety.

Of course, there was no assurance that the British would merely pass through on their way to Concord. They might want to search Lexington in an attempt to find Hancock and Adams; or they might take some other action, in which case, it would be up to the Lexington company to do its best to defend the town. But there was no use speculating on the many possibilities; the Lexington men would have to wait and see. Parker dismissed the men, telling them to stay within hearing of the drum, in case it became necessary to call them out.

The thing that bothered Parker most at this time was the lack of information. There was no telling whether the British were still on the way or whether they had stopped, turned back, or taken another route. The patrol that Sergeant Munroe sent out to follow the British riders on the road to Concord had not been heard from, and of the several scouts Parker sent toward Boston only one had returned—with the report that he had gone as far as Cambridge and had seen nothing of the regulars. It is no wonder that, when a new arrival on the green at this time asked the captain whether or not the British really were on the march, Parker replied, "I don't know what to believe. . . ."

Then suddenly Parker saw a rider break into view on the hill on the south side of town, and he soon recognized Thaddeus Bowman, the last scout he had sent out to reconnoiter the road. Bowman rode hard down the hill and into town and reined up alongside Parker with some startling news: The British *were* on the road, and no more than a half hour away. He had seen them on this side of Menotomy, a large column of redcoats in full equipment and marching fast—he had just enough time to pull his horse around and sprint away from the lead scouts. Bowman was a bit off on his estimate: the head of the column at that moment actually was less than fifteen minutes away, and time was running out for Parker and his Lexington men. Parker had his drummer sound the alarm.

Seventy-six men of the company responded to the call and gathered in two long ranks on the green, about a hundred yards behind the meetinghouse. They faced toward Boston, and Parker took his place in front of them. A Woburn man with the whimsical name of Sylvanus Wood came along, told Parker he had heard the alarm signals, and asked to join the company. Parker needed all the men he could get and he was more than willing to accept Wood as a volunteer.

The men were still getting into formation when Parker looked down the road and saw the regulars coming over the hill toward the town. It must have been a heart-stopping sight as that seemingly endless column poured into view, the six light companies out in front with flankers off about a hundred yards to either side, and the grenadiers now only about a quarter mile behind. There were only minutes left now for a decision—Parker could stand fast, or order his men to fall back off the green and relinquish it to the British.

Since one o'clock in the morning, after he had consulted with his men and then dismissed them to rest and wait, Parker had been thinking about this moment. He was aware that this was not the first column of redcoats ever to march out of Boston, and if Revere and Dawes were correct about the number of troops, it was not the biggest, either. Whole brigades had been on the roads lately, although not out as far as Lexington, and not at night.

He knew also what the other companies of militia and minute men had done when faced with a British force on the march to their towns. In February a handful of men at Marblehead had stopped Colonel Leslie and the whole 64th Regiment; a few weeks later the Cambridge minute men tore up the planking of the bridge there and (it was said) stopped the 1st Brigade. The same brigade was turned away from Watertown when the militia rolled two cannon up to their bridge over the Charles. He also knew that in the dozens of marches through the countryside in the past months, the regulars very often had marched within firing distance of groups of provincials, some of them armed, as at Watertown, and had not fired. The well-publicized remark of John Felt at Salem, "You have no right to fire without further orders!", influenced provincial thinking on this point, as events at Lexington and later in the day at Concord were to prove. (Jonathan Harrington of Parker's company said, many years later, "We supposed their guns were loaded only with powder . . .")

There was no bridge at Lexington, no barrier to defend, but on the other hand there was nothing in the town the British could consider an objective of their march. If they were coming to capture Hancock and Adams they would, indeed, "miss their aim." Those two men had been warned and had left town at least an hour earlier. If the troops intended to pass through on the way to Concord, Parker knew that there, too, they would find no success. Most of the cannon and supplies had been removed to places of greater safety. There was no need to attempt to prevent the British march, which would achieve nothing, like all the other marches.

There is no doubt, of course, that the last few moments before contact were filled with confusion and that many considerations influenced Parker's decision. Not the least of his worries was the knowledge that armed opposition to the King's troops could be the proof of a charge of rebellion, punishable by death. Although the whole story will never be known, it seems clear that Parker did intend some kind of confrontation with the oncoming British; but a point worth remembering is that he was not blocking the road to Concord; he had positioned his men within musket range of the road, but not on it, and in formal parade-ground formation, not in ambush.

He wanted to maintain the honor of the company and the town. He thought that with the formation and place he had selected, he still had certain options—a discussion with the British leaders, a graceful falling back, keeping the British column under observation—left open to him. Finally, he could not bring himself to believe that, without further provocation, the regulars would attack his parade-ground formation. He was mistaken, for many reasons.

As the British column, marching fast, neared the fork of the road in front of the meetinghouse, the leading company saw the provincials drawn up on the green and instead of continuing down the left fork to Concord, it angled off to the right of the meetinghouse, down the Bedford Road, and onto the green, heading straight for Parker's company. The bulky meetinghouse obscured a view of the green, making it difficult for Pitcairn to judge just how many provincials were assembled there, and also made it hard for Parker to see what the advancing British column would do.

Pitcairn let his column go to the right, and galloped around to the left of the meetinghouse, thus momentarily separating himself from his men. He was never able to regain full control of them; Smith, coming up from the rear, finally restored order.

Pitcairn always insisted that he did not want his men to fire, but rather to surround and disarm the rebels, and this probably is true. But he had lost control of them. Riding with him as he came around the meetinghouse, barking orders at his leading companies, were more than half a dozen officers—Major Mitchell, Captain Cochrane, Captain Lumm, Lieutenant Sutherland, Lieutenant Adair, Ensign DeBerniere, and the other officers in the patrol.

The regular troops were not accustomed to being led by Pitcairn. This made it even more important for him to be in a good position to see his men and, especially, to be seen by them. Now he was out on the left flank, surrounded by a bevy of hangers-on, when the attention of the troops was focused on the armed men to their front.

Parker, seeing the British turn toward him, started his men off farther to the north, away from the Concord Road. In the words of Pitcairn, "when I arrived at the end of the village, I observed drawn up upon a green near 200 of the rebels; when I came within about one hundred yards of them, they began to file off toward some stone walls on our right flank—the light infantry, observing this, ran after them. . . ." Lieutenant Gould afterward also wrote, "On our approach, they dispersed. . . ." Parker's men were trying to get out of the way, but there was to be no escaping Pitcairn, who was now shouting conflicting orders, telling the rebels to disperse and calling on his men to surround them and keep them from dispersing.

If Pitcairn had let him, Parker might have been able to back his men out of the way. This very well might have happened, except for the many small incidents and situations that occurred in the hours just before the two forces met: the boasting of several provincials and the sound of alarm guns in the night, which worked on the excitable nature of some of the regular officers who had spent too much time in garrison; the conglomeration of officers from various units at the head of the column, serving more to impede Pitcairn and confuse the troops than anything else; the buildings which blocked a good view of the green until the last moment and made Parker's seventy-seven men look like 200; the organization of the British column which put a major of marines in command of six companies of light infantry from six different regiments, but not in command of the column as a whole; the poor tactic of failing to halt the British column and flank some companies out to bring the formation on line, but instead driving on in a tight column, so that the leading British company, thirty-two men strong, was marching straight at seventy-seven armed rebels, but with orders not to fire (although

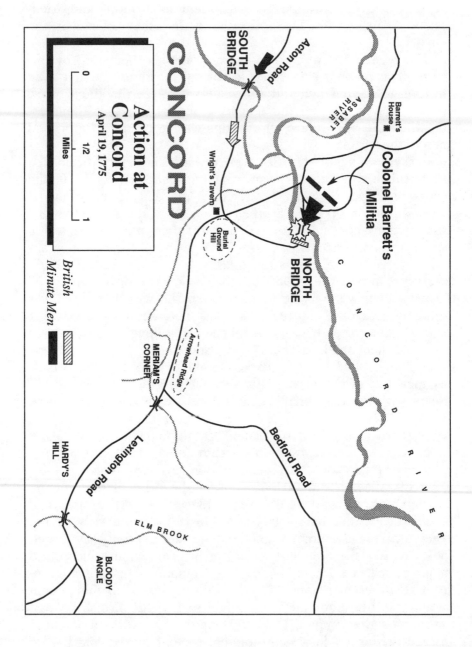

CONCORD

Action at
Concord
April 19, 1775

0   1/2   1
Miles

British
Minute Men

SOUTH
BRIDGE

Action Road

ASSABET RIVER

Barrett's House

Colonel Barrett's
Militia

Wright's Tavern

Burial
Ground
Hill

NORTH
BRIDGE

CONCORD RIVER

Arrowhead Ridge

MERIAM'S
CORNER

Bedford Road

HARDY'S
HILL

Lexington Road

ELM BROOK

BLOODY
ANGLE

at least two officers remembered Pitcairn's orders as "mind your space" and "keep your ranks," rather than "don't fire"). In such a situation, it little matters that Pitcairn insisted the men lacked discipline and fired without orders. The soldiers have taken the blame for this for too long, and though Pitcairn died gallantly in the action at Bunker Hill a few weeks later, it must be said that as an experienced marine battalion commander he should have done better than he did at Lexington.

To consider further the kind of pressures that influenced Pitcairn's concept of the situation at Lexington, it may be added that he had rather explicit views on the Massachusetts rebels and their recent activities. In a letter written to a superior in England only six weeks earlier, he had said,

> Orders are anxiously expected from England to chastize those very bad people. The General had some of the Great Wigs, as they are called here, with him two days ago, when he took that opportunity of telling them, and swore to it by the living God, that if there was a single man of the King's troops killed in any of their towns he would burn it to the ground. What fools you are, said he, to pretend to resist the power of Great Britain; she maintained last war three hundred thousand men, and will do the same now rather than suffer the ungrateful people of this country to continue in their rebellion. This behaviour of the General's gives great satisfaction to the friends of Government. I am satisfied that one active campaign, a smart action, and burning of two or three of their towns, will set everything to rights. Nothing now, I am afraid, but this will ever convince those foolish bad people that England is in earnest.

After Lexington, the people were convinced.

No one will ever know who fired the first shot. It is hard to imagine that a small group of soldiers trying to get out of the path of a much larger unit would turn and fire point-blank at it, but much stranger things have happened. A sniper, off to the flank, might have found the target so inviting that he forgot his orders "not to fire unless fired on." Some witnesses insisted that a British officer fired his pistol, and it does not stretch the imagination much to see Major Mitchell finally finding some use for his.

Once the firing started it was hard to stop. The companies in the rear of the column flanked up without orders and became intermingled, so that the company officers were less effective. Within a minute or so Pitcairn had completely lost control of the six companies, which overran Parker's line and spread out among the houses. The firing was not just a volley or two but a rather healthy skirmish, at least on the part of the British. Parker's men got off a few rounds, but the initial surprise and the momentum of the regulars drove them back in confusion. Lieutenant Sutherland's horse bolted and carried him 600 yards down the Bedford Road, and when he finally regained control and got back to the green, Lieutenant Colonel Smith had arrived but was unable to stop the melee. Smith ordered Sutherland to find a drummer and have him sound "cease fire," something which Pitcairn and his flying squad of officers apparently had not considered.

The affair must have lasted ten minutes or more. When the drum sounded and the smoke cleared and the British troops were once more assembled in their correct formations, they could count only a single casualty in their ranks: one soldier slightly wounded. Pitcairn said his horse was also hit in two places, but he continued to ride the animal until it threw him and ran away later in the day.

Among the minute men, eight were dead and nine wounded— one in every four men was a casualty.

Chapter 15

The March to Concord

Sorting out the individual companies and getting them ready to march again took about thirty minutes. The soldiers, according to one lieutenant, "were so wild they could hear no orders," and in pursuing the rebels they had gone through the yards and out into the fields north and east of the town. The formation took place on the green, just about where Parker and his men had made their stand, and the regulars had to step over several of the provincial dead in order to get to their place in ranks. Smith spent this time in conference with Pitcairn and the other members of his semiofficial staff.

In the group surrounding Smith, some of the officers were anxious to cut the expedition short and return to Boston. They did not like the looks of things. The state of alarm in the countryside was obvious, and the town of Concord was certain to be warned, ready, and full of rebels. As one member of this group later said, "Several of the officers advised Col. Smith to give up on the idea of prosecuting his march, and to return to Boston, as from what they had seen, and the certainty of the country being alarmed and assembling, they imagined it would be impracticable to advance to Concord and execute their orders."

For Smith it must have been interesting to hear such conservative advice from officers who had led the dash into Parker's

129

lines and had presided over the action while he himself came up from the rear calling for a drummer "to stop the slaughter." Smith told them that he had his orders and he intended to carry them out; this ended the discussion.

With DeBerniere and the rest of the collection of guides and scouts leading the van, the column moved off toward Concord. It was now about 5:30. Smith ordered security parties to move a hundred yards out on the flanks—squads from the light infantry companies, hiking through the fields and swamps bordering the roads, climbing stone walls, skirting warily through the quiet farmyards, keeping a watchful eye on the woodlines at the edges of the fields. The leading companies marched at a slow rate in order to allow the flankers to stay abreast of them.

The road led out of the town to the northwest, up Concord Hill, down the other side, across a little valley, and up Fiske Hill. These hills were not much more than small knobs less than a hundred feet above the surrounding ground, but nevertheless they gave the road an abrupt slope at some points.

As the last of the companies marched over the crest of Fiske Hill, a lone British soldier left the column and sat down by the side of the road. His name was Samuel Lee, and he had just decided that his soldiering days were over. He laid his Brown Bess against a tree and waited. It was not long before he saw a provincial soldier, another loner like himself, working his way cautiously up Fiske Hill with his musket at the ready. The provincial was Sylvanus Wood, Captain Parker's Woburn volunteer, who had been trailing the British column since it left Lexington and who now captured the first of Gage's regulars as a prisoner of war. Lee offered no resistance and was marched back to Lexington in triumph. The appearance of Lee in his high grenadier's hat followed by Wood, only five feet tall and carrying two muskets, must have been a sight to see in Lexington at that hour.

Other British soldiers had straggled from the column before the skirmish at Lexington Green, and several of these men now wandered up the road into town looking for the column, not realizing that their comrades in arms had ruthlessly smashed the local militia company less than an hour earlier. These men, four of them, were quickly taken prisoner and marched to the center of town, where dead men were still lying in the streets and yards where they had fallen, and where a large crowd of militia men and townsfolk attended to the task of caring for the casualties and for the distracted wives and children, many of whom had witnessed the events of the morning from the windows of their own homes. The captured soldiers were all well treated, a good indication of the general character of this small town that had suffered so severely at the hands of the regulars.

Beyond Fiske Hill the British column followed the road to Concord. The route curved sharply, first to the south, then back northward to avoid a small but steep hill called The Bluff. It then continued on to the west into the outskirts of Lincoln.

Suddenly the quiet of the morning was broken by several shots off to the flank of the column—snipers in the woods were attempting to find the range. Smoke drifted out of the trees a few hundred yards away, and a rider galloped along the crest of a ridge in the distance. Smith's men were growing uneasy. They sensed that they were not the only soldiers on the march for Concord that morning.

This, of course, was quite true. A five-mile circle drawn around the marching column of regulars would have encompassed seventy-five companies of minute men and militia, most of them mustering more men than a regular British company. At this time nearly every one of those provincial units was either in the process of assembling or on the march to meet the British column at Concord.

Concord was the shire town and the leader of all activities in Middlesex County. The town was the geographical center around which the county regiments were located, every one of them containing at least one company raised in Concord or in a town bordering on Concord. These regiments alone totalled 6,000 men. Not a soldier of Gage's army understood how well these regiments were organized—not even Gage himself, even after the several contacts with the rebels over the past few months. Almost to a man the regulars simply refused to believe that an army had been created under their noses, and now, unwittingly, they were marching directly into the center of six regiments of that army.

Two regiments were already partially mustered in Concord; one of these was Colonel James Barrett's militia, with companies from the towns of Concord, Bedford, Lincoln, Acton, Sudbury, East Sudbury, and Framingham. Of this regiment, the first three towns mentioned had four companies assembled before dawn in Concord. While Colonel Barrett took command there, his staff officers were assembling the rest of the regiment. Lieutenant

Colonel Ezekiel How organized four companies to the south at Sudbury, preparing to march to Concord, and Major Francis Faulkner supervised the muster at Acton of two other companies (which met in his yard and prepared their equipment while the womenfolk cooked meat for them to carry).

There was another regiment from the same towns; this one was Colonel Abijah Pierce's minute men, only recently organized by splitting off volunteers from each of Barrett's companies and electing new officers. The regimental major, John Buttrick, was at Concord with three companies while Pierce's second-in-command, Lieutenant Colonel Thomas Nixon, assembled seven companies as he marched up through Framingham and Sudbury. One company from Acton was preparing to come in on its own. The ten minute man companies known to be in Colonel Pierce's regiment averaged forty-seven men each; the rolls of Colonel Barrett's regiment are less complete but indicate that it was about the same size.

Beyond Concord to the north and west Colonel William Prescott commanded a regiment that was split into militia and minute men, but although the new companies were complete, the new regimental commander and staff had not been elected, and Prescott was still in control of ten companies of militia and seven of minute men (from the towns of Ashby, Townsend, Pepperrell, Shirley, Groton, Westford, Littleton, Carlisle, and Stow).

On the right flank of the marching British column, and still within the limits of Middlesex County, were two more strong regiments, one of militia (formerly the 2nd Middlesex Regiment of Foot) under Colonel David Green, and a sister regiment of minute men under Colonel Ebenezer Bridge, each with companies formed or forming in the towns of Dunstable, Dracut, Chelmsford, Tewksbury, Billerica, Wilmington, Woburn, Reading, and Stoneham. Thirteen companies are known to have belonged to Green, and Bridge had at least nine. Over the county line farther to the east there were two regiments from the towns in the north section of Essex County, commanded by Colonels James Fry (minute men) and Samuel Johnson (militia), and a large regiment close to Boston, the minute men of Colonel Timothy Pickering. All of these units were stirring with the news of the alarm.

In the wake of the British march, in the towns through which the column had passed, was a militia regiment under Colonel Thomas Gardner. The Lexington company belonged to this unit, as did companies in Menotomy, Cambridge, Watertown, Medford,

Waltham, Weston, Newton, and Charlestown. This was the old 1st Middlesex Regiment of Foot, commanded until the recent elections by General Brattle, and it had not yet split off its minute men into a separate regiment.

South of the Charles River but within easy striking distance of the British line of march were three Norfolk County regiments commanded by General William Heath, Colonel John Smith, and Colonel Lemuel Robinson. A Norfolk minute man regiment, led by Colonel John Greaton, had been formed out of companies from the three militia regiments.

To the west, in Worcester County, there was a military organization more powerful than that of any other county in the province, including Middlesex County—three minute man regiments under Colonels Jonathan Warner, John Whitcomb, and Ephraim Doolittle; three militia regiments under Colonels Artemus Ward, Nathaniel Learned, and Jonathan Ward; and two mixed regiments of minute men and militia commanded by Colonels Asa Whitcomb and Nathaniel Sparhawk. These units were for the most part well trained, ready, and waiting. Although very few Worcester County companies were close enough to arrive in time to intercept the British, all of them marched hard toward Boston that day, and took part in the later siege.

Other units farther south and west raised the over-all total to twenty-eight complete regiments of ten or more companies, and nineteen still in the formation stage, putting the combined strength of minute men and militia at forty-seven regiments, containing more than 14,000 men. All of these units had been on edge for the past four days, since receiving the messages from Doctor Warren informing them that the British planned some kind of move immediately, with Concord as the likely goal.

This was the situation at seven o'clock that morning as the British column marched along through the rolling countryside, the quiet fields and woods betraying little sign of the activity in the surrounding communities. Colonel Smith was now past the spot where Revere had been taken prisoner. The head of his column tramped by the home of William Smith, commander of the Lincoln minute men, now waiting at Concord, crossed the Bedford-Lincoln Road, and marched over the bridge at Elm Brook. Again, puffs of smoke appeared in the distant tree line, followed by echoing reports of muskets. Snipers were once more taking pot shots at the regulars. The column continued on over Brooks' Hill and across the Concord town line. The village itself was now about

two miles away. It was 7:30 in the morning, and the sun was
bright.

Chapter **16**

The Regulars at Concord

Concord, with its low, rolling meadows and its protecting ring of wooded hills had always been, paradoxically, both a beautiful quiet haven and a place of danger and impending violence. Early in the history of the colony this sunny open circle in the wilderness was selected to be the site of the first inland town, but the settlers who came so eagerly to these promising fields soon found themselves in an embattled outpost, open to attack by marauding Indians and also, because of its location, a key base of operations in the frontier defense system. One of the town founders, Major Simon Willard, became a leading military figure in the colony, commanding a 300-man expedition against Ninigret's Indians in 1654, and leading a column to save the town of Brookfield in King Philip's War. In the bitter fighting around Sudbury and Groton in 1676 and in the later patrols to the northeast, the town lost a number of good soldiers. On the casualty lists of these actions and the sporadic fighting leading up to the French and Indian War, the same family names are found again and again: Barrett, Buttrick, Hosmer, Prescott, Davis. Concord sent three companies to Crown Point in the French and Indian War and also several men to Rogers' Rangers; a number of these veterans were members of the Concord militia and minute man companies on this April morning.

135

The main part of town lies in the flat, nearly circular meadow about a mile in diameter, part of the valley where the Sudbury and Assabet Rivers come together from the south and west to form the Concord River, which then flows northeastward out of town through wide meadows and grasslands. Around the edges of Concord stand low but abrupt hills, rising about sixty feet above the valley floor, and in the center of this ring of hills are two pieces of high ground. Nashawtuc Hill stands 100 feet above the fork where the rivers meet, and a long ridge, shaped like an arrowhead, runs eastward from the center of town for about a mile, finally coming to a sharp point at Meriam's Corner. The arrowhead points directly at Lexington; in fact, the road to Lexington follows along the southern base of this ridge as it leaves Concord. As DeBerniere put it in his report, "The town of Concord lies between two hills that command it entirely."

It was a little before two o'clock when Prescott galloped into town with the news Paul Revere had been unable to bring: the British were on the way and not far behind. The town's alarm bell rang out, warning the tired Concord soldiers.

And tired they must have been. All the previous day and far into the night they had been moving military supplies out to the neighboring towns: they carted four cannon to Stow and six more to various hiding places on the outskirts of town; others they hid in cellars and barns. All night wagons trundled the roads between Concord, Acton, Sudbury, and Stow in a desperate move to prepare for the march of the regulars. Colonel Barrett, who was responsible for all the provincial army goods stored in Concord, spent the night traveling from place to place in town, checking that the supplies were well hidden, and when he received word of the alarm he turned his horse back toward the center.

At Wright's Tavern he found men beginning to gather. Some were militia men from his own regiment, others were from Colonel Pierce's minute men. Barrett sent a rider to scout down the road toward Cambridge, to see if he could discover what the regulars were doing. He ordered several others out to alarm Carlisle, Acton, Westford, and other neighboring towns to the north and west. He wanted to ship more of the military goods out of town and to continue dispersing and hiding the rest, but the men were tired and he suspected that the coming day would be a long one. He therefore dismissed the men, just as Parker had done in Lexington, telling them to rest while they could and to listen for the alarm. And as at Lexington, very few men went home and very few slept that night.

Barrett himself stayed in the center of town waiting for further word. The scout he sent toward Cambridge returned about 3:30—with no definite news. Many riders and many rumors were abroad, but the roads were empty of troops. At daybreak, about a half hour later, Barrett sent saddlemaker Reuben Brown down the road toward Lexington with orders to report any sign of the regulars.

Minute men and militia began to drift into town, just as they had mustered for the practice alarm a month earlier. The Concord militia companies of Captains George Minott and Nathan Barrett and the town's minute man companies under Captains Charles Miles and David Brown assembled at nearly full strength. They were joined by a Lincoln company from Colonel Barrett's regiment under Captain Samuel Farrar and a Lincoln minute man company commanded by Captain William Smith. Two Bedford companies, Captain John Moore's militia and Captain Jonathan Wilson's minute men, were among the earliest arrivals; not only had two of Parker's Lexington men alerted them to the march, but also they had seen the undeniable evidence of Josiah Nelson's saber cut when they mustered at Fitch's Tavern. Their ensign carried Bedford's own military flag, a cavalry guidon from the French and Indian War, bearing the motto VINCE AUT MORIRE —Vanquish or Die.

A number of men from neighboring towns rode or walked in, reporting that several companies were on the road to Concord or preparing to march. Major John Buttrick of Concord, the ranking officer then present from Colonel Pierce's minute man regiment, formed the six companies on the green near Wright's Tavern. The sun was up now, but the daily activities of the town were suspended while all waited and watched.

By six o'clock Reuben Brown reported back from Lexington with chilling news: the redcoat column was attacking Captain Parker's men on the green there. Colonel Barrett did not want to believe his own ears. "Were they firing ball?" he asked—the same question that was to occur to so many provincials on that day. "I don't know," answered Brown, who had spurred for Concord at the first shots, with the echoes of prolonged firing ringing in his ears. "I don't know, but I think it probable."

Now, while everyone sought to question Brown and while the various companies of the two partially formed regiments milled around waiting for orders, more individuals arrived with conflicting reports of the British activities, but with the general agreement that many redcoats were on their way to Concord. In this tense and confused atmosphere all sense of unity and discipline might easily have slipped away except for the firm and cool leadership of Barrett and Buttrick.

Barrett issued his orders. The company of minute men under Captain Brown would march down the Lexington Road as far as Meriam's Corner. Paralleling them along the flat-topped ridge the two Concord militia companies would advance until they arrived at the point of the arrowhead, overlooking Meriam's Corner and abreast of the minute men. The two militia commanders sent out on this mission were, incidentally, Barrett and Minott—the son and son-in-law of their regimental commander. Their orders were to watch for the British column, and fall back ahead of it to the center of town. The remaining companies and the men from units not yet completely organized would take positions of defense on the ridge above the burial ground at the base of the arrowhead, overlooking the town and commanding the main crossroads at the center.

Barrett himself went to this position. From there he could see along the top of the ridge running away eastward to Meriam's Corner and also down the Lexington road in the same direction. At this time he had about 250 men. Barrett intended to slow down the redcoat column and to present the British with the fact that they were opposed by an organized force, but he did not want to become engaged.

The three outposted companies had barely arrived at their assigned positions when the first red and white ranks broke into sight on a slight rise about three quarters of a mile down the Lexington Road, marching to a muffled cadence of fife and drum which grew more distinct as the twenty-one companies came into full view, three men abreast, the column stretching back into 1,000 yards of precisely arrayed muskets and glittering bayonets, of white crossbelts and brass, of scissoring white leggings and flashing red sleeves. The Concord men on the hill and down on the road watched in silence.

Riding slightly ahead of the column were several officers, who reined up as they spotted the provincials in the road and on the hill to their front. The hesitation was only momentary; the column marched on until the leading troops came up to a small creek that crossed the road a hundred yards from the base of the hill.   Here the ten companies of light infantry angled off toward the hill and quickly formed an assault line, while the grenadiers passed to their left and continued in column down toward the town.

On the road, Captain Brown faced his company about and marched back toward Concord only a few hundred yards ahead of the grenadiers—so close, in fact, that his fifer and drummer were able to pick up the British cadence.   It was, said one member of Brown's company, "grand musick."   The companies on the hill waited until the British light infantry was fully deployed and climbing the slopes toward them, then fell back in good order on Colonel Barrett's position at the other end of the ridge.

Colonel Barrett watched his picketed companies drawing back as the redcoats pressed closer, and made his plans for the next move.   In this effort he was not without the advice of his fellow townsmen and his officers, some of whom suggested a fight to the death on the spot, but Barrett made another of the many decisions which, taken in aggregate, show quite clearly that his election as a regimental commander was indeed a fortunate event in the history of the town of Concord.

Barrett ordered his troops to withdraw 400 yards to the north, to another section of the arrowhead hill mass; he moved from south to north along the base of the arrowhead, leaving the town side to the British but still maintaining possession of part of the ridge and keeping the British troops in sight.   This he managed to do without making contact, holding his men always just out of musket range.

The light infantry advancing along the ridge were surprised to see the provincials pull back.   "We expected they wou'd have made a stand there," wrote Lister, "but they did not chuse it." The soldiers swarmed over the hilltop and took possession of it, cutting down a liberty pole and flag that had been erected there.

Barrett had given up one good position, and now his anguished men watched their flag go down; his next decision, however, was to be even more difficult.   The light infantry moved off the hill and into the center of town to join the grenadiers, and the British officers grouped together in conference.   It was apparent now that they would not be satisfied merely to march into town and make a show of force, as they had often done in the towns around Boston during the previous winter.   Barrett and the other leaders became more and more convinced that the British meant to search the town.

It is hard to realize what a prospect such a search presented to the provincials without some idea of what was actually stored in Concord at that time. The possession of powder, cannon, and other supplies of war might have meant arrest for revolutionary activities, as everyone concerned was well aware. Within the town, scattered through the cellars and attics and outbuildings of at least twenty-five houses, the provincials had concealed ten tons of musket balls and cartridges, thirty-five half barrels of powder, 350 tents, fourteen medicine chests, eighty barrels of beef, eight and a half tons of salt fish, seventeen and a half tons of rye, 318 barrels of flour, 100 barrels of salt, twenty bushels of oatmeal, nineteen sets of harness, and hundreds of spades, axes, canteens, wooden spoons and dishes, plus candles, matches, butter, reams of cartridge paper, and other stores— besides, of course, a substantial number of cannon and gun carriages of varying sizes. The major part of the collected supplies for the Provincial Army, minus that which had been hastily carried away in the past twenty-four hours, was stored in the homes of Concord. This is what Barrett knew he had to defend.

But the supplies were well hidden, and at that point there was no knowing how thorough the British search would be. He decided to keep his men out of musket range and to see what more the redcoats intended to do.

Barrett's problems were further complicated at this point by the growing number of non-participants—women, children, and old men—gathering about his position and beginning to block the roads below. He ordered some men to lead these townfolk out across the North Bridge and toward Punkatasset Hill, a little over a mile away to the east. Many, however, lingered behind. A number of people gathered in the yard of the Reverend William Emerson's home adjacent to the bridge and remained there throughout the action that followed.

In the center of Concord Colonel Smith conferred briefly with his officers and outlined the plan for searching the town. As it turned out, the orders clearly showed Smith's confidence in the officers and men of his own regiment, the 10th Foot.

Captain Parsons, commanding the light company of the 10th, was to seize and hold the North Bridge and to proceed to Barrett's farm and destroy the equipment there. For this task he was given command of seven of the light companies, including his own—one third of the men in Smith's column. Among the companies assigned to him was the 52nd, commanded by Captain

Brown, who had made the earlier reconnaissance to Concord. As an additional guide Parsons was given Ensign DeBerniere, also of the 10th Regiment.

A second detachment was ordered out to secure the South Bridge, block entrance into town from that direction, and search the nearby houses. The three companies sent on this mission were to be led by Captain Mundy Pole, commander of the grenadier company of the 10th.

This meant that Colonel Smith, Major Pitcairn, Major Mitchell, and several unattached captains and lieutenants were left to supervise the operations of the eleven companies in the center of town, while the other half of the force was split up and sent out in the charge of two captains. In view of the fact that Smith knew he had 200 or 300 armed rebels prowling about his flanks, his use of the officers does not seem too sound, until one remembers that the last time he let Pitcairn and Mitchell out of his sight for a minute, he found himself in the middle of a wild exchange of musketry, searching for a drummer to sound "cease fire." He may well have had more faith, at this moment, in men who though of lesser rank were better known to him. And in view of what happened later, Smith's keeping his volatile majors under his thumb may have been the most sensible move he made on that morning.

Captain Parsons marched immediately with six of the seven companies assigned to him (those of the 10th, 4th, 5th, 38th, 43rd, and 52nd, probably in that order in column). He left the 23rd Company behind to find Lieutenant Grant and his chaise of engineer tools and bring them along as soon as possible. Captain Pole set off for the South Bridge with three companies, probably his own grenadiers of the 10th, plus the light companies of the 47th and 59th, leaving the remaining light company (of the marines) in town with the other ten grenadier companies.

Colonel Barrett saw the column under Captain Parsons start out of the town toward him, and he immediately ordered the provincials to withdraw again, this time across the North Bridge to the high ground on the opposite side of the Concord River. Many townspeople had to be cleared off this hill, where they had congregated in small knots to watch the troops. Barrett and Buttrick tried to make them move further eastward, out of the area where fighting might occur, but many drifted back and stayed close by the provincial positions. As soon as his men were across the river, Barrett turned the command over to Major

Buttrick and told him to form the companies out of range; he himself would go to his farm to warn of the immediate approach of the troops, make a last minute inspection of the dispersing of the supplies, and arrange to keep newly arriving provincial units from running into Parsons' column. He set off at a gallop not far ahead of the British troops.

Major Buttrick took charge, appointing Lieutenant Joseph Hosmer as his temporary adjutant, and moved the militia and minute man companies to high ground about 1,000 yards on the far side of the North Bridge, between the two roads leading into town from the north and east, and in a good position not only to observe the British movements but also to pick up reinforcements as they arrived from Carlisle, Chelmsford, and other towns on that side of Concord. Here for the first time Major Buttrick divided the men into the two regiments to which they belonged, placing the minute men on the right and the militia on the left as they faced the town.

At this time Lieutenant Colonel John Robinson, second-in-command of Colonel Prescott's minute man regiment, galloped in along the Carlisle Road and informed Major Buttrick that the two Westford companies of that regiment were not far behind him. As his mixed command continued to grow, Buttrick anxiously watched the actions of the British, wondering whether they would march to the west, toward Colonel Barrett's farm, or eastward toward his own position, two hills removed from the bridge. As it turned out, the British did both.

Captain Parsons passed over the North Bridge and halted his column. He had seen the rebels on the second hill away to his right, and their growing strength made him hesitant about the force he needed to leave behind not only to keep the rebels out of the town but also to protect his own line of withdrawal. He first dropped off two companies, those of the 5th and the 43rd Regiments, to whom he said simply, "Remain at the bridge." He then marched on a short distance, about one-eighth of a mile, and again halted, apparently to reconsider the situation. Here he placed his own company in command of Lieutenant Waldron Kelly and sent it up on the first hill overlooking the bridge and about 400 yards from it. On Kelly's left flank and about 500 yards farther along the road he placed the company of the 4th Regiment on another knoll, and a little farther on he ordered the 38th Regiment's light infantry company up on a flanking hill. Then he marched on with only the company of the 52nd Regiment, the one commanded by one of his guides, Captain Brown. But before he was out of sight of the bridge, Parsons again re-considered his plan, recalled the 38th Company from its hill, and took it with him down the road. He was not too far along when he halted for the fourth time and again changed his mind. He sent back orders for one of the companies at the bridge, the 5th Regiment company, to rejoin his column. The company from the 23rd Regiment, which he had left back to bring up the tools, was also hurrying to join him, leaving Parsons ultimately with four companies to search a few farm buildings and only three compan-ies to hold open the route and block entrance to the town.

It cannot be said that Captain Parsons failed to consider all possible ways to use his troops; in fact, at one time or another he tried them all. Of the three companies finally left to "remain at the bridge" or in the immediate vicinity, there was no plan for coordinated action. Captain Walter Laurie, at the bridge with his company of the 43rd Regiment, did not have command of the two companies on the hills in front of him and did not know what orders they had been given. Neither of the two companies on the hills (10th, Lieutenant Kelly; 4th, Captain W.G. Evelyn) was aware of the orders to the other, though both knew what Captain Laurie was supposed to do. Lieutenant Sutherland, walk-ing up to see what was going on in the company of the 4th, was surprised to find that the light company of the 38th, his own regiment, had been ordered off to rejoin Parsons, leaving him behind.

When Major Buttrick saw the British companies coming up to take isolated positions on the hills, he resolved to move down closer to them. With his reinforcements he now outnumbered them; the tables were turned, at least for the moment. He set his two regiments, now ten companies in all, in motion toward the British companies of the 4th and the 10th. They pulled back off the hills (Sutherland, trying to join Parson's column, had to turn back to the bridge and was almost cut off) and Major But-trick took up a new position on the ground vacated by the com-pany of the 10th. This piece of ground was fifty feet higher than the bridge and 400 yards away. From here Buttrick could look down on the three redcoat companies now gathered on the near side of the bridge. The two groups warily watched each other.

Parsons marched on to the Barrett farm, two miles west of the bridge on the road to Acton. The route ran generally along the north side of the Assabet River, with wooded low hills on his right and open fields sloping down to the river on his left. On Barrett's land a stream, Spencer Brook, came down from the north, and here the Barrett family operated a small sawmill and a grist mill (probably some of the power was used to assist in the manufacture of weapons as well.) The main part of the farm was a field about 1,000 yards long and running up from the river 500 yards to the first hills. The road ran down through the center of the field, parallel to the river, and the colonel's house sat about in the middle of this open space. As Captain Parsons and his two companies broke into the open and marched toward the house, Colonel Barrett was guiding his horse along a path through the woods on the high ground north of the road, circling back toward the bridge. He had done all he could at the farm.

Barrett had made a final check of the supplies hidden in and around his house. In addition to six half-barrels of powder, he had stored a part of almost every wagonload of supplies that had been sent to his care at Concord, plus a number of cannon and some of the new carriages. The cannon had been laid in furrows and buried, and some of the powder placed in the attic and covered with feathers. To warn the militia and minute men arriving from the west and direct them away from the British detachments at the South Bridge and at his farm, Colonel Barrett sent his son Stephen to a crossroads on the west border of the town.

By the time Colonel Barrett got back to his men, the two regiments were in their new positions overlooking the three British companies at the North Bridge, and waiting for further orders. Barrett spoke briefly with Buttrick, Robinson, and the other officers, and again decided to wait for the next move of the British. Perhaps he felt that the major part of the search would be conducted at his own farm. So far, it was still possible that the British would do no more than make a demonstration of military power and a perfunctory search. And Barrett knew that the longer he waited the stronger his own forces would grow.

It was not long after this that Barrett was joined by the reinforcements he had been looking for. Captain Isaac Davis arrived with thirty-eight minute men from Acton. Several squads of men were now present from Littleton, Chelmsford, Carlisle, Westford, Groton, and Stow. The Acton company under Captain Joseph Robbins arrived to take its place in the militia regiment, reporting that Captain Simon Hunt's minute man company was close behind.

The men under Barrett were now formed in ranks along the hill as follows: from their own right, the minute man regiment, with Major Buttrick still the ranking officer and commanding, Lieutenant Joseph Hosmer acting adjutant, the minute man companies of Miles (Concord), Brown (Concord), Smith (Lincoln), Wilson (Bedford), Davis (Acton); then to the left of these, the militia regiment, Colonel Barrett commanding (and ranking officer on the field), the companies of Minott (Concord), Barrett (Concord), Farrar (Lincoln), Moore (Bedford), Robbins (Acton). In addition there were a number of unattached soldiers—in all about 500 men present under Barrett's command.

At the bridge the three British companies totalled less than 100 men. The companies stood in column on the west side of the bridge and the officers talked together while the rebels above them also were in conference.

The regulars were forced to establish a temporary command of their own and they did so, agreeing that Captain Laurie, the ranking officer, should take charge of all three companies. Laurie asked Sutherland if he thought the situation warranted sending to Colonel Smith for assistance, and Sutherland, looking at the 500 men above on the hill ("Their disposition appeared to be very regular and determined. . . ."), said yes. Lieutenant Robertson of Laurie's company was sent back to town immediately.

But Laurie made no plans, nor did his brother officers suggest any. They all waited for the return of Parsons, and in the meantime pretended that the rebels were not there. This was hard to do. Perhaps the strain—standing for half an hour at the bottom of the hill with their backs to the river while two regiments of well-armed rebels stared down their throats from a good position only 400 yards away—was unnerving enough to the men in the ranks to be considered one of the causes of the debacle which was to follow.

Time passed while Barrett, Robinson, Buttrick, and the company commanders, standing in a tight group, watched the British and discussed the possibility of attacking them. Barrett stuck to his original plan: let the British make the first hostile move. He wanted to allow for the possibility, no matter how slim, of avoiding an encounter. But the men, who probably considered that things had become hostile enough for them, were restless.

It was about 10:30.   While they talked, Adjutant Hosmer glanced toward the town.   Through the trees he could see a plume of smoke rising over the cluster of houses in the center of Concord.   He turned to the colonel, who was still absorbed in discussion.

"Will you let them burn the town down?"

Chapter 17

The Bridge Fight

The Concord townhouse was stuffed full of military supplies, including heavy gun carriages, tents, cartridge paper, spades, and a large number of other wooden articles that were part of the "twenty seven hogsheads of wooden ware" sent from Charlestown by David Cheever of the Committee of Supplies. The grenadiers, discovering this cache, stacked some of the combustible supplies outside to burn. When these were put to the torch, the wind carried sparks against the building and soon smoke began to drift out of the eaves. An old woman who lived nearby, Mrs. Martha Moulton, up until this time had fretted over the fact that she was forced to provide food and water for the soldiers and even chairs for Lieutenant Colonel Smith and his staff, who spent some of their spare moments resting on her front lawn. But now her feelings of personal inconvenience disappeared as she saw the smoke issue from the townhouse. She ran from soldier to soldier, begging them to save the building, until finally, perhaps remembering their commander's admonition against unwarranted destruction in the town (though this was not private property), the grenadiers carried buckets of water into the building and put the fire out. Ironically enough, it may have been while the soldiers were engaged in this constructive act that the provincial officers, seeing the smoke rise over the townhouse, misinterpre-

147

ted its meaning and were galvanized into action.

Far from trying to burn down the town, the British, as this gesture at the townhouse indicated, were doing their level best to make their search of the town as fair and gentlemanly as possible. In examining the houses, store, barns, and other buildings, the grenadiers were willing to accept the word of the townspeople present that certain places contained no supplies belonging to the rebels. The people of Concord took full advantage of this deferential attitude, saving many supplies by lying to the troops in one way or another about the contents of rooms, of barns, even of chests and barrels.

Besides three cannon, some gun carriages, tents, wooden articles, and some barrels of flour, the grenadiers destroyed very little of the huge amount of rebel stores in the town. It seems clear that they had no heart for ruining a lot of equipment and food which they were not sure belonged to the rebel army. Most of the obviously military equipment such as cannon and ammunition had been spirited away before their arrival, and in every house they were faced with the prospect of deciding whether or not to confiscate and destroy such items as flour, beef, harness, medicine, molasses, and candles. It is hard to believe that the grenadiers, after their months of exasperating contact with the wily Bostonians, were naïve enough to be fooled by as many townsfolk as the legends tell us; perhaps it is more accurate that they chose to overlook many rebel supplies rather than chance the destruction of private property, and if so it is to their credit. Besides, they had marched all night and the day ahead was sure to be a long one. The soldiers spent a good deal of time simply trying to buy breakfasts at the houses they were to search. The fact remains, however, that Colonel Barrett and his men believed the British were bent on destroying the town.

Barrett, as always, tried to keep open as many options as possible. He agreed that it was now necessary to march into the town, but he still felt that this might be done without bloodshed. He ordered Major Buttrick to lead off with his regiment and to march over the bridge and into the town, but he did not try to anticipate what would occur beyond the first obstacle—the bridge.

With this order the conference ended and all officers quickly took their positions. Buttrick, out in front of his regiment on line, spoke to the men. In the words of Amos Barrett, who was in the ranks, the major "said if we were all his mind we would drive them from the bridge. . . . We all said we would go."

The minute man regiment under Buttrick's orders faced to the right into column and started down the road to the bridge; a last-minute change by Buttrick had placed Captain Isaac Davis and his Acton company first in order of march.

Davis was without a doubt the most energetic of the company commanders in the minute man regiment. A gunsmith by trade, he had taken care that all his men were well armed; every man in the company had a good musket, a bayonet, cartridge box, canteen—this was one of the many provincial companies to be complete in accouterments. The men under Davis were good shots, too. Davis had built a firing range out behind his house, where twice a week from November to April he had led his men in firing and drill. Needless to say, the fighting spirit of Isaac Davis rubbed off on his men. His own weapon, a product of his shop, was perhaps the best musket on the field that day.

Everyone knew Davis well, and knew of his energy, his determination, and the pride he had in his spirited company. When Davis, characteristically, volunteered to lead the march, no one was surprised, and Buttrick placed him in the van where his marksmen with their solid line of bayonets could be more effective.

Davis was no hothead, but a man of quiet conviction. His wife, many years later, recalled as a very old woman the man she had known in her youth, on the day of the battle: "My husband said but little that morning. He seemed serious and thoughtful; but never seemed to hesitate as to the course of his duty. As he led the company from the house, he turned himself round, and seemed to have something to communicate. He only said, 'Take good care of the children,' and was soon out of sight."

There was a small swamp between Buttrick's position and the British. To get to the bridge he had to march his column down to the right as far as the river, then turn left along the bank and approach the bridge over a low causeway built out into the swamp, which was now flooded with the high water of spring.

Marching with Major Buttrick and Captain Davis at the head of the lead company was Lieutenant Colonel Robinson. Though only a handful of individuals from his regiment had yet arrived on the field, he asked Buttrick if he could go along. Buttrick offered him command of the minute man regiment but he of course declined, saying he wished only the honor of accompanying the column. He was a soldier much like Sutherland of the regulars; he hated to miss a good fight.

As the double file of provincial soldiers marched past Colonel Barrett, who had reined up at the front of the column before it moved off, the men heard him repeating to each company, "Don't fire first . . . don't fire first." Amos Barrett remembered, "we were all ordered to load, and had strict orders not to fire till they fired first, then to fire as fast as we could."

Down at the bridge, Captain Laurie still had done nothing. This may not have been indecisiveness on his part, since to move the three companies back to the Concord side of the river would not only go against the spirit of his orders, sketchy as they were, but also might be the sign of weakness that would touch off an attack by the rebels. Having received a message from Lieutenant Colonel Smith (hurried to him by the mounted Captain Lumm) he knew reinforcements were on the way. As soon as the rebels began to march, he "agreed with all the gentlemen in opinion that it was better to cross over the bridge" and defend on the other side, using the river to full advantage.

The British officers were much impressed with the provincial formation approaching them. "They began to march by divisions down upon us from their left in a very military manner," recorded Lieutenant Sutherland (he meant to say "right" rather than "left"). "They moved down upon me in a seeming regular manner," wrote Laurie.

The regulars retreated back across the bridge according to the order they found themselves in—the 47th, which had been there all along, went first; the 10th, which was on the closest hill and had arrived back earliest, went next; the 4th, farthest away, went last. Thus when they had crossed over and faced about, the 4th was then in front, facing the oncoming provincials, and the 47th was in the rear behind the 10th.

Laurie now had two or three minutes to give his orders for the defense of the bridge. His plan was good. Laurie shouted for the 4th and 10th to take up the "street firing" maneuver, and for the 47th to split and move up to protect the right and left flanks. "I determined to repass the bridge with the three companies, retreating by Divisions, to check their progress, which we accordingly did, lining the opposite side of the river with one company, to flank the other two in case of an attack. By this time they were close upon us."

If this had been carried out correctly, Evelyn's men of the 4th Regiment, formed in three ranks, would have fired a volley, then marched by files around both flanks of Kelly's 10th Regiment company to form again in the rear and load while Kelly's company fired a volley. (For a company volley, the front rank knelt and the rear rank stepped up almost even with the standing second rank and in the gaps between men; each rank contained twelve men when at full strength.) The 4th and 10th would thus have alternated, giving way slowly and pouring volley after volley into the packed ranks of the provincials trying to get across the bridge, while the 47th placed half a company on each flank, firing at will and falling back on line with the front company to keep the provincials from getting around the sides of the formation.

This, of course, is not what happened, for a number of reasons, the first of which was that long, unnerving wait.

As the leading ranks of the minute man regiment closed on the bridge the British got their last man across and began to tear up the planks—a rather futile gesture in terms of the time left at that moment for such efforts—and Major Buttrick, urging his troops to quicken their pace, called to the regulars to leave the bridge alone.

That he would call to them in this reproving manner seems to be another indication that Buttrick was still not sure there would be shooting, but a few seconds later three quick musket shots convinced him that the fight was on, and a volley from the front company of regulars cut down Captain Davis and one of his men, Abner Hosmer. Both were killed instantly; two or three others were wounded.

"Fire!" shouted Buttrick, "For God's sake, fire!"

There had been a pause just after the first three shots, while the minute men stared at the smoke blowing through the ranks of redcoats and made themselves realize that they were actually under fire. "God damn it," muttered Timothy Brown in disbelief, "they are firing ball!" But the crash of the volley and Buttrick's shouted command broke the spell and the men took aim and opened fire at a range of about fifty to seventy-five yards.

The response from the provincial ranks was a ragged but very strong volley and then a continued succession of shots as the men loaded and fired at their own rate. The provincial fire took a heavy toll. Four of the eight British officers were wounded— Lieutenants Sutherland, Hull, Kelly, and Gould—and a sergeant and six privates went down, one of the soldiers dead and another dying.

One reason for the heavier fire from the provincial side was the position of Buttrick's column of two's with respect to the British, whose three companies were formed in nine ranks, ten or twelve men wide. The causeway as it approached the bridge was almost parallel to the river, while on the British side the road was perpendicular to the bank, running straight away from the river. This meant that Buttrick's men, strung out along the river, could fire from almost any position in their column while only the front three ranks of the regulars, at best, were able to fire. Almost every man in the provincial column had a clear shot at the bridge. The first volley from Captain Evelyn's 4th Company was less than thirty-six rounds. The answering volley by the Americans might well have been triple that.

The Americans also were able to return a heavy fire because they had not been badly shaken by the British volley which might have crippled the column except that the men fired too high, a universal sign of poorly trained marksmen under pressure. Only six provincials were struck, and all were hit high; three in the head (Abner Hosmer, killed; Joshua Brooks, grazed; Ezekiel Davis, grazed), one in the chest (Davis, killed), one in the shoulder (Jonas Brown), and one in the neck and side (Luther Blanchard, who died some time later, possibly as a result of these wounds). Amos Barrett in fact commented, "It is strange that there were no more killed, but they fired too high."

One volley was all that Laurie was able to get from his men. Immediately on the exchange of volleys, the British column dissolved and fell back in confusion toward Concord, leaving the bridge in the hands of the provincials. As Lieutenant Lister put it, "The weight of their fire was such that we was oblig'd to give way then run with the greatest precipitance."

For Lister it was the heavy fire that broke the ranks of his regulars; Laurie was more specific in his report of those few moments: "I imagine myself, that a man of my company (afterwards killed) did first fire his piece, tho' Mr. Sutherland has since assured me, that the country people first fired. A general popping from them ensued. The company of the 4th Regiment gave afire, as did a few of my own from the flanks, after which the whole went to the right about, in spite of all that could be done to prevent them."

In stalling for time Laurie had waited too long. There was not enough time for his orders to be translated into specific actions for the men in the ranks; not enough, even, for the junior

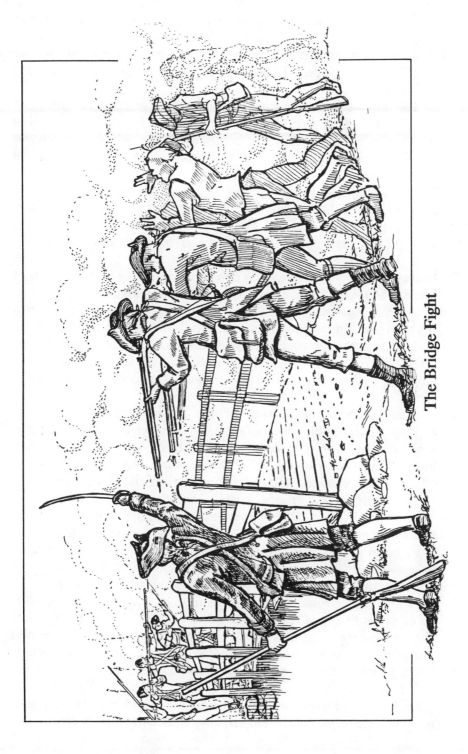

The Bridge Fight

officers to understand fully what he had in mind. Lieutenant Barker later noted that "the three companies got one behind the other so that only the front one could fire." Since this is just what Laurie intended, Barker seems to be one of those who did not get the word.

Lieutenant Sutherland, as always, quickly grasped the intent of Laurie's orders and tried his best to help carry them out. Seeing that the men of Laurie's own company in the rear of the column were hesitant to move up on the flanks, he leaped over a stone wall into the field next to Reverend Emerson's house and urged the men to follow him down the left flank of the column (Laurie himself was probably with the flankers on the other side). Only two or three men heeded the orders of Sutherland, who was a stranger to them, and those who did found themselves facing across the river toward the whole column of rebels on the causeway, 100 yards away. When this column fired, nearly all of these men on the flank were hit, including Sutherland.

A glancing ball struck Sutherland in the chest, raking open a flesh wound and spinning him around. When he recovered, he looked to see the column broken and in flight. Musket balls whistled around him in a hail of fire. He, too, fell back, not stopping even to check the fallen soldiers who had accompanied him.

Laurie's plan for defense of the bridge had failed. It was rendered impossible not only by his own error of waiting too long, but by lack of proper training, discipline, and experience among his officers and men, and by the element of surprise which the well-drilled and determined provincial forces created in their march on the troops. The narrow roadway restricted the "street firing" drill Laurie wanted to conduct, but if the men had gone about it unhurriedly and with some precision it could have been done; after all, the maneuver was planned for use in narrow streets, and this was an ordinary open farm road.

Captain Laurie is by no means fully responsible for the poor showing of the regulars at this point. Laurie's commander left three companies scattered with rather vague orders; Parsons himself had been placed in a job which required decisions he seemed not prepared by experience to make; Smith kept his more senior officers out of the key positions; the companies in this provisional group were not accustomed to working together. Nevertheless, three regular companies should have been capable of holding that narrow bridge at least temporarily, and this they did not do.

And Captain Laurie was the officer in command.

The loss of control in the three British companies was quite complete as the men ran back from the bridge. With half the officers wounded, the rest were helpless to do more than follow after the troops, and it was fortunate for Laurie that Smith arrived at the moment the men came running around a curve in the road near Elisha Jones's house, about 200 yards from the bridge. Lister did not mince words in his account of the action at this point: ". . . fortunately for us in consequence of the Message sent to Lt. Col. Smith he had considered to send the 47th Co. of Grenadiers to our assistance, though too late to be of any service at the bridge, yet they served as a cover for us to draw up our scattered companies again, we then retired in regular order to Concord. I mean the 10th and 43rd Companies with the 47th grenadiers. I don't know that the 4th Co was collected again that day, some of them joined our Co and was permitted to remain some time. . . ."

The growing force of provincials had not gone unobserved by Colonel Smith. On the ridge above the burial ground in the center of Concord, he stood with Major Pitcairn and watched through his spyglass the line of provincials in position above the bridge, and when Captain Laurie's message arrived, Smith decided to proceed to the bridge with reinforcements and to take charge there himself. He ordered two grenadier companies, the company of the 47th Regiment and one other, to stop work and make ready to march under his command. A few minutes later, he set out for the bridge, arriving just in time to see Laurie's troops falling back in disorder.

This new tactical move placed Smith temporarily in command of only two of his twenty-one companies while direction of the rest devolved on Parsons (four companies), Laurie (three), Pole (three), and Pitcairn (nine). With five officers now in command in various places and all of them out of touch with the others, perhaps the best that can be said is that, tactically, it at no time got any worse than this throughout the battle.

Chapter 18

Concord Surrounded

As the British gave way, the minute men and militia did not push the attack. Some of the provincials, probably the minute men under Major Buttrick, crossed the bridge and followed the regulars a short distance, then took positions on a slope overlooking the road about 300 yards on the Concord side of the bridge. The rest of the provincials returned to the hill they had started from, carrying their wounded.

Smith, who for the second time that day found himself hurrying to the sound of firing, halted with his two companies of grenadiers on the road and, as he had done at Lexington, stopped the confused and intermingled companies of light infantry and reestablished some control over them. Captain Laurie, the wounded Lieutenant Sutherland, and the other officers from the bridge gathered around the colonel to tell him what had happened and to explain the retreat of the three companies.

As they talked, the two forces, regulars and provincials, faced each other at a distance of about 250 yards. The five companies now commanded directly by Smith were reorganized in a column, the grenadiers leading, ready to march in the direction of the bridge. On the slope of the hill to their right front, just out of musket range, about 200 of the minute men under Major Buttrick waited to see what the next command to the regulars would be.

Amos Barrett's account is again the most vivid record of these moments:

> We soon drove them from the bridge. When I got over, there were two lay dead, and another almost dead. We did not follow them. There were eight or ten that were wounded and a running and a hobbling about, looking back to see if we were after them. We saw the whole body coming out of the town. We were then ordered to lay behind a wall that run over a hill and when they got near enough, Major Buttrick said, he would give the word to fire. But they did not come as near as he expected before they halted. Their commanding officer ordered the whole battalion to halt and officers to the front. There we lay, behind the wall, about two hundred of us, with our guns cocked, expecting every minute to have the word—fire; . . . if we had fired, I believe we would have killed almost every officer there was in front, but we had no order to fire and they were not again fired on. They staid there about ten minutes and then marched back and we after them.

The British were probably not as close as Amos Barrett remembered many years later, but at all events Colonel Barrett did not intend to resume the fight unless he had to, and Major Buttrick knew this. They let the British march back into town, and taking positions once more on the north end of the base of the arrowhead ridge, about 400 yards north of the burial ground, they continued to observe the British moves.

Buttrick, from his position, could look back across the river to the high ground he had marched from a few minutes earlier, part of the hill on which his own house was situated. There he could see Colonel Barrett and the militia regiment, another 200 men, assembled in their original positions. Buttrick knew that the British force on the road in front of him was now nearly equal to his own, and there were still four companies of regulars that had marched to Barrett's farm and were now no doubt on their way back to the bridge. He was in a good position to repel any attack by the regulars, but he would be risking a lot to attempt to charge down on the column below. If there had been any doubt earlier as to whether or not the British would fire on the minute men and militia, there was little left now. Buttrick decided to await the next move of the British, which he fully expected to be an assault up the hill against his line of minute men.

Over the years there has been comment on Buttrick's failure to push into the town as he had been ordered to do. In the confusion after the first firing he did well to get half the column (his own regiment, the first in line) across the river and up on the best terrain on the other side. While the British fell back in confusion toward Concord, he picked a high place dominating the road and occupied it. That in itself was tactically as good a move as any of the regular officers had been able to make in Concord up to that point. Further attack toward the town would have been foolhardy. Besides, he did not have to drive the regulars back. Smith was convinced that with the provincials on the hill above him, he could not remain where he was without tempting them to repeat the attack they had made only a few moments earlier.

It was a bad spot for Smith, and he knew it. He could not pull back to the town without abandoning the four companies under Captain Parsons that were still across the river at Barrett's farm, but if he marched forward to join Parsons the rebels would surely attack him—in fact, they might do so at any minute, right where he was. He decided to return to the center of Concord, thus easing the pressure at least for the moment, and take the chance that Parsons might be able to get past the rebel force without drawing fire. A withdrawal to the town would also give him the opportunity to prepare a force strong enough to extricate Parsons, who would not be able to push through the rebels by himself if they decided to stop him. Smith faced the troops about and marched back to town.

As soon as he arrived at the center, Smith took Major Pitcairn and clambered up the burial ground hill to watch for the return of Parsons. For the tired colonel, puffing and perspiring as he peered through his field glass at the road on the other side of the river and waited for some sign of the four companies under Parsons, these must have been difficult moments. It is probably well that he did not know what the rest of the day held in store for him.

Below him in the town there was a bustle of activity as his men prepared to go out to Parson's assistance or to begin the return march. Smoke still drifted across the town from a number of small fires, each marking a place where the grenadiers had discovered military stores hidden away, but all searching for supplies was now halted and soldiers were sent to confiscate horses and buggies to carry their wounded companions back to Boston.

From his hilltop lookout Smith now perceived a new threat: the rebel companies that had confronted him at the North Bridge were on the move again, climbing up the slope of the arrowhead ridge just to the north of his own position. He would soon be flanked on the north, and if the rebels continued eastward they could cut off his route back to Boston. He immediately ordered three light infantry companies—those that had come back with him from the North Bridge—to get up on the arrowhead ridge and keep the rebels off it until he was ready to march. This they did, moving from one high place to another as the provincial companies continued to drift eastward along the north side of the town, toward Meriam's Corner and the Lexington Road.

Colonel Smith sent a messenger to Captain Pole at the South Bridge, telling him to pull back into the town where his three companies could reinforce the grenadiers there. Pole complied with the order, calling his men down from their vantage points on Lee's Hill and other high ground on the far side of the bridge, assembling them, and marching back along the Mill Dam into the center of town. As he left the bridge, provincial troops watching his movements at a distance began to edge closer to the river on that side of Concord.

Every time Colonel Smith brought his glass to bear on the hill beyond the North Bridge the force of rebels there seemed to have grown, even though companies of that group were continually being sent across the bridge to reinforce the provincial concentration on the near side of the river, north of the town. Parsons would have to pass close to both of these rebel forces in order to get back to the main body of regulars, and with every minute that slipped away the possibility of his getting through before the road and the bridge were effectively blocked grew dimmer.

On the south side of town where Pole had been positioned, there was now some new activity: armed rebels in large numbers —at least 100 of them, possibly more—had crossed the South Bridge and were moving through the swampy ground on the near side of the river, also heading for the Lexington Road east of Concord. After Captain Pole had abandoned the bridge there was no way to stop this movement across it. The situation that General Gage had foreseen when he wrote Smith's order was not taking place: rebels were crossing both bridges and surrounding the town.

The men moving along the south side of the town were Sudbury and Framingham minute men, four companies comprising the rest of Colonel Pierce's regiment, being led into the battle area by the second-in-command, Lieutenant Colonel Thomas Nixon. The arrival of these four companies brought the strength of the provincial forces surrounding Concord to two complete regiments, and for the first time since the beginning of the operation Colonel Smith's column was outnumbered by the militia and minute men maneuvering directly against it. Colonel Barrett held his militia regiment waiting above the North Bridge, except for four companies under Lieutenant Colonel How, at that moment trailing Captain Parsons as he withdrew from Barrett's farm. Major Buttrick commanded the minute man regiment now moving eastward on the north side of town, except for the companies crossing the South Bridge under Nixon. To Smith, of course, the band of rebels lacked organization and was simply milling about the town, but if their military appearance did not bother him, as it bothered Sutherland and the other lieutenants, their numbers did.

Smith peered down the road toward Lexington and Boston—as he had done a dozen times in the last few minutes. It was now eight hours since he had sent his message to General Gage requesting help, and nothing would have looked better at that moment than a flash of red and white in the distance, announcing the approach of one of the brigades from Boston. But the road remained empty, no matter how many times he scrutinized the point where it disappeared into the woods to the east.

He turned back to watch for Parsons, and at long last caught sight of the companies marching along on the far side of the river, heading toward the North Bridge about half a mile farther on. Smith and Pitcairn watched Parsons draw closer and closer to the bridge. There was no way to warn him of the earlier firing, and it was easy to see by his tight column formation that he was unaware of trouble. In the town the word passed through the ranks that Parsons was on the way in, and the troops waited in tense silence for the sound of ragged volleys out to the north.

As Parsons neared the bridge he was surprised to see that the companies he had placed there were gone, and that the rebel force had moved down to a knoll overlooking the bridge. As he marched closer, he could pick out another strong formation on the opposite side of the river; sensing that there had been trouble, he increased his rate of march and crossed the bridge at a very rapid pace—almost a trot—not even bothering to stop to pick up his own soldiers lying there, even though he noticed that one of the men was "not quite dead." This dying soldier had been wounded in the first firing and then, as he tried to rise, struck in the head by a hatchet-wielding provincial. When Parson's men saw his battered and bloody head, the word spread that the rebels were scalping any regular soldiers they could get their hands on. This atrocity—for such it was—had an effect on the bitterness of the fighting that later occurred, just as the early morning massacre at Lexington fired the provincials with an insatiable spirit of revenge. From this point on, the fury of the long battle could only grow more and more intense.

Colonel Barrett, still with his troops on the hill above the North Bridge, now galloped a few hundred yards down the Acton Road to greet his second-in-command, Lieutenant Colonel How, coming in with the four companies from Sudbury and Framingham. How, jaunty in his dress epaulets and saber, had circled around the west side of town, avoiding the South Bridge, and had trailed the regulars under Parsons as they marched back from Barrett's farm. He reported happily to Colonel Barrett that the British had discovered nothing of consequence except a few of the newly made gun carriages, which they had burned. How was anxious to get after the redcoats, and Barrett decided to move the remainder of the militia regiment across to join Buttrick and the minute men. Lieutenant Colonel How crossed the river and moved eastward toward Meriam's Corner, thus making almost a complete circle around the town with his companies.

At Meriam's Corner, just below the east tip of the arrowhead ridge, the old road from Bedford comes in from the north to join the Concord-Lexington road at right angles. The Meriam house sits back from the intersection about sixty yards, and the fields on all sides offer a clear view in every direction except back toward Concord, where the road into town disappears behind the ridge.

It was down the road from Bedford that parts of two new provincial regiments now marched to augment the units already there. Companies of Colonel David Green's militia regiment and from the minute man regiment under Colonel Ebenezer Bridge, some from towns more than fifteen miles away, came down the road in quick cadence, marching to the sound of fife and drum.

As they hurried along, mounted messengers riding out from Concord kept the leaders informed of the activities up ahead, so that by the time these reinforcements arrived east of the town they were aware that the British were preparing to march out along the arrowhead ridge and the Lexington Road.

Three militia companies from Green's regiment came in at this point under the second-in-command, Lieutenant Colonel William Tompson, also of Billerica, at fifty years old a veteran of Pepperrell's 1745 Louisburg campaign and of the French and Indian War. Tompson told his company commanders—Captains Solomon Pollard and Edward Farmer, and Lieutenant Oliver Crosby—to place their men to the left of the Meriam house on a line parallel to the Lexington Road and about 100 yards east of it.

Marching up on Tompson's left a few minutes later came Colonel Green with five more of the companies from the regiment —three from the town of Reading, captained by John Flint, Thomas Eaton, and John Walton, and two Chelmsford companies under Captains Moses Parker and Oliver Barron. This brought the greater part of Green's regiment up against the British. Missing were the Woburn companies; Green was not aware at that time that the Woburn men were only a short distance down the road toward Lexington, occupying positions where they could observe the exit from Concord.

Colonel Bridge halted his minute men just short of Lexington Road and put them into position around the Meriam house. Two of his companies were from Reading, under Captains John Batcheller and John Brooks, and one was from Wilmington, led by Captain Cadwallader Ford. The fourth company, out of Bridge's home town, Billerica, and formerly commanded by him, was now led by his old lieutenant, Jonathan Stickney, who had served with Bridge at Crown Point and Fort Ticonderoga in the French and Indian War. These Billerica men had a score to settle with the regulars; their fellow townsman, Thomas Ditson, had been tarred and feathered by the British troops in Boston only a month earlier, when he tried to buy a musket from one of the soldiers.

Almost as soon as they arrived, the new regiments were joined on their right by troops coming through the swampy meadows on the north side of town—companies from Pierce's minute men and Barrett's militia. These veterans of the fight at the bridge had been observing the movements of the British and they warned the men of Bridge's and Green's regiments that the redcoats were now in their marching formation, with the main column on the Lexington Road and the flankers out to both sides, and that they would arrive shortly at Meriam's Corner. The men from the twelve newly arrived companies stood in their long line on both sides of the Meriam house and waited for their first glimpse of the redcoats.

One of the captains standing with his company as it waited in firing position there was twenty-two-year-old John Brooks of Reading. Nearly every one of his fellow captains and almost half his men were veterans of earlier campaigns, but this was to be his first fight. Brooks was also a new man in town; he had just moved to Reading from Medford, where he had finished his medical studies under the renowned Doctor Tufts. Brooks set up his practice and also joined the minute men, where he found to his surprise that grizzled veterans twice his age wanted him to be the company commander. After some hesitance, he agreed to lead the company, a duty that immediately became an obsession, driving him to frequent trips into Boston, where he observed the drill exercise of the regulars in order to know what to teach his own men. When Bridge was elected regimental commander at a meeting of the minute man company officers, he asked Brooks to be his regimental major. Brooks declined, saying he had not enough knowledge of military tactics, but Bridge continued to insist. Brooks, a few days before the battle, told Bridge he "was still thinking it over." Possibly he became a major on the road to Concord that day; at any rate, he went on to become a regimental commander in the Continental Army, a major general in the postwar militia, and in 1816 governor of Massachusetts—but at this moment in 1775 he was concerned only with getting his men into good positions, 100 yards from the British line of march.

Chapter 19

Smith Marches from Concord

Captain Parsons, leading his four light infantry companies—150 men of the 5th, 23rd, 38th, and 52nd Regiments—back to Concord, passed within 200 yards of Colonel Barrett and his militia in order to get across the North Bridge. He then had to march down the road under the muskets of Major Buttrick and the minute men to reach the town. This he did, traveling as fast as he could in a parade-ground formation without flankers or scouts, simply hoping for the best and trying not to provoke the rebels. Not a shot was fired, indicating that Colonel Barrett's policy ("don't fire first") was once more in effect, and that the provincials were at that time still determined to fight only defensively.

The arrival of Parsons was all that Smith was waiting for. It was now past noon and there was no sign of any reinforcement from General Gage. The rebels, plainly outnumbering his own troops, had now completely ringed the town, with fresh groups arriving from all directions. It was seventeen miles back to the boats, and if he waited much longer he would not arrive before dark. As for the decision to march, there was no alternative. Smith had only thirty-six rounds of ammunition per man and no supply wagons. If the rebels attacked him and drove him into a defensive position he could not hold out for even the rest of the

164

afternoon. He had to march, and soon. The rebels, if they were allowed time to block his route, could force him to attack to clear it, and this he could do only a few times before running out of ammunition.

As soon as Parsons was safely into town, Smith put away his field glass, came down off the burial ground hill, and told his officers to prepare to march. His column was lined up just as it had been earlier that day when it marched into Concord, the grenadier and marine companies each in three files on the road and the light infantry in skirmish formation on the ridge to the left of the main column. Smith made only two changes: on the right flank, one or two companies of light infantry marched as security south of the road (there was only a squad or so out there on that side when Smith marched into town) and at the end of the column, just ahead of the rear guard, several of the confiscated buggies carrying the wounded were placed in line.

On Smith's order the column began its march toward Lexington. The light infantry on the ridge to the left kept a wary eye on the rebels off to the north side of the road, the grenadiers and marines marched along the road, and the light infantry on the right flank moved through the back yards of the houses south of the road. All went well for the first fifteen minutes, until the light infantry on the left came to the end of the ridge and started down into the fields at Meriam's Corner.

A small stream crossed the route of march at this point, and as the companies of light infantry came down off the ridge they angled to the south, toward the Lexington Road, in order to cross the bridge there rather than wade through the stream. This squeezed them in on the main column, leaving the left flank dangerously open, but it also probably prevented a major battle from taking place at that point. If the companies of light infantry had continued straight ahead, they would have run directly into the waiting regiments of Green and Bridge, reinforced by Barrett and Buttrick. Indeed, it may have been more than the little stream that turned the light infantry southward at that point.

The first sight of the regulars momentarily awed the provincial companies of Reading and Billerica and Wilmington; minute men and militia stared at the companies of light infantry, resplendent in their red coats and tricorner hats, marching down the slopes and crossing 100 yards to their front. In the words of a private in one of the Reading companies, the Reverend Ebenezer Foster, "The British marched down the hill with very slow but steady step, without music or a word being spoken that could be heard. Silence reigned on both sides."

As the light infantry turned away toward the bridge, the minute man and militia companies edged forward, drawing closer and closer to the column. Here again, as at Lexington and at Concord, there is disagreement as to what happened next. From the provincial point of view, the British fired on them and they returned the fire. Private Foster says, "As soon as the British had gained the main road and passed a small bridge near the corner, they faced about suddenly and fired a volley of musketry upon us. They overshot; and no one to my knowledge was injured by the fire. The fire was immediately returned by the Americans, and two British soldiers fell dead at a little distance from each other in the road near the brook." Ensign Jeremy Lister of the 10th Regiment's light infantry, who was wounded at this point, described the opening fire quite differently: ". . . immediately as we descended the hill into the Road the Rebels begun a brisk fire but at so great a distance it was without effect, but as they kept marching nearer when the Grenadiers found them within shot they returned their fire just about that time I recd a shot through my Right Elbow joint which efectually disabled that Arme, it then became a general firing upon us from all quarters, from behind hedges and walls."

With these opening shots the long, running ambush began. The fire of the regulars was once again too high, and not a man among the provincials was hit. One of the British officers in Smith's command later wrote that his troops were overeager at Meriam's Corner, that they "threw away" most of their fire "for want of that coolness and steadiness which distinguishes troops who have been inured to service." Most of his soldiers, he states, had never been in action before; they thought that a few brisk shots in the direction of the provincials would frighten them away. Actually, the British volley seemed to have the opposite effect. Until the regulars fired, the new minute man and militia companies were uncertain about attacking the troops of the Crown, but the first volley roused them to action and they peppered the column with a continual fire. The provincials also were heartened by the ineffectiveness of the British fire. "This gave the rebels more confidence," wrote the British officer, "as they soon found that notwithstanding there was so much, they suffered but little from it."

As the British column quickened its pace and marched on, the companies of provincials drifted eastward, trying to keep up. Men ran through the fields trying to reach positions where they could get another shot at the redcoats, and in the skirmishing all order was lost at least temporarily, making the battle an individual affair for each of the minute men and militia soldiers. The amount of control that company commanders were able to maintain has always been problematical. They tried, and several of them fell during the next few miles of the battle, including Jonathan Wilson, the Bedford captain, who was killed, and two of the four Concord company commanders, Barrett and Minott, who were wounded. Miles was also wounded later, at Charlestown.

Smith's troops ran the gauntlet at Meriam's Corner, and although a harassing fire continued on the left flank and the rear, the British officers began to feel that breaking off contact with the provincials who had virtually surrounded them in Concord would be a fairly simple task. They were soon relieved of this illusion by five companies of minute men waiting in ambush on the right hand side of the road at Hardy's Hill, a mile or so from Meriam's Corner. As the British came up this hill, their attention diverted by the constant sniping on their left flank, they ran into John Nixon and the rest of Colonel Pierce's regiment, including the companies that slipped across the South Bridge at Concord after Captain Pole moved his regulars away from there.

Lieutenant Colonel Thomas Nixon, second-in-command of Pierce's minute men, was in charge of this group, but his older brother John commanded the largest company, fifty-three minute men from Framingham, and probably was the natural leader. There were four other companies present: one more from Framingham under Captain Nathaniel Cudworth and three from Sudbury commanded by Captains Simon Edgell, Micajah Gleason, and Jesse Eames. All of these men knew each other well, and of the six officers, three had served previously under John Nixon in hard campaigns of the past.

John Nixon, forty-five years old, was a veteran of Pepperrell's 1745 Louisburg campaign, in which he served as a private; when the French and Indian War began he moved up to lieutenant and then captain of a company in the Crown Point expedition of 1755-1756. Thomas, seven years junior to his brother, began as a private in John's company and worked his way up to ensign and finally lieutenant. Simon Edgell, now forty years old, had been a private and then a sergeant in the same company. There had been another company, again commanded by John Nixon, created for the march to Fort Ticonderoga. Edgell had joined this company as a sergeant. In a sister company on this expedition, Micajah Gleason (sixteen years old at the time) and Jesse Eames served together as privates. Finally, when General Amherst went into Canada in 1759 John Nixon commanded a third company, with brother Thomas once more his lieutenant and with young Gleason in the ranks as a private. Fate now placed all of these men together, commanding units side by side, waiting to open fire on troops carrying the flag they had so willingly served on earlier battlefields.

No matter how much the redcoats may have been disliked in Massachusetts, the psychological impact of aiming and firing into the ranks of the marching regulars, symbols of the King and protectors of the colonies, has to be taken into account in considering the actions of newly arriving companies along the whole route of the battle. The many instances of apparent delay and confusion of provincial companies may have been in great measure caused by a reluctance to fire until the regulars committed some obviously hostile act. In the case of Nixon's men, they knew of the bridge fight, they saw the fires in the town of Concord, and they heard the volleys at Meriam's Corner.

At Hardy's Hill the woods came right down to the road as it cut across the north side of the hill below the crest. The minute men were able to position themselves on higher ground than the regulars from the first slope all the way across the hill to Brooks' tavern, where the road turned downward into the little swampy valley of Elm Brook. This spot was one of the most advantageous in the area, and the ambush was organized in plenty of time by veterans of this kind of fighting. It was here that the British met the first heavy volume of musketry when the five companies, 215 men, opened a ragged but continuous fire.

To make matters worse for Colonel Smith, the firing from Hardy's Hill encouraged the provincials from Meriam's Corner who were harassing the other side of the British column. Private Foster noted, "We saw a wood at a distance, which appeared to lie on or near the road where the enemy must pass. Many leaped over the walls and made for that wood. We arrived just in time to meet the enemy. There was on the opposite side of the road a young growth of wood, filled with Americans. The enemy were now completely between two fires, renewed and briskly kept up. They ordered out a flank guard on the left, to dislodge the Americans from their posts behind the trees; but they only became better marks to be shot at."

Smith managed to fight his way through the minute man position with the loss of only two men killed and several wounded, but now his flank guard had been driven in on both sides and could no longer keep fire off the main column. The light infantry was now only a few yards off the road, the men were beginning to march blindly and fast, and Smith was having trouble, once again, with his control of this provisional unit, led at company level by junior officers of eleven different regiments and the marine battalion.

Chapter 20

The Bloody Angle

Beyond Hardy's Hill the Lexington Road dipped down to cross Elm Brook, then climbed the slope of another hill and, just below the crest, bent sharply to the left and ran northward for 500 yards before turning back to the east again. All along the British right flank in this section the woods came right down to the road, and the heavy underbrush made any pursuit of the regulars along that side very difficult. On the left of the road, where the hill and the brook continued down, the land was divided into small pasture fields by several crisscrossing stone walls.

The turn in the road was a great disadvantage for the British at this point—it forced them to march into a corner—but there was nothing Smith could do about it. He could not let his column leave the road and travel cross country; they did not know the area well enough, and if the command bogged down in swamps or heavy brush it would be finished. He could not even take a short cut across the angle in the road, because to do so would mean marching downhill over broken ground into the valley of the little brook and then up steep slopes to the road again. Smith stayed on the road, and as he turned left to march along the eastward leg of the angle, all the provincial units that had been struggling over the walls and through the fields and brush on his left flank caught up with him again and were able to get good positions for another shot at his column.

In the four regiments pouring through the fields on the left flank there were over 1,500 men, and a good percentage of these managed to plunge through Elm Brook and scramble up the hill to get within range of the easterly leg of the road, a place which has come to be called The Bloody Angle.

The British were lucky at least in one aspect of The Bloody Angle—the road, as it ran along the side of the hill, was "sunken" between dirt banks on the downhill as well as the uphill side. As the minute men and militia opened fire from the downhill side, the regulars were able to protect themselves by bending down as they hurried past this point, letting much of the fire go over their heads. Because of the angle they were also able to deliver flanking fire from the rear of their column on the provincials attacking the leading companies.

The British increased their fire as the provincials closed in on them and the fighting became very heavy. The Bedford company came up the hill firing, with tough old Cornet Nathaniel Page, a local hero of the French and Indian War, waving the company's cavalry flag. Captain Wilson was killed here, and his nineteen-year-old lieutenant, Edward Stearns, took over the company and led it the rest of the day. Another company commander, Chelmsford's Oliver Barron, of Green's militia regiment, was wounded in this firing, as were several other provincial soldiers.

Colonel Smith was about half way through this first turn in the road, with his officers concentrating on the rebels coming uphill at them from the left, when there was a sudden increase of firing up at the front of the column, where the route turned back toward Lexington. Within a few seconds the regulars were staggered by a second powerful ambush as 197 fresh provincial troops waiting in concealed positions close to the road opened fire from both sides at point-blank range. This was the rest of Green's militia regiment, three companies under Captains Joshua Walker, Jonathan Fox, and Samuel Belknap, all of Woburn, with their fellow townsman Major Loammi Baldwin in overall command.

Only thirty years old, Baldwin already had acquired a middle-aged spread and several double chins to go with it, but for all his chubbiness he was a bundle of energy. He had been a member of Colonel Phips's cavalry since 1768, and he later commanded a regiment in the Continental Army, but at this moment he was bouncing from place to place flailing about with his saber as his companies poured a rapid fire into the British ranks.

The town of Woburn had been slow to conform to the Provincial Congress plan for organization of minute men; only two days before the battle, it was voted in the town meeting to organize a minute man company for Bridge's regiment out of the three companies in Green's, but this probably had not yet been accomplished. When an excited messenger from Medford carried the news of the alert into town early that morning he caught the Woburn men in the process of reorganization, but under Baldwin's leadership the town companies were quick to assemble and march— Baldwin had them all on the road before dawn, heading for Lexington as fast as they could travel.

They were just too late, arriving only a few minutes after the British column marched on toward Concord. Too late, that is, to help Captain Parker in his fight, but just in time to see the results, including the body of their fellow townsman, Asahel Porter, lying beside a stone wall north of the green. Porter had been on his way to the Boston produce markets when the British advance guard picked him up near Menotomy. When the firing began at Lexington he had been released and ordered, perversely enough, to walk, not run, away from the road. He ran, and the regulars shot him down. This at least was the story his companion told Major Baldwin and his men, and the effect on the Woburn soldiers is not difficult to imagine.

Baldwin and his men lent a hand to help Parker with his wounded, and cheered the arrival of little Sylvanus Wood with his big grenadier prisoner. Then leaving Parker to reorganize his company the Woburn men marched down the road to Concord after the British.

One thing that Baldwin had learned in Lexington that morning was that the regulars, if given the opportunity, would overrun his small unit without hesitation. He hoped to be able somehow to join with the rest of Colonel Green's regiment, which he knew would march through Bedford into Concord, but if he could not do so, he was resolved that the regulars would not catch him in open ground, where they could mass their strength against him. He kept his scouts well out, and approached Concord with caution.

The three Woburn companies halted on the high ground at the town line between Concord and Lexington, and Baldwin's scouts moved up to observe the British. They were too late for the fighting; Smith had withdrawn from the North Bridge and was maneuvering his light infantry to keep the provincials from closing in on the town while he waited for Captain Parsons to return from Barrett's farm. The Woburn men skirted Concord at a distance, watching the redcoats on the ridge and in the town. They learned, of course, of the fighting at the North Bridge, and they could see the smoke rising from fires lit by the regulars to burn equipment in various places around the town.

After he had made his reconnaissance, Baldwin decided to keep the British in sight until he was sure they would begin their return to Boston by the same route they had used on the way out, then to fall back and try to ambush the column somewhere in Lincoln. The site he had in mind was Elm Brook, because of the rugged ground, the woods, and the many stone walls in that area. He held his men outside of the town until he saw the British starting to march.

When the firing broke out at Meriam's Corner the Woburn men, surprised, stopped to watch the skirmishing from their position on the road about a mile away. Then they turned and marched out of sight of the British and hurried on into Lincoln. They crossed Elm Brook and climbed the hill to the angle, then "concluded to scatter and make use of the trees and walls for to defend us and attack them." The three companies got down close to the road just about at the corner where it turns back toward Lexington. Here the road crosses the crest of the hill and runs along level for about 400 yards. There was a small schoolhouse on the left, and then several farmhouses and barns spaced about 150 yards apart. On the right the woods and brush continued as heavy as before, and as usual the low stone walls bordered both sides of the road. Most of the Woburn men found concealed firing positions in the woods on the right, or south, side of the road, but a few took cover behind the barns on the north side.

Although the woods and the crest of the hill hid the British column from sight, Baldwin's men heard the rattle of musketry at Hardy's Hill when Nixon's men opened fire, and then the growing fusillade as the men from Meriam's Corner made their attack against the west side of the angle. The two groups were so close that high rounds, missing the British and coming over the hill, were clipping through the trees above the Woburn men as they crouched in their positions, muskets cocked and ready.

Suddenly the British lead company, Smith's 10th Regiment of light infantry, still commanded by Captain Parsons, burst into view, trotting rather than marching. The men were looking back to watch the provincials downhill from the angle. Wary sergeants, shouting orders, tried to get scouts out behind the schoolhouse and into the farmyards as the second company in line, Captain John G. Battier's light infantry of the 5th Regiment, with some of the men of the shattered 4th Regiment company mixed in with them, came over the crest of the hill. The men of the three companies under Baldwin squinted down their musket barrels at red coats and white crossbelts.

There was a scattering of shots and then a crescendo of fire as almost 200 muskets of the Woburn men opened up, ripping into the British ranks. The two leading companies of regulars took the full shock of the fire, and in the next few minutes eight or more soldiers were killed and about twenty wounded. All of Battier's lieutenants were hit almost immediately—Hawkshaw in the cheek, Cox in the arm, Baker in the hand.

The first companies recoiled, but the momentum of the column drove them on. The smoke blew across the road as the regulars began to return the fire. With more companies pouring over the hill, officers tried to organize sallies out to both flanks to take the pressure off the main body. On the right Baldwin's men held their own, some getting off ten or more successive shots at the redcoats trying to struggle through the underbrush and fallen trees, but on the left the provincials around the buildings were swept back. Daniel Thompson was killed there, and three other Woburn men were wounded. The firing during the ambush at this part of the road took place at a range of fifty yards or less. Lieutenant Barker, now the only unwounded officer of the 4th Regiment's riddled company, said of this part of the march, "the country was an amazing strong one, full of hills, woods, stone walls, etc., which the rebels did not fail to take advantage of, for they were all lined with people who kept an incessant fire upon us, as we did too upon them but not to the same advantage, for they were so concealed there was hardly any seeing them. . . ."

The British were now under fire from all sides. The Woburn companies engaged the front half of the column, the large number of men from Meriam's Corner continued to work against the left flank and rear, and the minute men under the Nixon brothers were still firing from the woods along the right side. At this time six new companies, the first to arrive from Colonel Prescott's mixed regiment of minute men and militia, caught up with the rear of the column and got into the fight along the

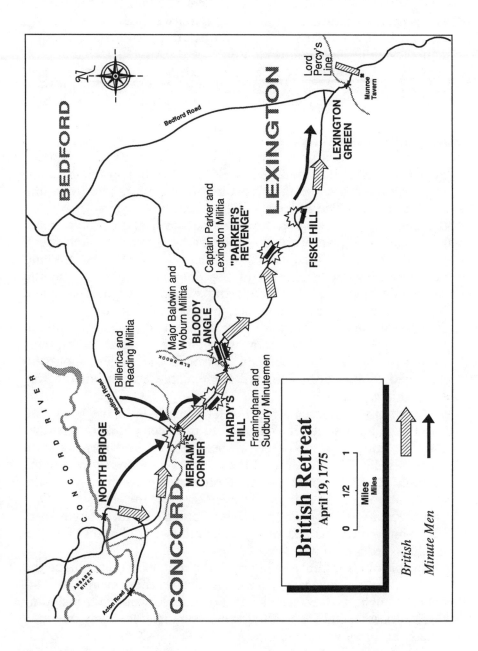

British Retreat
April 19, 1775

NORTH BRIDGE

CONCORD

MERIAM'S CORNER

HARDY'S HILL

BLOODY ANGLE

BEDFORD

LEXINGTON

LEXINGTON GREEN

FISKE HILL

"PARKER'S REVENGE"

Lord Percy's Line

Munroe Tavern

Billerica and Reading Militia

Major Baldwin and Woburn Militia

Captain Parker and Lexington Militia

Framingham and Sudbury Minutemen

CONCORD RIVER

ASSABET RIVER

ELM BROOK

Bedford Road

Acton Road

British

Minute Men

Miles

0   1/2   1

road near the bridge at Elm Brook. Three of these companies were from Westford, commanded by Captains Bates, Minott, and Underwood; two came from Stow under Captains Whitcomb and Hapgood; the sixth was Captain Henry Farwell's Groton company. As one British soldier wrote home after the battle, "it seemed as if men came down from the clouds."

In The Bloody Angle, as at the North Bridge, the pressure on the regulars was so great that they were unable to pick up their own wounded. They hastened on, firing almost at random into the woods, unable to pick out targets, wanting only to get away from the incessant fire.

It took the British nearly a half hour to drive the Woburn men back from the road, get their flankers out again, hold off the swarm of provincial companies in the rear, and push the column through The Bloody Angle and out the other side. Minute men and militia trying to circle to the north of the column and get ahead of it again were slowed down by the swamps and rough ground where the land breaks off sharply into the brooks and pools forming the beginning of the Shawsheen River. On the south side of the hill, the woods and swamps marking the source of Elm Brook hindered attempts to bypass the column.

Several men who knew the lay of the land, especially minute men from the Lincoln company, were able to move ahead on their own. One of these was William Thorning, an excellent shot, who managed to stay even with the front of the column all the way along this section.

Of the three houses along the left-hand side of the road, one was the home of the Lincoln minute man company commander, Captain Smith, and the other two belonged to the Hartwells, both sergeants in Smith's unit. These Lincoln men were moving through their own back yards, sniping at the column, while the regulars poured fire into the windows of the houses. One grenadier fell, badly wounded, in Captain Smith's front yard. The family later carried him into the house and cared for him until he died a few days later.

In this bitter and bloody ambush the men of Woburn made the regulars pay a heavy toll to pass that corner of the road—between eight and twelve dead and a score wounded, including three officers—and for this Baldwin's command lost only one man killed and three wounded. Except at Meriam's Corner, where two regulars were killed and a number wounded without inflicting any casualties on the provincials, there was to be no part of the battle at which the ratio of casualties was so lopsided in favor of the provincials.

The British at The Bloody Angle apparently were caught completely by surprise. They seem to have assumed that if they could get over the crest of the hill there and outrun the gathering forces coming up on their rear and flanks, there would be a clear path open to them toward Lexington and Boston. Baldwin and his men had seen to it that this path was not clear.

Nixon's ambush at Hardy's Hill a few minutes earlier contributed to Baldwin's success at the Bloody Angle by driving in the flank guard on the right side. The heavy force from the regiments of Barrett, Pierce, Bridge, and Green running along in the low fields on the left of Smith disorganized the flankers on that side, who could not make the long swing on the outside of the angle in time to flush the Woburn men out of their ambush positions. Some of the British killed and wounded may have been in the flank fights going on before and during the main ambush.

Then the British rear guard, firing and moving by squads to try to keep the provincials back, finally cleared through the ambush. The Bloody Angle was taken over by the 2,000 men of the now disorganized provincial regiments, all trying to crowd down the road at once, completely intermingled as a result of the nature of the land and the kind of fighting that had been going on. Confusion reigned. Baldwin could not have congratulated his men for a job well done—he could not find half of them; in fact, at Lexington, hours later, he was still trying to round them up. All along the road lay dead and dying British soldiers and scattered pieces of equipment, and over the whole area an acrid pall of smoke drifted back westward from the firing up front.

The shouted orders and the haloos of men looking for their units and the general chatter of the excited mass of minute men and militia was suddenly stilled by yet another explosion of musketry in the distance toward Lexington. Smith's battered regulars had run into another heavy ambush.

Chapter 21

Parker's Revenge

As soon as he got past The Bloody Angle with the front half of the column, Smith put his flank guard out once again. The land was now much more open, with ploughed fields and pastures on both sides of the road, interrupted occasionally by clumps of woods and small swampy areas. The column began to climb a gentle slope as the marching regulars passed by the spot where earlier on the morning of that same day Paul Revere and his companions had been challenged by Major Mitchell and his patrol. The woodline Revere had so desperately tried to reach and the fields through which Prescott had galloped at full tilt in the darkness were now occupied by breathless provincial soldiers running hard to get ahead of the redcoats for another shot at them.

Heading toward the Lexington town line Smith knew the column was still moving much too fast (already the fatigued light infantry companies out on the flanks stumbling through the fields on the right and left were falling behind and unable to provide protection for the men up front). But Smith had to keep up the pace, if for no other reason than to pull the tail end of the column through The Bloody Angle. From front to rear, Smith's twenty-one companies took up half a mile of road, even in this tight formation, which meant that his leading elements would be across the line into Lexington before the last regulars got by Captain Smith's house at the end of the ambush site.

Every time Smith turned in his saddle to look back through the dust of the marching column, he could see the puffs of smoke drifting away along both flanks of his trailing companies as they tried desperately to fight clear of the provincial sharpshooters. Speed was essential to escape, even at the expense of order and security up forward. Smith decided to keep up the pace and take his chances on the road ahead.

In fact, there was not much else that the baffled and angry colonel could do. There was no way he could attack and defeat the rebels, who appeared out of nowhere and disappeared quickly when his light infantry formed to move out against them. The only place at that moment where the rebels were gathered in large numbers was in the road at the rear of the column, and to turn back and attack them would require a change of direction that was a practical impossibility at that time. "Notwithstanding the enemy's numbers," Smith later reported rather plaintively to General Gage, "they did not make one gallant attempt during so long an action, though our men were very much fatigued, but kept under cover."

Smith was not only tired and exasperated—he was worried. With the powerful rebel force, apparently increasing every minute, on his rear, he knew that a rebel roadblock at one of the defiles in the road up ahead might mean the end of his expedition. If the provincials could manage to hold up the column for even a few minutes, the grenadiers in the rear would become so heavily engaged with the armed horde bearing down on them that Smith would not be able to extricate them to continue the march. A five-minute halt might mean a battle to the finish. Smith therefore allowed a pace that in any other circumstances he would have considered reckless. It was a gamble, and Smith, as it turned out, was always a loser.

The speed increased, the flanking companies fell back, and the provincial soldiers, most of them hardy individuals who had run through the woods for a mile or more to get ahead of the column, began to close in again. Near the Nelson house, where twelve hours earlier the minute man Josiah Nelson had been sabered by Mitchell's patrol, a field on the north side of the road recently had been crisscrossed by irrigation ditches, and several provincial marksmen hidden there began to snipe at the regulars coming down the road.

The stone walls lining the main road were often an advantage to the regulars, especially in the many places where the roadway was worn down below the level of the surrounding land. The walls effectively shielded them from much of the fire placed on them, and they were too close to the road to be used by the provincials, who maneuvered behind the pasture walls that ran through the fields, usually parallel or perpendicular to the road.

These provincial soldiers were now able to get in close because the return fire from the regulars in the front of the column had slackened considerably. These British companies had borne the brunt of the fighting at the North Bridge, at Hardy's Hill, and at the Woburn ambush. They were low on ammunition now, and many of the officers and sergeants were wounded or dead. It was becoming more and more difficult for the remaining leaders to get their men to fire back at puffs of smoke in the woods or out in the fields. The men staggered along, racked by fatigue and thirst, seeming almost mesmerized by the road stretching ahead toward Boston and safety.

The firing from the irrigation ditches ceased when the flankers finally came up and drove the handful of provincial soldiers out, but shortly afterward these same snipers were harassing the column from the next field, a pasture full of large boulders. The exhausted flank guard attacked once again, and in a series of sharp skirmishes around these boulders, two more regulars were killed. Unfortunately for the rest of the column, the flank guard, maneuvering against this small group and chasing the snipers into the woods, fell behind and left the north flank wide open. One of the men who unintentionally drew off Smith's flankers was William Thorning, the Lincoln minute man and keen shot who knew this area well. After the flankers finally continued on, Thorning returned to his post by the boulders and continued to bedevil the passing regulars with his accurate fire.

Just beyond this field of boulders the road crossed a small brook at Nelson's Bridge and curved slowly around to the south in order to avoid a wooded ledge about forty feet high extending down from Pine Hill on the north to border the road for a hundred yards. This was the "bad spot" mentioned by Brown and DeBerniere in their report to General Gage after the spying trip they took to Concord a month earlier. It must have seemed ominous to Smith at this point, and even more so to DeBerniere himself, who was marching with the leading troops of the front company as they crossed the flat open space toward the hill.

The flank guard on the left was still engaged around the boulders and Smith had no protection forward at that point. He had committed himself to speed, and now his men hurried blindly across Nelson's Bridge, hardly looking at the hill only fifty yards to the front. This was Smith's most vulnerable moment, of all the hours and miles of marching—and Captain John Parker of Lexington was waiting to take full advantage of it.

John Parker had performed a miracle of leadership, regrouping and reanimating his company after the regulars overran it in the dawn attack that left twenty-five percent of the men killed or wounded. Somehow he was able to transform the scattered and demoralized soldiers into a fighting unit again, determined to avenge the loss of their comrades by meeting the British on their return from Concord. The brave men marched westward out of town at ten o'clock that morning, the fifer playing *The White Cockade* as they headed for the Lincoln-Lexington line.

The British might return by the same route they had used on the way out, or they might pass south of the town, through Waltham. Parker gambled that they would come back on the shortest route—through Lexington—and he hoped to give them a proper reception this time. He may have heard some news of the activities at Concord, but it is more likely that he made his plans for battle on the basis of what he learned in his first encounter with the British troops. Parker had been maladroit in his attempt to meet and deal with the regulars while in a parade ground formation earlier that morning, but when it came to preparing an ambush, Indian style, his awkwardness disappeared. Besides, the intentions of the British now were obvious, and there was only one thing to do: fight them as hard as he could.

Parker selected the hill east of Nelson's Bridge as his ambush position. It was the first hill inside the Lexington line, and in the absence of further orders he felt that it was still his primary duty to defend the town. The hill would provide him a clear view of the regulars as they came down the road, while at the same time concealing his men. The slope of the hill was quite abrupt, spotted with outcroppings of ledge, and covered by trees and tangles of brush. The approaches from the west and from the south were across 200 yards of open fields, and to the north Pine Hill rose 100 feet above the road, making any attempt to flank his position quite difficult and slow. He placed his men, upwards of 100 of them now, on a line about halfway up the slope and well hidden. Each man cleared an opening in the brush

—just enough to get a good view over his musket barrel down the road to the west. Then began the long wait.

There was none of the confusion and hesitation of the earlier battle; the issue was now crystal clear. The Lexington men knew firsthand the power of the regulars and their willingness to use it. They had experienced the stunning shock of a point-blank volley from the redcoats drawn up in line, and had seen their comrades bayonetted by the charging troops. Beaten and swept aside into the fields and woods north of Lexington Green, they had listened and watched as the regulars fired a victory volley and gave three cheers, while men of Lexington died in the grass a few yards away. Better than anyone else these bitter Lexington men knew they were at war.

At one o'clock a horseman galloped in from Concord to tell Parker that the British had fired on the Concord men and were now on their way back toward Lexington. It was not long until sounds of firing echoed in the distance, sometimes single shots, then heavier exchanges. From their hill positions the men of Parker's command could see a thousand yards or more down the road, and they strained to catch sight of the first rank of redcoats.

The earliest sign of the oncoming battle was the thin white smoke drifting up through the trees on both sides of the road in the distance, marking the heavy volume of fire around The Bloody Angle. Shortly after this the men of Parker's company could pick out the figures of minute men and militia running through the fields. Then, much more quickly than they expected, the battle was upon them. The harried regulars burst into view at a curve far down the road, marching very unevenly as the soldiers tried to return the fire they were receiving from the flanks. A large number of the redcoats were wounded, some of them half carried along by their comrades. Hatless officers gestured with their sabers and shouted orders that were carried away by the wind.

The redcoat column continued its headlong pace toward the hill where the Lexington men waited, muskets cocked and aimed at a spot in the road just over the Nelson Bridge and directly in front of their position. Parker's troops watched the left flank guard on the north side of the road come up over a little rise behind Nelson's farmyard and turn away to engage the provincials in the field of boulders. On the south side the right flank guard continued on, splashing heavily through the creek and clambering over a stone wall into Jacob Whittemore's ploughed field directly south of the ambush hill and about 200 yards away.

Smith had no scouts out to the front. The energetic Lieutenant Sutherland, who served as Smith's eyes and ears far ahead of the leading companies on the march out, was now bouncing along in a buggy at the rear of the column, a shallow but ugly and painful wound across his chest (it was thought, at that time, that he was dying). Lieutenant Adair was serving with one of the marine companies, and Surgeon's Mate Simms, the part-time point man of the 43rd, was very busy with his primary job.

The first of the redcoats to come over the Nelson Bridge was Captain Parsons with the ragged remains of his company, including Ensign Lister, in great pain because of his smashed elbow and almost severed right arm, and Lieutenant Kelly, also with one arm useless since the fight at the North Bridge. Smith was riding with them at the head of the column, well recognized by Parker's men as they squinted down their musket barrels at him.

Behind them Battier's company with its three wounded lieutenants came across the bridge, followed by the light infantry of the Royal Welch Fusiliers, who were also providing the flankers out to the right, and then Captain Laurie's 43rd Regiment company, missing Lieutenant Hull, who had been badly wounded at the North Bridge.

Parker let the British come right up to his position and start to pass before he opened fire with a volley that swept across the first three or four companies from their left side. Lieutenant Colonel Smith was struck in the thigh and unhorsed, Captain Parsons was hit in the arm, and a number of the soldiers went down under this first fire. Major Pitcairn rode up and took over, organizing a return fire and bringing up grenadier companies from the rear of the column to circle to the north and attack Parker's right flank. On the south, the British flank guard turned in through the fields and crossed the road to come in on the left of the Lexington company's position.

All this took time, and the companies of regulars began to pack tightly into this section of the road as the pressure on the rear built up. Parker's veterans kept firing as fast as they could as the grenadiers and light infantry closed in on them. Jedediah Munroe, bandaged from a wound received in the earlier fighting on the green, was hit again and died on the hill.

The regulars drove Parker back, first to the top of the hill, then down the east side, where his men finally were forced to

scatter in the woods. But while the British prepared and executed this assault, hundreds of provincials once more were able to
catch up with the column and circle around to get ahead of it
near Fiske Hill, the next piece of high ground on the road.
Parker forced Smith and Pitcairn to waste precious time: the
companies that had fired on the grenadiers at Meriam's Corner,
three miles back, were now in front of the column again, among
them the Reading men commanded by John Brooks.

Worse still for the regulars, the thing Smith feared most was
happening—the tail end of the column was becoming pinned down
by the provincial fire, and all along the road the companies,
wedged in closely, were intermingled and disorganized. Wounded
men, fearful of being left behind (and possibly scalped, the fate
they thought their comrades at the North Bridge had suffered),
were leaving their units and struggling up toward the front of
the column. Those who could no longer walk were begging for a
chance to hang on a saddle girth. Colonel Smith found a horse
and got up on it, then turned it over to Ensign Lister, the
officer he had counseled not to come along on this trip in the
first place. Lister, seeing three soldiers more badly wounded
than he was, dismounted and gave the horse to them. They
hobbled away, using the horse half as a shield and half as
support. Another horse, wrote Lister, "was shot dead close by
me, that had a wounded man on his back and three hanging by
his sides. . . ."

Pitcairn, once he saw that the attack against the rebel
ambush had relieved the pressure on his front and his left flank,
began to look for a way to get the column organized and moving
once again. Just a few hundred yards farther down toward Lexington the road curved around the small hill called The Bluff. If
he could position a force on The Bluff, he could use it as a
strong point to hold back the rebels while the column rallied on
the far side. He ordered his marines, the men from his own
command, up on The Bluff, and riding hard up and down the
length of the column, saber flashing, he urged the flagging
companies to get around behind the protection of the little hill.

The idea worked. For the first time since The Bloody Angle,
the pressure against the exhausted companies in the rear was
lifted as the marines held back the rebels for a few minutes. On
the Lexington side of The Bluff, Pitcairn managed to put the
column in some kind of marching order and get them started up
Fiske Hill. He paid for the few moments of relief with heavy

casualties among the marines who held The Bluff. Among them Captain Souter was wounded in the leg and put out of action, Lieutenant Potter was wounded and captured, and several of the men were killed or wounded.

In the end, the extra time was as helpful to the provincials as it was to Pitcairn. He had no sooner put the column in motion once again than a volley of fire raked the lead companies. Pitcairn's horse reared, threw him, and galloped away, leaving the major sprawled in the road, shaken but unhurt. To the British troops this volley was a message telling them that they had not escaped the grip of the provincials and that every inch of the road would be contested in Lexington as it had been in Lincoln. From this point on, neither Pitcairn nor the wounded Smith was able to exert any control over the twenty-one mauled and dispirited companies of light infantry and grenadiers.

The collapse, when it came, was rapid and complete. Fiske Hill was a steep climb with the road hemmed in by woods on both sides, and the unseen enemy lashed the redcoat ranks with musket fire from fifty yards away. More fresh companies had arrived, including Captain Samuel Thatcher's Cambridge men from Gardner's Militia Regiment, a sister company to the Lexington unit, with a strength of seventy-seven men. At least five regulars lost their lives trying to keep the road open across Fiske Hill. The fighting was all at very close quarters. At the Ebenezer Fiske house James Hayward of Isaac Davis's Acton minute men met a regular in the yard near the well. They fired simultaneously at point-blank range. The regular died instantly and Hayward survived him only a few hours. Near here Noah Eaton of Framingham pointed his musket at a regular in the act of loading his Brown Bess and said, "Surrender or die." The regular handed over his weapon and Eaton led him away, never telling him that he, too, had an empty musket.

In the little valley between Fiske Hill and Concord Hill a wounded British soldier sat down by the side of the road; he could go no farther. Other wounded men joined him, until in all six men were left behind as the column hurried on (the men were carried to nearby houses, where three died that day; the other three later were transferred to the Buckman Tavern and cared for there).

In the ranks of the companies climbing the slope of Concord Hill, just outside Lexington, the men would no longer listen to orders, or else were too apathetic to hear. They made no

The Minute Men in Action

attempt to return the heavy fire of the rebels, but simply disregarded it. Every officer and sergeant knew the end was only minutes away, and in a final and hopeless gesture, a handful of the junior officers attempted to stop the rout by threatening to kill some of their own men. Ensign DeBerniere, who by some miracle had survived to guide the leading elements through this six-mile inferno, later described the final moments of Smith's disintegrating command:

> . . . we at first kept our order and returned their fire as hot as we received it, but when we arrived within a mile of Lexington, our ammunition began to fail, and the light companies were so fatigued with flanking they were scarce able to act, and a great number of wounded scarce able to get forward, made a great confusion; Col. Smith (our commanding officer) had received a wound through his leg, a number of officers were also wounded, so that we began to run rather than retreat in order—the whole behaved with amazing bravery but little order; we attempted to stop the men and form them two deep, but to no purpose, the confusion increased rather than lessened: at last, after we got through Lexington, the officers got to the front and presented their bayonets, and told the men if they advanced they should die: upon this they began to form under a very heavy fire.

DeBerniere was a bit inaccurate as to the place this occurred— he could not have been "through Lexington" because Smith's men saw the reinforcements before they passed Lexington Green—but the situation he describes is unmistakable. The column was finished. The British return fire had weakened and died away, and the rebels, stronger than ever, were moving in for the kill. Only a miracle could save what remained of Smith's force.

At that point the miracle happened. The officers pointing muskets at their own troops were astounded to see the men break into a wild spontaneous cheer, and turning toward Lexington they saw, on the hill at the far side of town, the long, perfect lines of red and white—a regular brigade drawn up in a line of regiments, filling the whole hill with soldiers. Above the ranks flew the colors of the famous regiments—the King's Own, the Royal Welch Fusiliers, the 47th Foot, and Major Pitcairn's marines. There was a puff of smoke from the center of this long battle line followed by the dull report of a cannon—the Royal Artillery was in the field.

With the sight of nearly a thousand British reinforcements, the sound of the boom of the cannon and of the great cheer from the parched throats of Smith's men, the provincials were stopped in their tracks. The firing ceased. The Massachusetts men watched in numb silence as victory was wrested from their grasp, and Lieutenant Colonel Francis Smith, weary to death, blood-spattered, and covered with dust, hobbled painfully across Lexington Green, staring at the relief force waiting for him in the distance. He was saved.

Chapter **22**

Percy's Relief Column

Gage fretted about the conduct of the expedition from the time he began to write and rewrite the order; if he had been present to see the confusion at the foot of the common when Smith and the column left Boston he might have been even more worried about the fate of the operation. As it was, neither Gage nor Major General Haldimand, his commander of troops, nor any of the three brigade commanders saw fit to observe or supervise Smith's departure. Later in the evening, when it became clear that "the town was a good deal agitated and alarmed at this movement," Gage decided to place Brigadier Earl Percy's First Brigade on alert as a possible reinforcement for Smith. He sent an aide with written orders for Percy to stand by with his brigade at four o'clock the following morning, ready for further instructions. This message was delivered to the quarters of Brigade Major Moncrieff. Moncrieff, unfortunately, was not at home, and when he did arrive he failed to notice the message left for him and went to bed. Thus when four o'clock came around, nothing happened—Percy's brigade slept soundly.

At five o'clock that morning the messenger Smith had sent back from Menotomy finally arrived at the Province House, and requested that the general be awakened. He informed Gage that Smith considered the situation very dangerous, with the country-

189

side alerted and very active, and that Smith requested immediate reinforcement. It is likely that Smith and Gage had discussed this possibility beforehand and agreed that such a request would be answered by ordering one of the brigades out immediately. Gage sent word for First Brigade to form up with full battle gear at the accustomed place on Common Street (now Tremont) east of The Mall.

But First Brigade, from the commander to the last private soldier, was still asleep. Officers were scattered through the town in homes where they had been billeted and the troops were in tents on the common and north of Beacon Street. The order from brigade headquarters, signed at six o'clock and requiring all units to be in formation by 7:30, did not reach the separate regiments until about seven o'clock.

Moving with "the utmost expedition" the regiments managed to get their men to the assembly area at Common Street by the appointed time—except for the marines. In the hasty delivery of orders to all the troop units, someone forgot that the marine commander, Major Pitcairn, had been sent with Colonel Smith, and the marching orders for the marines still lay on Pitcairn's desk at his rooms almost next door to Paul Revere's house in North Square.

Percy rode up and down the column, impatient for some sign of the marines. When assembly time passed by with still no marines, he sent his aide out to the north end of town to their barracks, and there the error was discovered and the battalion was told that the whole brigade was formed up and waiting for them. It is not difficult to imagine the scene at the marine barracks during the next half hour.

The advance guard of First Brigade, a captain and fifty men from the 4th (King's Own) Regiment, was standing down near Frog Lane (Boylston Street) at the south end of the common. Behind them came the rest of the 4th, minus the light infantry and grenadiers that were already out with Smith (all Percy's regiments, for that reason, had only eight companies present). The 4th was commanded by Lieutenant Colonel Maddison, who led the expedition that took the powder from Quarry Hill and caused the Powder Alarm. Next in line, in front of Percy's own quarters at Winter Street, was the 47th (Lancashire) Regiment, Colonel Nesbitt commanding. This was the unit that had tarred and feathered Billerica's Thomas Ditson. After the 47th there was a space left for the marines about opposite the Burying Grounds (though called a "battalion," the marines at 400 strong were larger than any of the regiments in Boston). The 23rd Regiment (Royal Welch Fusiliers), with its leading company at School Street, stretched back to "Scollay's buildings" where the rear guard was placed (another fifty men, probably drawn from the 23rd). The two brass six-pounders of the Royal Artillery initially were located between the 4th Regiment and the advance guard but were later moved to the middle of the column.

Hugh, Earl Percy had been a colonel commanding the 5th Regiment (Northumberland Fusiliers) until Gage made him an acting brigadier and put him in charge of First Brigade (Percy's old regiment was placed in Second Brigade under Brigadier Pigott). Though only thirty-two years old, Percy already had now commanded the brigade for almost a year and within three months would be promoted to major general. He had been a regimental commander in his middle twenties, he was a veteran of Minden, and he was respected as a cool and competent battle leader.

Percy loved magnificent horses, and he had the money to buy a few. He was the son of an influential earl, which may in some measure account for his rapid rise in the army, but this did not divorce him from his soldiers. He always had shown a deep interest in the welfare of his men and they liked him for it. When the 5th Regiment was sent from England to Boston, Percy paid £700 to help the soldiers who wanted to bring their wives along. In the practice marches Percy often left his horse behind and marched along with the men, even though he was bothered by attacks of gout which later forced his retirement from an active military and political life.

Percy could be strict with his troops, and he had a reputation for fairness among the citizens of Boston. John Andrews in his letters describes an incident in which two officers of the 38th Regiment insulted two women. The husbands went to see Percy. As Andrews relates: "They then both went and press'd a complaint to Lord Percy: what satisfaction he gave 'em, can't learn, but from his disposition to punish every misbehavior, either in officers or soldiers, I am perswaded he will do them justice." One of the indications of his strong personality is that he was often described as "handsome" and "imposing," while actually he was thin, long nosed, and so weak-eyed that he could not see to write by candlelight.

He was not happy about his orders to reinforce Colonel Smith. He had very little sympathy for the "extremely violent & wrong headed" people of Massachusetts, but he did not want to march against them. His father, in the House of Lords, voted against the Stamp Act and disliked the idea of strong military forces intimidating the colonies. At the time Gage was contemplating a march to Worcester, Percy wrote home to say, "I should imagine . . . from some informations which I have received, that it will be necessary to detach a brigade up farther into the country; for I understand the people are beginning to be a little troublesome there. As I cannot say this is a business I very much admire, I hope it will not be my fate to be ordered up with them."

This was, however, to be his fate. The orders from Gage were not detailed; he was told only to march "to support" the earlier expedition. Beyond the sketchy news that Smith's column had been discovered almost immediately, and that the countryside was alarmed and assembling, nothing had been heard from Smith.

Percy, however, was not worried. He was still of the opinion that the provincials, as fighters, were a "cowardly lot," unlikely to be of any real concern to the regular troops, and that while his troops should be prepared to fight there was no need to become overexcited. Colonel Samuel Cleaveland, commanding the 4th Battalion, Royal Artillery, told Percy that his two field pieces going with the brigade had only twenty-four rounds apiece in the side boxes, and suggested that Percy take along an extra wagon, located nearby and already loaded with 140 rounds for the six-pounders. "Lord Percy refused to take it, saying it might retard their march," wrote Cleaveland, smarting under criticism that he had allowed the brigade's artillery to run out of ammunition, ". . . he did not imagine there would be any occasion for more than was on the side boxes."

At 8:30 the marines finally arrived (there is no record of the exchange of conversation between the troops as the marines, marching to their position in the column, passed by the Royal Welch Fusiliers, who had been waiting in the street in full equipment for an hour). Fifteen minutes later, Percy gave the order to march and the column started down to Boston Neck, flags flying and fifers playing.

Percy ordered a slow rate of march. In view of the unknown situation he did not want to tire his men or to give the idea that this was an emergency. The pace all the way to Lexington averaged three miles per hour—definitely not a forced march, but one calculated to keep the men fresh and ready to fight.

The route Percy selected, actually the only one open to him

unless he wanted to ferry his troops, horses, wagons, and cannon across the Charles, was the road through Roxbury and Brookline to the bridge at Cambridge. This route was well known to all his men; they had used it on several regimental practice marches and on the brigade march three weeks earlier. Once across the river and through the town of Cambridge, he could follow Smith's trail through Menotomy and Lexington to Concord.

All the way through Roxbury, across the Muddy River at Brookline, and on to the Charles River Bridge, the column marched through an empty and quiet countryside. Shutters were pulled tight on the houses, the farm fields were vacant, the people were gone from the streets and yards, and only an occasional barking dog greeted the approach of the regulars. The soldiers marched uneasily through this silent world, and many later mentioned the strange impression it conveyed to them. Percy noted in his report that "all the houses were shut up, and there was not the appearance of a single inhabitant. . . ."

Percy sent his engineer, Captain John Montresor, with four volunteers out ahead of the column to secure the bridge at Cambridge, keep the rebels from blocking it, and repair it as necessary. Arriving there Montresor saw that Percy's concern for the bridge was well founded: the planking had been torn from the stringers. The rebels made the mistake of leaving the planks close by and on Percy's side of the river.

Lord Percy wanted the bridge completely repaired; he was so concerned with the bridge that he had requested wagonloads of lumber to accompany his column, to be used in case the timbers at the bridge site were destroyed. After the column got across, Percy ordered the supply wagons to be left behind until the twelve-man wagon guard finished replacing the roadway of the bridge.

The column marched on, past the empty and silent brick buildings of the Harvard Yard and through the town of Cambridge. Not long afterward Percy turned westward on the Lexington Road. They were now, for the first time, following in the footsteps of Smith's column. There are many anecdotes telling of encounters and conversations between Percy and various people in Cambridge, but in his report he says he saw no one until his brigade reached Menotomy. At this little village three miles beyond Cambridge Percy received his first information of Smith. One of the Loyalists in the town told him "that there had been a skirmish between His Majesty's troops and the rebels at Lexington and that they were still engaged." Percy increased his pace up the long hill from Foot of the Rocks toward the high ground south of Lexington.

A short distance farther on, a light buggy came down toward the column, and when it was stopped by the advance guard Percy found that it was Lieutenant Gould from his own brigade (who had been with Smith as an officer in the 4th's light infantry company). Gould, wounded in the foot, confirmed the news of the fighting and had much to add. Smith's command was in serious danger, he told Percy. The rebels had surrounded the column with a strong force, well armed, and were mounting fierce attacks against it. The regulars were "retiring, overpowered by numbers, greatly exhausted and fatigued, and having expended almost all their ammunition." Where were they now? Gould did not know. Somewhere beyond Lexington. Percy pushed on.

Behind Percy's brigade the bridge was finished and the two supply wagons, with their twelve-man squad as a guard, started forward to catch up with the column. At the same time, in Menotomy, a group of old men, too old to be fit for active service, gathered in the main street of town after Percy marched on toward Lexington. Their purpose was not merely to speculate on the events of the day, however. All of them were armed. David Lamson, a half-Indian who had fought for the English in the French and Indian War, was the natural leader of this group, which included Ammi Cutter, Jason and Joe Belknap, James Budge, and Israel Mead. All of them were aware of what had happened at Lexington early that morning although they did not know of the running fight now going on up ahead. They were watching for stragglers from Percy's column, or for any opportunity to do damage to the British.

This opportunity presented itself when a mounted provincial messenger called out that a wagon and a squad of British soldiers were coming up the road from Cambridge. The old veterans realized that this must be part of the supply train, attempting to reach the rest of the column, and they huddled together to plan an ambush.

The men crouched down behind a stone wall on the north side of the road and waited. When the wagon drew abreast of them they leaped up and fired, killing the driver and the horse. The guard of soldiers surrendered and were taken off singly out of the British line of march. A second wagon, following soon after, met the same fate. The captured wagons remained hidden for most of the day in a spot just north of the road, where passing soldiers from several of the towns replaced their powder supply and availed themselves of what equipment they found in the loads. Eventually the wagons were taken to Danvers, the horses to Medford, and the captured soldiers to the jail at Ipswich.

Lieutenant Gould soon passed this spot—or tried to do so. The old men stopped his buggy at gunpoint and captured him. Finding that he was wounded, they took him to Ammi Cutter's house, where Mrs. Cutter looked after him until a doctor could be found.

Percy's column, with the brigadier riding in the lead on his fine sorrel, topped the ridge just south of the town of Lexington at 2:30 P.M. All along the road for the last ten or fifteen minutes the men had been listening to the steadily increasing sound of firing—not volleys, but raggedly spaced shots—and when Percy saw the town across the flat ground a mile ahead, he decided to halt on the hill and form a line by fanning out to the right and left of the road. This was quickly executed, the soldiers leaping over stone walls and running through the fields. The 4th Regiment straddled the road, with the 47th on its right flank and the 23rd on its left. The marines were held back as a reserve on the road behind the 4th, and the artillery was wheeled up in the center.

From their line the soldiers could look out over the town to the hills half a mile beyond it to the northwest. Directly ahead, about a thousand yards away, the meetinghouse dominated the fork where the road divided and ran off to Concord on the left and Bedford on the right. Down in front of Percy's position lay a swamp to the south of the road and open fields to the north. It was a good defensive position; from every side except the rear the land sloped downhill and was fairly open.

The sounds of firing up ahead continued to grow louder and louder, and drifting smoke appeared on the hills beyond the town. Suddenly the first few redcoats broke into view on the crest of the hill. As more and more of Smith's men appeared, a great cheer echoed across the town, and the firing on the flanks slackened a bit. The cheers continued as each company cleared the crest and saw the brigade waiting ahead.

Percy took one look and ordered his cannoneers to load. Even though he had been warned by Gould, he could not believe his eyes. Smith's wracked column was in full retreat, with rebels swarming along both flanks. There was no sign of order or precision, neither in the formation nor in the firing. The regulars were almost running, trying to stay ahead of the rebels, and very few of them were firing. They were now in the center of town, crossing the green. Percy directed the artillery to put a few rounds off on the flanks of the column. At the first boom of the cannon another ragged cheer went up from the oncoming regulars, and the provincials scattered and fell back. Percy's ranks opened and the regulars struggled up the hill and poured through, faces grimy, uniforms torn and bloody and blackened with dirt and gunpowder, their hoarse voices calling for water. Their comrades in the brigade fired volley after volley at the rebels, keeping them at a distance.

Gage had sent his own aide-de-camp, Lieutenant Rooke of the 4th Regiment, along with the column to act as a messenger between Percy and himself. At this point Percy called Rooke over and told him to ride for Boston with the word that the brigade had found Smith and would be coming back probably heavily engaged. In a reverse of the ride of Paul Revere and William Dawes, Rooke galloped toward Boston alone, taking to the fields and woods whenever rebel companies came in sight. In fact, he followed almost the same route Revere had taken, crossing back to Boston over the Charlestown ferry at about four o'clock that afternoon.

The sense of relief that Smith's men must have enjoyed as they caught their breath in the comparative safety of Percy's lines is evident in the words of a soldier in one of the riddled companies: ". . . we had no firing in front then which was the effect of our meeting the 1st Brigade a little on this side of Lexington under the command of Lord Percy who made one of the best dispositions I ever saw and soon drove back the Enemy, we now began to entertain very sanguine hopes of our returning in safety to Boston." Of Smith's command at this time Percy said simply, "I had the happiness of saving them from inevitable destruction."

Chapter 23

Lexington Surrounded

The men from the battered column passed into the lines of the brigade and Smith received directions from Percy to move his companies a few hundred yards down the ridge to the Munroe Tavern, where he could rest his men and treat the wounded. The tavern was just off the road on the south side, an easy spot to defend because of the high ground in that area, and well protected by the 23rd Regiment's left flank companies curving around below it on the border of the swamp. Smith made this building his headquarters. His men, grouped in their company formations, lay down under the nearby trees to rest, and his wounded were carried inside the tavern to be attended by Mr. Sims and the surgeons.

Smith's passage through Percy's lines to safety was not without incident; as he came limping through, the minute men and militia were close on his heels. There had been a momentary pause as the pageantry of Percy's brigade impressed itself upon the provincials, but then a large number of them surged ahead again, took up the fire, and harassed Smith's column until the last company fought its way into the waiting ranks of the relief brigade. In fact, this last sally at Smith's rear guard carried some of the provincial units in against Percy's left flank, by the swamps on the south side of the road, where the Royal Welch

Fusiliers were waiting and watching their fellow soldiers taking punishment from the provincial sharpshooting.

The British soldiers, forced to stand their ground and look on helplessly while the rebel fire continued, became so furious that they broke their ranks, dashed out into the swamp, and tried to pursue the rebels, who withdrew into the woods. One of the regulars in that action later admitted, "Revenge had so fully possessed the breasts of the soldiers that the battalions broke, regardless of every order, to pursue the affrightened runaways. They were however formed again, tho' with some difficulty, and it would have been scarcely possible but for a morass which lay between us and the enemy."

With the assistance of the "morass," the volatile regulars were brought under control by their officers, who knew that a disorganized pursuit of the rebels into the woods and swamps would be playing directly into enemy hands, besides being contrary to orders. The line at the foot of the hill was restored and remained in place guarding the swamp approaches on the north during the rest of the time. Percy was not interested in attacking to punish the rebels. He knew he would be fortunate to maintain a coordinated defense on the return to Boston.

The activity on the left flank settled into a sniper's war, with the minute men and militia skulking through the woods, always attempting to edge close enough to get a shot into the British lines, and the regulars a bit embarrassed about running for cover to avoid the fire, yet not wanting to stand in formation and be shot. The British solved the knotty problem of military convention by pulling back their lines somewhat and putting out a handful of good shots to advantageous points where they could return the sniping of the provincials. Thus, in a characteristic compromise they maintained the dignity of their colorful ranks, standing in the open (but back a bit and close to the stone walls) while their marksmen, "lying on their bellies like rebels," fought the battle. It was a good move. It saved ammunition, used a minimum force to keep the rebels at their distance, and kept the companies formed and ready in case the rebels massed for an attack.

Over on the right flank, north of the road, the situation was about the same. Beyond the Woburn Road, which ran off to the eastward just below the positions of the 47th Regiment, Estabrook Hill rose 100 feet higher than the surrounding ground and dominated the zone. Since the regiment did not choose to occupy the hill, the regulars were forced back from the Woburn Road, leaving the long stone walls there to be manned by the rebels in force. The good protection for the rebels here and the proximity of the two forces led to a warm exchange of fire during the hour that the 47th defended this position.

On the main road, beginning at the place where it entered the British position and extending back to the Munroe Tavern, there were several houses that overlooked the British positions and would offer excellent fields of fire for rebel snipers. Percy, who by now had heard Smith's story of the rebels who fired from the buildings around Lexington Green that morning and at The Bloody Angle that afternoon, decided that the houses would have to go.

He sent word to Colonel Maddison, and squads moved into the farmyard of Deacon Joseph Loring and set fire to the house, barn, and corn house. The stone walls around the house were knocked down to keep rebel marksmen from using them to get up close to Percy's cannon, which were in position nearby. Farther down the road toward the tavern, two more houses and two attached shops were also destroyed by fire.

This burning of the houses, obviously intended as a precaution against sniping, had other effects on the British troops. Before the buildings were destroyed they were ransacked for items of value, and this act weakened the inhibitions of many soldiers who had been instructed by Smith to leave personal property strictly alone. To many, the destruction meant that the old orders no longer counted, and from this point until the end of the battle the conduct of the regulars worsened to the extent that several of the officers later made note of it in official reports.

With the threat of sniping from the building now eliminated, Percy was satisfied with the troop dispositions curving back along both flanks. Some of the provincials had begun to move north and south of the ridge, obviously intending to get on his rear and hinder his withdrawal, but for the moment at least the situation was well in control. He rode back along the main road to Munroe's Tavern to confer with Smith, Pitcairn, and his regimental commanders, Maddison, Nesbitt, and Bernard, to decide on a formation for the return.

At the tavern he found that even an hour's rest was going to be barely sufficient for the exhausted grenadiers and light infantry. On both sides of the road for hundreds of yards men were lying in the grass in a dazed half-sleep. The kitchen of the large square inn had been tapped for everything that could be called food or—more important—beverage.

Nearly every room in the building was filled with Smith's casualties, some of whom would have to be left behind when the brigade moved on. Surrounded by these exhausted and wounded men, Percy, Smith, and the other officers stood in conference. Smith discussed the attack in Lexington earlier that day, insisting that this was an aggressive assault by the rebels and that it had triggered all the other attacks. He felt that if he had been able to get by Lexington in the morning, the rest of the fighting in all probability could have been avoided. He recounted the attack at the North Bridge, emphasizing the "scalping" episode, word of which had already spread through the regiments of First Brigade, and he described the fighting between Concord and Lexington, complaining that the rebels refused to do battle in a soldierly fashion, choosing to keep under cover rather than to form up in close ranks and march against him. This he considered ungallant.

Percy listened and made his own evaluation. His men had started with thirty-six rounds apiece, the cannons with twenty-four. It was now after three o'clock, already too late to get back to Boston before dark if he returned by the same route he had come out, through Menotomy, Cambridge, Brookline, and Roxbury. The route of withdrawal was certain to be contested by at least some of the rebel units. If they did manage to block the road to Boston and make him fight his way out, Percy knew that he might lose more soldiers than he had saved by halting. He also knew that the halt would rest the rebels as well as Smith's men, and that new units were joining the rebel ranks every few minutes. In addition, he now was forced to assume that his supply wagons were lost and probably captured. Nothing had been heard from them since the brigade passed through Cambridge four hours earlier, and the road in that direction was now closed off by the rebels.

Percy, with the deliberate coolness so characteristic of him, decided to wait another half hour and to march at 3:30. Once the decision had been made, Percy informed his regimental commanders of the order of march. He then returned to the slope of the hill facing toward Lexington to watch the movements of the rebels.

Percy's leadership was without doubt the most important element in the successful extrication of Smith's column from its disastrous situation and also in the well conducted, though bloody, retreat to Boston. The comments of Smith's officers show that the sight of Percy riding around the position revived their spirits and made every man feel that the confusion and disorder was over. Tired and shaken troops became confident once again, and a military professionalism that had been lacking since the beginning of the operation was now increasingly more evident.

Percy's leadership, however, did not deter the provincials. Their steady movement around the north and south flanks of his defensive position was continuing, and a large group of rebels had assembled by the meetinghouse on the green. Percy had his cannoneers fire a few rounds in their direction to break up the group, and in the firing one of the balls struck the meetinghouse itself, passing completely through it. This enraged the Lexington soldiers, who had placed inside it the bodies of the men from town killed earlier that morning. Colonel Baldwin, who felt little concern for the house itself, was moved by the affair for another reason: he happened to be standing close to the rear wall when the cannonball came crashing out and sailed on leaving a trail of splintered clapboards and timbers flying in its wake. Like the other provincials he moved quickly away from the building and out of the area.

But this shot was one of the only rounds fired that day actually to cause any damage. Most of the rounds bounced off into the fields or rattled through the woods, and the provincials quickly became accustomed to the firing; in fact some of them, including Captain Davis's Acton company, ridiculed the ineffectiveness of the guns. One veteran of the battle later told Ezra Stiles (who recorded it in his diary) that Lord Percy "applied his field pieces but found them of no use the fire being lost on the *dispersed*, tho' *adhering* enemy." The reason the guns did not do much damage is that the regulars had to conserve the little ammunition available. Percy at this time may well have wished he had taken the advice of Colonel Cleaveland on carrying along the extra wagonload of rounds for the guns—but in view of the fate of the other wagons, perhaps it was just as well for the British that they had not done so.

The situation was growing better for the provincials and worse for the regulars with every passing minute, just as it had for Smith a few hours earlier, when he waited on the ridge at Concord while the rebel force around him grew and grew. The companies of minute men and militia, under the pressure of the alarm, had hastened away from their home towns before their

Minute Men Awaiting British

assembly was complete; they were now being augmented by the arrival of latecomers, straggling in by twos and threes.

At Lexington at this time facing the British there were the four complete regiments (those of Colonels Barrett, Bridge, Pierce, and Green) plus four others with about half their strength present (those of Colonels Gardner, Greaton, Prescott, and Davis, the latter commanding General Heath's old regiment). Only a few miles away and closing in on the town were companies from the regiments of Pickering, Fry, Johnson, and Robinson. Mounted messengers and guides, some sent by the regiments and some self-appointed, were stationed at every important crossroads to give news of the battle and suggest the best routes into the fighting area. William Tudor of Charlestown writes in his diary, "Rumor on rumor: men & horses driving post up & down the roads. . . . By 10 we heard of 2 or 3 redgements marching from Boston under the command of Lord Percy, with field pieces. . . ."

One of the minute man regiments that tried in vain to catch up with the battle was commanded by Colonel Fry, of Andover. Thomas Boynton, a soldier in Captain Ames's company of that regiment, described their attempt to join the fight: ". . . about the sun's rising the town was alarmed with the news that the Regulars was on their march to Concord. Upon which the town mustered and about 10 o'clock marched onward for Concord. In Tewksbury news came that the Regulars had fired on our men in Lexington, and had killed 8. In Billerica news came that the enemy were killing and slaying our men in Concord. Bedford we had the news that the enemy had retreated back; we shifted our course and pursued after them as fast as possible, but all in vain; the enemy had the start 3 or 4 miles." This constant receipt of information on the battle was also mentioned by one of the minute man officers with Colonel Fry, Lieutenant Benjamin Farnum, also of Andover, who chronicles the "quick march" to within about five miles of Concord, where "meeting with the news of their retreat for Boston again . . . we turned our course in order to catch them . . . but could not come up with them."

In many of the provincial companies, and especially in the minute men, the commanders had made arrangements to have a supply wagon follow the unit when it marched (in Malden, small boys rode out with full saddlebags to replenish the men), and at Lexington, because of the halt, these supplies caught up with the companies and were an additional help to morale.

The disorganization of this growing force of minute men and

militia, now approximately 2,000 men, has always been overemphasized—to the point of assuming that there was no organization at all. There was without doubt a vast confusion in and around Lexington, engendered by the earlier attempts of the rebel regiments to intercept the British and by a lack of overall command. The initial effect of the cannon fire that greeted the provincials on their arrival in the town contributed to the breaking up of regiments, as did the rough ground and woods they had just passed through on Concord and Fiske Hills, and the loss of several good company commanders. Additionally, the provincials had no desire to mass in regimental formation and attack the regulars. They continued to fight as they had up until this point —under control of their company officers, with regimental officers directing groups of three or four companies wherever possible. Lieutenant Colonel William Tompson controlled the Billerica companies of Green's regiment; Captain John Nixon and his brother Thomas kept the Framingham and Sudbury minute men together, while Lieutenant Ezekiel How led the militia companies from those same towns. Several other regimental officers, who like the Nixons were to go on later to regimental commands (or higher) in Washington's army, were providing field leadership— among them John Brooks, James and William Prescott, Loammi Baldwin, Ebenezer Bridge, John Greaton, Thomas Gardner, William Bond, and John Robinson, all of whom were at this time commanders or staff officers of minute men and militia regiments present on the battlefield.

The idea that the 2,000 men fought only as individuals against the British at Lexington has little in the way of support. Many of the provincial soldiers who recorded their description of the battle saw nothing but action of single men or small groups, but the senior officers spoke of regimental organization. Thus Major Francis Faulkner "was organizing his regiment to work upon the flank of the enemy so soon as he should move again for Boston." The British soldiers said that their opponents were "much scattered, and not above 50 of them to be seen in a body in any one place" on the field at Lexington; since the minute man and militia companies averaged about fifty men apiece, this again points to company-size battle units, working their way into positions on Percy's front, flanks, and rear, keeping their formations spread so as not to present a target for the cannon, and slipping in as close as possible to harass the redcoats with sniper fire. They knew that time was on their side—the regulars were expending their ammunition and the day was wearing on. Soon Percy would be faced with the necessity to resume the kind of tormented march that Smith suffered, which was just what the provincials wanted.

At this time Brigadier General William Heath arrived to lead the Massachusetts forces in the field, and to prove himself peculiarly fitted for that job at that moment.

There were six generals in the Provincial Army at the time, although none actually had commanded in the field. All had been appointed about two months earlier. The senior general, Jedediah Preble, declined to serve; Artemas Ward, a former minute man regimental commander, was sick in Worcester County; Seth Pomeroy, the third ranking general, was on his way from Worcester with his minute man regiment; John Thomas was down in Plymouth County; and the most junior of the generals, John Whitcomb, also a minute man regimental commander, was on his way from Worcester and would arrive later in the day, in time to join Heath.

Heath was at this time respected by his fellow soldiers as a tactician with an all-encompassing knowledge of military affairs. Like his contemporaries Timothy Pickering and Henry Knox, he was a theorist who had acquired his reputation through his knowledge of the military literature of the time. Knox owned a bookstore well stocked in military works and frequented by British as well as American officers in the years before the war; Pickering contributed essays to the press and wrote a book on tactics and drill; Heath wrote "addresses to the public" for a local newspaper, signing himself "A Military Country-man." At the opening of the war Knox was twenty-three, Pickering was twenty-nine, and Heath was thirty-eight. None of the three had any combat experience, but all rose quickly to positions of responsibility in Washington's army—and there the parallels ended. Knox became one of Washington's irreplaceable leaders and the father of American artillery; Pickering moved into staff positions, becoming first adjutant general, then quartermaster general, of the army; Heath was unable to apply his rather aphoristic military knowledge to the problems confronting him later in the war, and was shifted to positions where a general was needed in name only.

But Heath's mistakes came later; at Lexington, he was in his element. If his weakness lay in his inability to grasp the scope of a large military action, he was nevertheless a genius of the minor plan, moving a gun here, catching a prisoner there, deceiving a sentry somewhere else. His memoirs are full of detailed and anecdotal appreciations of the acts of small groups, while the battles in which he was involved as a senior leader seem always to be garbled by just such fixation on incidents of lesser consequence.

But at Lexington, where organization of the battle to a level where regiments could be directed by a brigade headquarters was completely out of the question, Heath's firm grasp of the tactics of the skirmish line and his tendency to see any battle as a series of isolated little fights was just what the provincials needed. Where a general accustomed to a staff, or at the very least to a planned and coordinated operation, would have been lost, Heath was quite at home, happily—and effectively—walking about the battlefield, helping regimental commanders to pull their people together, advising company commanders on the best use of terrain, moving units down on the flanks of the British and on toward Menotomy in the rear, and above all simply being present. His encouragement—the presence of the fat, bald, popular young general that everybody knew and liked—was enough.

With Heath in the field every man felt that this combat action was approved at the very highest level, a fact which until then had been in some doubt. Heath was not only a general in the Provincial Army, he was a member of the Committee of Safety, the action committee in control of the army (which had been given specific authorization by the Provincial Congress to call out the militia and minute men in case of danger). And accompanying General Heath was a fellow member of the committee, the well-known patriot Dr. Joseph Warren, who was to die a few weeks later as a major general on Bunker Hill.

Warren, who was described by a contemporary as "perhaps the most active man in the field" during this day, had been involved in the battle since the night before, when he sent Paul Revere and William Dawes on their way to Lexington to warn Hancock and Adams. He had little knowledge of military operations and was regarded as more an inspirational leader than a tactician, a man whose presence spurred the soldiers. Quotations attributed to him are characteristically encouraging and optimistic: "Keep up a brave heart . . . they have begun it . . . we'll end it. . . ." Warren and Heath made good partners, one cheering the men, the other providing specific tactical advice at the action level, and both lending dignity and official sanction to the fighting.

In another of the many coincidences of the day, Heath and Warren had been together at a meeting of the Committee of Safety in the afternoon of April 18, while Smith's troops were preparing their equipment for the march. The discussion at that meeting concerned the imminence of just such a march and the need for redistribution of supplies to spread out the large and tempting amount stored at Concord. The meeting was held at a tavern in Menotomy, right on the line of march of the regulars, and Heath on his way home to Roxbury about sunset rode by Major Mitchell's patrol near Cambridge.

Heath continued home and went to bed. At six in the morning he was awakened and informed that the British were on the march, "that they had crossed from Boston to Phips's farm, in boats, and had gone towards Concord, as was supposed, with intent to destroy the public stores." Heath immediately set out for Menotomy to find the rest of the Committee of Safety, but the march of the British had dispersed the other members, Orne, Lee, and Gerry, who had stayed the night at the inn. There was no one to make decisions for the guidance of the minute men and militia.

The next best thing was to join the army in the field, and Heath, taking a roundabout route through Watertown to avoid the British, arrived in Lexington after the battle there began. (He stopped in Watertown long enough to find a militia company and send it to block the bridge at Cambridge, another of his sound if minor decisions.) It was near Watertown that Heath ran into Warren, who was coming out from Boston to join the fighting provincials, and who like Heath had guessed that the road through Watertown—the long way around to Lexington—was less likely to be watched by the British. The two remained together for the rest of the day.

By the time they got to Lexington the houses near the British lines had been set afire, sending a pall of smoke over the town and "opening a new and more terrific scene" as a background for the occasional firing from the field pieces on the hill. Practically every contemporary account of the battle from the provincial side mentions their arrival, another indication of the importance that was attached to their presence as a nod of approval from the Provincial Congress and as a unifying force for the fifty-odd companies of militia and minute men then surrounding Percy.

Chapter 24

Percy Retreats

"**A**s it began to grow pretty late, and we had fifteen miles to retire, and only our thirty-six rounds, I ordered the Grenadiers and Light Infantry to move off first, and covered them with my Brigade. . . ." Percy's calm control is evident, even after the vicissitudes of the battle, in the words of his written report to Gage. It was 3:30 and the time had come to order Smith's battered and bandaged command to move out. Wounded soldiers, weary to the bone from more than seventeen hours of marching and fighting, forced themselves to their feet and shuffled into ranks in front of the Munroe Tavern. Major Pitcairn had assumed command of his marine battalion, leaving the wounded Smith to direct the march of the twenty-one companies. Smith's headquarters at this time was probably one of the commandeered buggies (his thigh wound now was so painful that he could hardly have walked).

With the mission of protecting the flanks now turned over to Percy's brigade, Smith put his grenadier companies in the van. They had taken less punishment than their compatriots in the light infantry and were in better shape. The ragged light infantry followed, several companies nearly stripped of officers and sergeants (wounded officers in Smith's column alone at this time included Smith himself plus two captains, eleven lieutenants, and an ensign; of these, two lieutenants, Knight of the 4th and Hull of the 43rd, later died). The leading company was now Captain Mundy Pole's 10th Regiment grenadiers, followed by the grenadiers of the 4th, commanded by Captain John West, and the 5th Regiment's company under Captain George Harris (afterwards Lord Harris). Embittered by the day's events, Harris fervently wished that the Americans would stand up and fight so his men could give them what they deserved, but he was to suffer the further frustration of fighting the same elusive enemy for the rest of the afternoon, losing half of his men killed or wounded before he reached Boston again. Behind these three companies Smith's column moved eastward once more, this time at a very slow pace to allow the wounded to keep up.

The right flank promised to be the most dangerous one, at least for the first part of the return march, and here Percy placed five of the regular companies of the 4th Regiment (Lieutenant Colonel Maddison). The road, in traversing the ground from Lexington to Menotomy, skirts the north edge of a three-mile broken ridge that terminates at high ground then called Peirce's Hill (now Arlington Heights). For most of the three miles the land on the south side (the British right flank) was wooded and sloping up from the road, in some places rather abruptly. The job of the companies of Maddison's regiment would be to move along this slope, often 100 feet above the road, with the rebels sure to be above them on still higher ground.

On the north side of the road the British left flank was open and flat for the first mile or so, with swampy meadows coming almost up to the road in many places. After the first mile, the meadows gave way to Mill Brook, a small stream running along parallel to the road, thirty or forty feet below it and 200 or 300 yards off. There the woods and brush bordering the creek provided convenient ambush spots for small groups of rebels. For this side of the road Percy ordered three companies of Lieutenant Colonel Nesbitt's 47th Regiment out to secure the flank.

Percy thought the greatest threat of all would be from the rear, where by far the largest number of rebels had gathered. He did not believe that the front of the column would have any problem brushing aside the few rebels who had managed to get around to that side of his position (he was soon to feel quite differently about his estimate). In his rear he left the 23rd Regiment, Royal Welch Fusiliers, Lieutenant Colonel Bernard's command. Marching between Smith's column and the rear guard would be Pitcairn's 400-man battalion of Royal Marines, which Percy planned to alternate with the 23rd as rear guard. The field pieces rolled along just ahead of Bernard's force, where they could be put to work quickly if needed against the rebels in the rear.

The order of march was Percy's only major mistake that day, and like most of the errors of Smith, Pitcairn, Laurie, Mitchell, and of course Gage himself, it grew out of a faulty evaluation of provincial military strength and organization. Percy had marched through the quiet and shuttered towns all the way from Boston only a few hours earlier, and he simply could not believe that the provincials would be able to throw a significant force into that area before he withdrew through it. After all, he had delayed at Lexington only an hour. He went through Menotomy at 1:30 and he would return through the town at about 4:30. What could the rebels do in three hours? Percy up to that moment remained convinced that a lack of organization and a poor state of training among the provincials—minute men or no minute men—would make it impossible for them to react in time to cut him off from Boston. He was soon to change his mind and, with a candor characteristic of him, admit that he had made a serious mistake—and urge brother officers not to do the same. But at the moment he was in the saddle near Munroe's Tavern, watching the departure of Smith toward Peirce's Hill, and as he thought, the safety of the Menotomy plains.

The brigade took thirty minutes to get all its companies on the road to Boston. In the meantime, as the 4th and 47th pulled off the line, Bernard moved his 23rd regiment into rear guard position across the main road. "We immediately lined the walls and other cover to our front with some marksmen," says Mackenzie of the 23rd, "and retired from the right of companies by files to the high ground a small distance in our rear, where we again formed in line, and remained in that position for near half an hour, during which time the flank companies and the other regiments of the Brigade began their march in one column on the road toward Cambridge."

As soon as Colonel Bernard saw the marines begin to move, he pulled in his marksmen and started his eight companies, 218 men, down the road behind the field pieces. This seemed to be a signal to the waiting militia and minute men, who surged in against the rear guard, and heavy firing began around the still-burning houses and from the high ground near the Munroe Tavern. "As soon as they saw us begin to retire," reported Percy, "they pressed very much upon our rear-guard. . . ." Bernard was forced to leapfrog his companies, backing slowly down the road by blocking with two or three companies, then allowing them to fall back under the protection of two or three more, and setting up in a new position further eastward on the road. It was a difficult series of maneuvers, and the regiment lost a number of men in the next four miles, finishing the march with thirty-six men killed, wounded, or missing—the equivalent of one complete company.

It was during this part of the march that the mounted provincial soldiers proved their worth. A few of the regiments had organized troops of horse: Captain Isaac Locker commanded Colonel Barrett's militia regiment cavalry troop, there was a troop from Groton in Colonel Prescott's regiment, and Captain Moses Jewett of Ipswitch led the horse troop of Colonel John Barker's Essex County minute man regiment (this troop marched but did not arrive in time). In addition, a number of individuals came on horseback even though they belonged to foot companies. These mounted men proved to be a scourge to the regulars because of their ability to slip in close to the route of march— often between the flank guards and the main column—then get off two or three shots and gallop away before the flankers or men from the column could close with them. An officer in one of the flank companies later wrote in exasperation, "Numbers of them were mounted, and when they had fastened their horses at some little distance from the road, they crept down near enough to have a shot; as soon as the column had passed, they mounted again and rode round until they got ahead of the column, and found some convenient place from whence they might fire again. These fellows were generally good marksmen. . . ."

There are a number of individual reports of provincial horsemen on that day. Nathaniel Cleaves and Benjamin Shaw of Captain Caleb Dodge's Danvers minute men in Pickering's regiment both lost horses that day, and Lieutenant Elisha Wheeler of Captain Moses Stone's company in Barrett's regiment had a horse shot out from under him. Perhaps the best-known horseman harassing the flank of the regulars on that march was Amos Wyman of Woburn, riding a large white horse. Several times he came in very close to the British main body and calmly dismounted to put a carefully aimed round into the redcoat ranks (several British soldiers gave him the honor of remembering him in their letters and reports). One mounted minute man, William Polly of Medford, was badly wounded while firing from horseback into the column, and died of the wound a week later.

The horsemen, however, were a minor if flamboyant part of the provincial effort as the minute men and militia attacked the moving column once again. A few individuals, among them William Thompson of Woburn, who had lost his brother at The Bloody Angle, became fatigued and dropped out of the fighting, but most of the companies continued on. This is evident in the distances each marched, later recorded on muster rolls. As Percy had anticipated, the firing on the column was heavier from the high ground on the south side, where the minute men and militia were able to take advantage of the woods and the rough terrain. The musket fire that the regulars received in the initial part of the retreat, however, was not at all comparable to the intensity of the earlier running attack against Smith, whose veterans now considered the firing as little more than a bother. To the men of First Brigade, who had been fired on only from the rebel snipers at Lexington, the scattered shots coming in seemed much more formidable.

The British flanking parties were now stronger and more aggressive than the security Smith used coming from Concord to Lexington. The soldiers took no chances on receiving musketry from the few houses along this part of the route. They fired into these, entered and searched them—and in the process confiscated any article that caught their fancy. The looting, absent from the conduct of the soldiers under Smith and embarrassingly prevalent after Lexington, began with the first houses encountered on the march; it was possibly abetted by the attitude of some British officers, some of whom were so angry at this point that they talked of burning every house and regretted that they lacked the time to do so.

After two and a half miles of marching without meeting any serious resistance, Colonel Smith started his men down the long slope of Peirce's Hill toward Foot of the Rocks, where the road descends to the flat ground around Menotomy, half a mile away. There were hopeful signs that the worst was over. The flanking companies were receiving an occasional shot, but the main column, moving quite slowly, was untouched.

General Heath and Dr. Warren at this time were still in the rear of Percy's column, where various provincial companies were putting pressure on the 23rd Regiment. As they neared the bottom of Peirce's Hill, just on the outskirts of Menotomy, Warren exposed himself recklessly while rallying the provincial troops, and a British soldier fired at him, the round coming so close that it knocked out a pin he wore to keep his hair back. This little detail duly impressed Heath and became one of his oft-repeated observations.

Then the tempo of the battle once more began to pick up— first a few shots at the leading scouts of the main body, then some firing from the tree line along Mill Brook down the slope to the left, then a heavy fire from the wooded high ground on the right flank. For Smith it was a familiar pattern; another big fight was building, and from the amount of activity on all sides, it seemed new units were entering the battle.

Menotomy was just a wide place in the road, a little village strung along for about a mile from Foot of the Rocks to Spy Pond, but it was a crossroads where routes coming into Boston from the north and west intersected, and it was an easy spot to reach for troops coming in from the eastern side of Middlesex and the south half of Essex counties. All roads, as it turned out, led to Menotomy when the purpose was to intercept the British.

It is no wonder that Percy and Smith were astounded by the number of troops the province was able to muster at Menotomy only three hours after Percy passed through the empty town; even today it is hard to believe that by the time Percy came across the slope of Peirce's Hill, there were as many minute men and militia waiting for him in Menotomy as there were to his rear and on the flanks. Two thousand provincial soldiers were now riding herd on him, and 2,000 more had stationed themselves between his column and Boston.

The thirty-five new companies waiting for Percy at Menotomy were from three regiments of minute men and one regiment of militia. Colonel Gardner's Middlesex militia, with the addition of a company from Watertown under Captain Samuel Barnard, one from Medford under Isaac Hall, and another from Malden under Benjamin Blaney, was now up to a strength of eight companies of foot and an "artillery battery" (from Weston) armed with muskets. Colonel Davis's Norfolk minute men of Heath's old regiment were reinforced by four companies from Dedham (Bullard, Daniel Draper, Ellis, Fairbanks), two from Roxbury (Child, William Draper), three from Brookline (White, Aspinwall, Isaac

Gardner), and two from Needham (Aaron Smith, Robert Smith). Some of these may have been up as far as Lexington before Percy began his retreat. Colonel Pickering's regiment was split into two sections, one under Pickering himself marching from Salem toward Charlestown, and the other already at Menotomy with no regimental officer in charge. These separated companies of Essex County minute men were commanded by Captains Epes, Flint, and Prince of Danvers; Captains Bancroft, Newhall, and David Parker of Lynn; and Captain Caleb Dodge of Beverly. Colonel Greaton's Norfolk minute man regiment was augmented by one company from Roxbury led by Moses Whiting and another from Dedham under Joseph Guild, bringing the strength of that regiment to seven companies in the field. The village of Menotomy also had its own company of minute men, commanded by Captain Benjamin Locke, probably attached to Gardner's militia regiment.

Chapter 25

The Menotomy Fight

The battle-worn vanguard under Colonel Smith passed Foot of the Rocks and entered Menotomy. The regulars, by now understandably shy of any kind of building, saw the feverish activity farther down the street as hundreds of minute men and militia scrambled for good firing positions in and around the houses, and knew that their fighting was far from over. The most costly of the series of tough skirmishes that marked the twenty miles from Concord to Boston was destined to take place in this little village now crowded with provincial soldiers and about to be inundated by three columns of redcoats—one down the road and one out on each flank.

The minute men and militia waiting in the town were operating under one great disadvantage: they had not seen the British column, and they assumed that it would come down the main road in a tight formation, just as the regulars had marched in all their earlier excursions out of Boston. The strong British flank patrols were a deadly surprise to many of the provincial companies that were situated too close to the road and were caught between the flankers and the main column. This mistake proved costly to several rebel units, including the company from Danvers commanded by Lieutenant Gideon Foster.

Danvers had three companies of minute men under Captains

Samuel Epes, Jeremiah Page, and Samuel Flint, and one company of minute men under Captain Israel Hutchinson, containing twenty-four men from Danvers and an equal number from Beverly. A second minute man company had just been formed, with Foster, who had been a second lieutenant in Epes's company, as its leader. The alarm had reached the town early that morning and all the companies were assembled and on the road by ten o'clock.

Marching almost at a trot the Danvers men covered the six-teen miles to Menotomy in less than four hours, changing their direction of march as they received word of the course of the battle. They arrived in Menotomy about two o'clock, after being diverted from the Concord Road by news they received in Woburn that the redcoats were in retreat. In Menotomy they found a confused mixture of minute men and militia companies with no over-all leadership and little idea of what to do. Some captains wanted to march around the British to Lexington, assuming that the regulars were preparing to attack that town, while others felt that the British would soon be returning by the road through Menotomy, and wanted to prepare an ambush there. In the end, each commander acted on his own. Some companies climbed the flank of Peirce's Hill to take positions overlooking Menotomy; others found concealed places along Mill Brook; still others attempted to make a circuit around the British.

Lieutenant Foster of the Danvers company looked over the land near the road and found a place where a hill on the south side afforded a good view of the route coming from Lexington. A long, low stone wall ran down from an orchard on the hill to the back yard of a house near the road (he later learned the house belonged to Jason Russell), providing a good measure of concealment and protection for his men. There were several other companies going into position in the same area, men from Lynn, Needham, and Dedham among them, but Foster decided there was room for his men, too. He crossed the road and ordered his men up the hill. Captain Hutchinson, following along with the other minute man company, was an older man and a veteran of much fighting in the French and Indian War. He stopped long enough to warn Foster that the orchard wall position was dangerously close to the road and too much exposed, and that a place in the wood-line farther up the hill might be better. Foster was not convinced. He pointed to the several other companies even closer to the road, and told Hutchinson that he intended to be near enough to give the redcoats a good fight.

Russell's yard was surrounded by a stone wall on all sides of the house, and many of Foster's men took places there. In the yard and on the opposite side of the street were men of the companies from Menotomy, Lynn, Needham, and Salem. At this time houseowner Jason Russell returned from conveying his family to safety and took his place in the yard with the rest of the men. Together the men of the several towns waited and watched the road over Peirce's Hill.

They could see the columns of smoke that marked the burning houses in Lexington and they heard the sporadic firing drawing nearer all the time. Finally the first of the redcoats appeared around the north slope of the hill. The men at the Russell house, concentrating their attention on the British to their front, did not notice the flanker companies closing in behind them. Perhaps it was Percy's cannon that kept all eyes turned to the main road.

Percy, who had burned the three houses at Lexington on the hunch that the rebels might try to infiltrate sniping parties into them, was not going to march through a double row of buildings in Menotomy without first clearing every one of them. He gave orders for one of the guns to unlimber and fire, and for the men of Smith's leading companies to form teams and storm the houses. The six-pounder went into action from the last piece of high ground overlooking the town.

As Lieutenant Barker of the 4th Regiment's light infantry noted, Smith's men "were now obliged to force almost every house in the road, for the Rebels had taken possession of them and galled us exceedingly, but they suffered for their temerity for all that we found in the houses were put to death." The first building to be entered was Tufts Tavern, on the left-hand side of the road at the outskirts of the town. With some of the regulars covering their advance, several soldiers rushed the entrance, and finding no one inside, carried away whatever articles they wanted and set the building afire.

Another house in the town proved to be the real beginning of the battle. This was the Jason Russell house. Old Ammi Cutter, one of the group of exempts who had captured the wagons earlier in the day, lived across the street from Russell, in a house on the other side of Mill Brook. He was out on the road at this time, one of the few men there who had already fired his musket at the regulars that day, and he saw Russell come out of the house, musket in hand. Russell was fifty-eight years old, and lame, and Cutter thought his old friend was carrying things a bit too far. He tried to tell Russell that the battlefield was no place for an old man, but Russell, who was piling bundles of shingles into a makeshift wall near his front door, answered simply, "A man's home is his castle."

Moving quickly, Smith's regulars attacked the house, and though repulsed with the loss of several men they were able to keep the minute men pinned down while companies of Colonel Maddison's 4th Regiment closed in from the back fields. Foster and most of his men along the stone wall in the orchard were driven back, but several of the minute men were cut off in the yard of the house as the British closed in. Foster himself described the action:

> Many of the men of Danvers went into a walled enclosure, and piled bundles of shingles which were lying there, to strengthen their breastwork; rumor had deceived them as to the force of the enemy; it was certainly their expectation here to have intercepted their retreat. Others selected trees on the side of the hill, from which they might assail the enemy. But they had little space for preparation; they soon saw the British in solid column descend the hill on their right, and at the same moment discovered a large flank guard advancing on their left. The men in the enclosure made a gallant resistance but were overpowered by numbers—some sought shelter in a neighboring house, and three or four, after they had surrendered themselves prisoners of war, were butchered with savage barbarity.

Possibly the last man to escape the trap was old Ammi Cutter, who begged Jason Russell to leave right up to the time the British closed in, then made a run for it, fell behind some logs, and lay still while British rounds chipped bark off all around him. The rest of the men, as Foster noted, retreated first into the yard, then inside the house. Russell, who was the last man to enter the house, was shot twice and fell dead in the doorway, where his body, bayonetted by other regulars who passed over him, suffered eleven more wounds.

Inside the house the fighting was as savage and brutal as anywhere in the battle that day. Two men from Lynn (the part that is now Lynnfield Center), Daniel Townsend and Timothy

Monroe, could not find the cellar and were trapped in a first floor room. Townsend leaped through a smashed window and was immediately shot dead by regulars waiting outside; Monroe followed him through the same window and somehow got away through the back field with every regular in sight firing at him. Lieutenant John Bacon of Needham, a fifty-four-year-old veteran of Pepperrell's 1745 Louisburg campaign, was killed in one of the rooms; as was Benjamin Pierce, a baker from Salem who had ridden hard all the way to Menotomy to become one of the only Salem men to reach the fight in time, and their only fatality.

Besides Daniel Townsend, three other men from Lynn were killed in the house—Abnego Ramsdell, William Flint, and Thomas Hadley—and three were wounded, including Monroe, who was hit in the leg. One Lynn man, Josiah Breed, was captured. Danvers lost seven minute men killed—Samuel Cook, Benjamin Doland, Jr., George Southwick, Perley Putnam, Jotham Webb, Henry Jacobs, and Ebenezer Goldthwait—all men in their early twenties. The final fighting in the house occurred on the cellar stairway, where at least one regular was killed by the men in the cellar, who were successful in defending themselves there against all attacks.

The number of British killed in and near the house is not known. Some of the men involved in the fight later insisted that the regulars had shot several of the men taken prisoner in the yard of the Russell house; Dennison Wallis, who was captured, reported that he broke away and ran because he saw the British preparing to shoot him and his companions. He was wounded several times and left for dead, but survived to tell the tale.

While some of the redcoats were swarming over the Nelson house, others pushed Foster and the remainder of the Danvers company back toward Spy Pond, a few hundred yards to the east toward Boston. Foster soon found himself in a desperate situation, with his back to the pond, the flanking companies on his left, and the main body of British coming down the road on his right. He elected to try to escape this trap by moving north along the edge of the pond and crossing the road directly in front of the main body, and by marching very rapidly he made it across without losing a man. The fighting around the Russell house delayed the column just enough to allow Foster and his men to get away. The men from Lynn and Needham pulled back to the north also, and moved across Mill Brook, where the tree line gave them some protection. Foster was not through yet. He placed his men in a new position on the north side of the road behind a wall and fired on the flankers of the 47th as they passed.

The Russell house was not the only place where the British were experiencing hand-to-hand combat at that moment. A regular and a Roxbury soldier, Dr. Downer, both with empty muskets, fought it out at bayonet point until the regular went down. At another place close by, Lieutenant Solomon Bowman of Menotomy, after an exchange of musketry, met a regular face to face in what should have been a bayonet duel except that Bowman had no bayonet. Swinging his musket as a club he downed and captured his opponent.

It was also in Menotomy that the British met their most formidable individual opponent, the aged Sam Whittemore, an old soldier who was out to stop the British even if he had to do it all by himself. Whittemore, who in his younger days had commanded a troop of dragoons for the Crown, was a tough customer, and always had been. The Middlesex Court Records for January 1741 show that he was hauled into court for expressing publicly his opinion that one Colonel Vassal was no more fit for selectman than his horse was; whereupon Colonel Vassal had him clapped in jail and sued him for defamation of character, claiming damages of £10,000. The court ruled that the words were not actionable, and when Whittemore heard the verdict he commenced an action against the colonel for "false and malicious imprisonment" and recovered £1,200 damages.

Now eighty years old, Whittemore was not the kind of man to be cowed by a mere 1,500 redcoats. Having heard that the British had marched through town, he spent the day preparing his own private arsenal, which included a brace of pistols, a saber, and a musket. Then he loaded himself with his gear and told his wife he was going up town to meet the regulars.

He joined the men going into position near Cooper's Tavern, where the road to Medford branches off to the north, and stationed himself 150 yards off the road, behind a stone wall that offered him a good view of the route to Boston. This location put him directly in the path of the flanking companies of Colonel Nesbitt's 47th Regiment, as well as in the way of the main body.

When the heavy firing began, Whittemore waited until the flankers were almost upon him, then fired his musket and dropped a regular in his tracks. He jumped up and fired off both pistols, killing at least one and possibly two more redcoats before a round hit him in the face and knocked him down. The men around him were driven back and the regulars, who lost several men getting across the Medford Road, leaped over the wall as Whittemore fell and bayonetted him again and again. Then they moved on, satisfied that they had killed at least one of their elusive tormentors. But with his face half shot away and thirteen bayonet wounds in him, Sam Whittemore survived and lived to be almost a hundred years old, always insisting that if he had to live that day over he would do the same thing again.

The repeated bayonetting of Russell and Whittemore is one indication of the fierceness that characterized the fighting at that point. To the British, the rebels were cowardly snipers who fired from hiding and who lurked along the edges of the column like wolves, ready to kill and scalp wounded men who had to be left behind; while to the minute men and militia the regulars were brutal ravagers who burned and looted their way across the countryside.

If the average British soldier still felt that the provincials were cowards and poor fighters—or at least was not willing to give them credit as soldiers—their commander was quite ready to concede that he had been wrong about the caliber of man that Massachusetts could put into the field. Writing a report the day after the battle Percy said,

> During the whole affair the Rebels attacked us in a very scattered, irregular manner, but with perseverance & resolution, nor did they ever dare to form into any regular body. Indeed, they knew too well what was proper, to do so.
>
> Whoever looks upon them as an irregular mob, will find himself much mistaken. They have men amongst them who know very well what they are about, having been employed as Rangers agst the Indians & Canadians, & this country being much covered with wood, and hilly, is very advantageous for their method of fighting.
>
> Nor are several of their men void of a spirit of enthusiasm, as we experienced yesterday, for many of them concealed themselves in houses, & advanced within 10 yds. to fire at me & other officers, tho' they were morally certain of being put to death themselves in an instant.
>
> You may depend upon it, that as the Rebels have now had time to prepare, they are determined to go thro' with it, nor will the insurrection here turn out so despicable as it is

perhaps imagined at home. For my part, I never believed, I confess, that they would have attacked the King's troops, or have had the perseverance I found in them yesterday.

Judging from Warren's close call, both Warren and Heath were in the thick of the fighting at Menotomy, just as they had been at Lexington, and again they were probably of more value as inspiring symbols than as over-all commanders, although Heath was slowly gaining a greater degree of control and his fascination with minor details of the battle was still helpful in this situation.

While the flanking companies were taking care of Whittemore and driving back the militia and minute men on the north side of the road, the process of clearing a route through the town continued with an attack against Cooper's Tavern, a hundred yards or so farther down the road. The regulars fired volley after volley into the building as a search party approached it, and in the firing or during the search two provincials, Jason Winship and Jabez Wyman, were killed. Others hiding in the cellar escaped unharmed in the hasty search.

Percy knew he was losing many men in this fighting, forcing one building after another, and he may have considered simply firing away at the houses with his field pieces, which could be brought up to point-blank range, but he was so low on ammunition that he had to save what little remained for emergencies. "We were most annoyed at a village called Anatomy," wrote one soldier, "having no shot to fire from our cannon on the houses which were all full of men. . . ." Besides lacking ammunition, Percy lacked time. He could not afford to stop even for a few minutes, not only because darkness was just a few hours off, but also because, like Smith earlier in the day, he was afraid his rear guard would become inextricably engaged with the mass of rebels following him.

There was one more large building in town, the Black Horse Tavern, and when this was cleared the British were able to march on across the Alewife Brook and into Cambridge. But the slow and hard-fought passage through Menotomy had cost Percy almost an hour of precious daylight. Worse still was the cost in men. The tired soldiers of Smith's command, expecting a more or less quiet march for the final miles of their eventful expedition, were the ones who faced the hard fighting all the way down Menotomy's main street, blasting a path through the stubborn companies of minute men and militia so that the column could continue on.   The regulars from Percy's brigade who were assigned to the flanks were also hard hit, as was the rear guard (Percy's description of the retreat as "a moving circle of fire" is quite appropriate).   In Menotomy the British lost forty men killed and about eighty wounded, or approximately half their casualties for the day's fighting.   One officer, Lieutenant Joseph Knight, was killed with the flanking companies of the 4th Regiment, and Lieutenant Hull of the 23rd was wounded again, this time fatally, when the chaise in which he was being carried dropped behind and was riddled with rounds by the provincials attacking the rear.   The commander of the rear guard, Lieutenant Colonel Bernard of the 23rd, was wounded in the thigh, and the regiment itself was so battered that Percy decided it was time to relieve it with Major Pitcairn's marines; the marines were thrown in at this point and suffered the heaviest losses of all the British units that day—a total of thirty-three killed and a large number wounded was the tally by the time Pitcairn got his men back to Boston.

In the ranks of the minute men and militia nearly every town that was present took casualties: Framingham, Newton, Beverly, Cambridge, Westford, Watertown, Salem, Danvers, Medford, Roxbury, Concord, Needham, Lynn, Dedham, and Menotomy. Twenty-eight provincials were killed, at least ten were wounded, and three captured.

Chapter 26

Charlestown

Percy crossed Menotomy River, finally escaping the village of Menotomy and entering the more open plains leading to Cambridge. There were only a few houses along the road in this area, making the job of the main body far easier, and the flankers were happy to see flat fields to the front. The firing abated a little as the provincials, lacking cover, were forced farther out away from the road, and the British companies were able to reorganize after the Menotomy battle. Squads of regulars that had become separated from their companies while clearing the buildings of the village now moved up the column and rejoined their units.

About a mile ahead of Percy the road forked, with the right side turning into Cambridge center and the left side continuing on to Charlestown. Beyond the fork, on the road entering Cambridge, a large part of General Heath's old regiment waited, now under the command of Colonel Aaron Davis of Roxbury. Advanced ahead of this regiment were a few men, possibly a company, in positions at Watson's Corner, about half way between Menotomy and Cambridge. Major Isaac Gardner of Brookline was in charge of the group.

As Percy's leading elements drew near the Watson house, the now familiar sequence was repeated—several men, taking cover around the house, were trapped between the flank guard on the south side and the main body coming down the road, and in a violent skirmish Major Gardner was killed, along with John Hicks and Moses Richardson of the Cambridge militia and William Marcy, a bystander.

At this time Percy gave orders to turn the column toward Charlestown rather than Cambridge. The most pressing reason for the change in route was his knowledge that there was a militia regiment waiting on the Cambridge Road, ready to turn that town into another Menotomy, but there were other reasons. Night was fast approaching, and the route to Boston through Cambridge was much longer than the route through Charlestown and across the ferry. It would be dark before Percy could get far beyond Cambridge, and he would still have to pass through Brookline and Roxbury. Also, Percy guessed correctly that the bridge across the Charles on the other side of Cambridge, the one he had been forced to repair on his way out, was probably by now dismantled again and would force another delay.

There is some evidence that Percy had at first planned to remain in Cambridge that night and resume his march the following morning, but that the unexpected pressure of the provincial forces in Menotomy and the blocked road to Cambridge made him change his mind, realizing that he would have to fight all night in a poor position if he tried to stay there. The road to Charlestown was much more open, and the hills of that town would provide him with a position he could defend.

Once he made his decision, Percy put it into action with the finesse which seems so typical of him. He moved his field pieces quickly to the front of the column, rolled them off the road into position near the fork, and opened fire on the militia regiment massed farther down the Cambridge Road. Under the cover of his fire, the column marched past the danger point and on toward Charlestown. When the militia tried to move up against the rear of the column a few minutes later, he fired another few rounds on them, breaking their formation into small groups (though as he noted, they still continued to come in on him).

There was yet one more formidable obstacle to pass before Percy could get his men to Charlestown. On the left side of his route, Prospect Hill, a sharply rising piece of high ground dominated the road for more than half a mile. Near the crest Percy's men could see another group of provincial companies standing in close formation, waiting to see what form of maneuver the

British would take. Here again, for the third time in a few minutes, Percy put his cannon to use, but this time it was also necessary to carry the hill itself before the column could pass along the road that skirted the steep slopes.

Colonel Nesbitt's companies were sent up the hill, supported by the cannon, and as they advanced in a skirmish line the provincial troops fired and fell back, leaving the ridge to the British. One Cambridge man, sixty-five-year-old James Miller, who lived in a house nearby, refused to retreat from his place on the hill. When his companions urged him to back away, he answered that he was too old to run and would stay where he was. Like Jonas Parker on Lexington Common earlier in the day, he held his ground and continued to fire on the advancing regulars until he was killed.

It was seven o'clock as Percy slipped his column into the shadow east of Prospect Hill and saw the high ground at Charlestown come into view, reddened by the last light of the setting sun. Behind him, 3,000 rebels tried vainly to pin down Pitcairn and his marines protecting the rear, and about a mile off to his left, a fresh new force from Essex County was closing in on another road leading into Charlestown.

Beyond the foot of the Prospect Hill there were several houses close to the road, and although the British did not receive any fire from these, they were careful to search and clear each one before passing. In the searching many of the regulars, realizing that they were now close to home, began to look for loot as earnestly as they looked for rebel soldiers. One regular was shot in a house at that point and fell dead across a drawer he had just removed from a bureau.

Percy tried to stop the soldiers from looting the houses, but too many sergeants and junior officers were out of action and the soldiers, many of them still separated from their companies, would not listen to orders. Lieutenant Barker of the 4th Regiment was one of the chagrined officers who offered no excuse for the conduct of the soldiers at this point. "Though they showed no want of courage," he wrote, "yet were so wild and irregular that there was no keeping them in any order . . . the plundering was shameful. . . ." Other officers, including Percy himself, complained of this lack of discipline.

General Heath was by this time able to exert a much greater measure of control over the minute men and militia, and after passing Prospect Hill he began to pull on the reins and slow down the companies attacking against the rear of the British. He knew that Percy would turn and defend the Charlestown hills and the narrow neck, and he did not want the momentum of the provincial attack to carry the troops up against such a strong British position. "As soon as the British gained Bunker's Hill," he wrote, "they immediately formed in a line opposite to the neck; when [I] judged it expedient to order the militia, who were now at the common, to halt, and give over the pursuit, as any further attempt upon the enemy, in that position, would have been futile."

Heath also mentioned the arrival of Pickering's regiment from the Salem area: "At this instant, an officer on horseback came up from the Medford road, and inquired the circumstances of the enemy; adding, that about 700 men were close behind, on their way from Salem to join the militia. Had these arrived a few minutes sooner, the left flank of the British must have been greatly exposed, and suffered considerably; perhaps their retreat would have been cut off."

But this fresh force, after marching all the way from Salem, halted on the crest of Winter Hill a little over a thousand yards from the road where the regulars could be seen in the dim light, marching on to Charlestown. George Washington was later to write, "If the retreat had not been as precipitate as it was—and God knows it could not well have been more so—the ministerial troops must have surrendered or been totally cut off. For they had not arrived in Charlestown (under cover of their ships) half an hour before a powerful body of men from Marblehead and Salem was at their heels and must, if they happened to be one hour sooner, inevitably intercepted their retreat to Charlestown."

Pickering's march is a story in itself, revolving around the circumstances of his tardy arrival on the battlefield. Captain Epes of Pickering's regiment had time to ride from Danvers to Salem, request permission to march against the British, ride back to Danvers, organize his men, and march to Menotomy before Percy's column reached that village in the retreat; yet Pickering was unable to move the shorter distance from Salem to Prospect Hill to intercept the regulars.

Pickering said that he was not aware of the alarm until Epes arrived at his office in Salem about nine o'clock in the morning. On hearing the news, he informed the selectmen of the town, who called for a meeting to decide what to do. The selectmen and other leaders agreed that there was little chance to intercept the British but decided that the companies from Salem should march in the direction of Concord in order to show their good faith.

The colonel set out with about 300 men (not 700, as Heath thought)—all of his regiment except the companies already at Menotomy and the Marblehead minutemen, who were held back by the Committee of Safety of that town on the grounds that two British warships were lying in the Marblehead Harbor.

Pickering seemed to be in no hurry. While the Danvers companies were practically running toward the battle, he halted his men at an inn in Danvers to rest for a half hour or so. It took him eight hours to cover the distance from Salem to Medford, where the news that the British were retreating to Boston made him quicken his pace toward Charlestown. Pickering later insisted that on reaching Winter Hill he reported to Heath, who told him the British troops "had artillery in the rear and could not be approached by muskets alone," but Heath, commenting on this action many years later (in 1807) said he did not remember discouraging Pickering's advance.

Pickering's comments at the council of war on the day following the battle show that as at Salem he was concerned more with arbitrating the disagreements with the Crown than with solving these problems by military force, and it may have been this desire to avoid bloodshed that caused his reticence on the road to Charlestown.

Percy marched along the final half mile into Charlestown in the gathering dusk, surveying the closely packed buildings of the town and wondering whether or not he would be confronted there by another force of rebels. He had already decided that he would not attempt a passage through the town and across the ferryway to Boston; the rebels were pressing too close to his rear for that, and he could not afford to let them get into the town with him. Instead, he would hold the high ground at Bunker Hill controlling the single entrance across Charlestown Neck, and wait until daylight came again before trying to pass through the narrow streets to the docks facing Boston. He was not ready to tolerate any attacks on the rear of his position from Charlestown while he defended against the rebel force across the neck, and he resolved to burn the town flat if he met resistance from that side.

The selectmen of Charlestown anticipated Percy's feelings on this subject. The townspeople had been fearful of trouble all day long, as reports of the battle came back from Concord and Lexington, and many inhabitants left for inland towns. The large majority, however, waited to see what might develop and were panicked by the sounds of firing as the British engaged the Cambridge men on Prospect Hill. A mass exodus from the town began, clogging the road over the neck with wagons filled with household belongings and excited families. Some of the townsfolk ran out in the marshes toward Medford, and others crowded the ferry across the Mystic River toward Malden.

By now it was dark, and the people remaining in Charlestown could see the flashes of musketry around the rear of Percy's column as it approached. Pinpoints of orange flame outlined a half circle that drew closer and closer to Charlestown Neck, and the long line of the column of regulars was sporadically illuminated by the return fire, silhouetting the figures of Percy's men in the darkness and smoke up and down the line.

When the British troops arrived at the neck they pushed their way across against the traffic leaving town and climbed the hill, where they immediately began to prepare positions. In one of the houses near the neck, a young boy looking out the window to see the soldiers as they passed was mistaken for a combatant and killed. Word spread quickly that the British were firing on the people of the town, increasing the panic, but Percy ordered everyone off the streets and quickly restored order.

It was a difficult situation for the selectmen of Charlestown. General Gage had warned them earlier in the day that if armed men left the town to fight his troops he would burn the place; now with Percy on one side and Gage on the other, they felt they had little choice but to go along with the British.

The selectmen sent a deputation to Percy, and in DeBerniere's words, "let him know that if he would not attack the town, they would take care that the troops should not be molested, and also they would do all in their power for to get us across the ferry." Percy answered that if the selectmen would keep the streets clear and would provide refreshment for the soldiers, he would see to it that the town was not harmed.

Percy now sent a note across to Gage in Boston, informing him of the general situation of the troops in their positions on Bunker Hill and requesting that ammunition be sent immediately. While he waited for a reply, he inspected his regiments along the slope of the hill and discussed with his officers the possibility of a rebel action against their position during the night. There was general agreement that an attack was not probable—the rebels would not be too anxious to meet the regulars under the disadvantage of such open and dominating ground.

Percy's selection of good defensive ground was fortunate for the regulars, who were not ready to do any more fighting. The wounded Ensign Lister of Smith's 10th Regiment provided a good picture of the conditions in the ranks of the light infantry: "A sergeant of the company came to me and informed me he had but 11 men and could not find any other officer of the company. . . ."

In a short time, Percy received an encouraging answer from Gage: "My Lord, Gen. Pigot will pass over with a reinforcement and fresh ammunition. The boats which carry him may return with the Grenadiers and Light Infantry who must be most fatigued, and the wounded. I propose sending over Capt. Montresor immediately with intrenching tools to throw up a sort of redoubt on the Hill, and to leave 200 men and guns in it, and it it's advisable during the course of the night, to bring your Lordship's men over. The fresh brigade may carry on the works. Fresh ammunition has been ordered long ago."

The rest of the night was uneventful. A slow trickle of reinforcements came across to bolster Percy's position, and the wounded were ferried over to Boston. When the reports were in, Percy found that the day had, indeed, been costly. Seventy-three regulars had been killed, 174 were wounded, and twenty-six were missing. Eighteen officers were among the casualties, including two regimental commanders, Smith and Bernard. General Pigott, commanding the Second Brigade, arrived at Percy's position with some of his men and took charge of the guard down near the neck and of the construction of trenches on the northwest slope of Bunker Hill.

Percy, relieved of these duties, took a well-deserved rest. He could afford to be satisfied with his own actions that day. He had brought back Smith's troops and his own brigade, about 1,500 men in all, against the opposition of nearly 4,000 rebels, and although he suffered twenty percent casualties, it was only through his leadership that the British column had not been more severely damaged. The start of the brigade from Boston had been marred by mistakes that caused it to get away three or four hours late, but there is no assurance that an earlier march would have helped either Percy or Smith; in fact, if the two had met in Concord rather than in Lexington, the whole column, far more unwieldy than Smith's 800 men, might have suffered a great deal more than it did.

As for the British at the end of the battle, the concluding words of Ensign DeBerniere's account perhaps most poignantly express the feelings of the officers and men: "The rebels shut up the neck, placed sentinels there, and took prisoner an officer of the 64th regiment that was going to join his regiment at Castle-William—so that in the course of two days, from a plentiful town, we were reduced to the disagreeable necessity of living on salt provisions, and fairly blocked up in Boston."

Chapter 27

The Aftermath

By the morning of April 20, the light infantry and grenadiers had returned to their units and Percy's First Brigade was settled in position on Bunker Hill, where it would remain until the 26th. Across the river in Boston General Gage showed evidence of the psychological strain that the long wait without any news of Percy or Smith had brought to bear on him. The rumors of the battle had all proved, unfortunately, to be true, and his now sensitive ear picked up a new rumor, indicating a plot to effect an uprising in Boston and kill all the British officers. On the basis of this tale, Gage ordered his men to remain fully dressed and under arms throughout the night of April 20. The plot, which never existed, merely inconvenienced the British troops.

Once all the reports were in, Gage was confronted with the task of preparing his own "circumstantial account" of the action to the authorities in London. Gage's version of the battle was a rather feeble composite of the reports that Smith and Percy turned in to him; the ability to produce carefully phrased official correspondence was one of Gage's strong assets, but he seems not to have had his heart in this one. He emphasizes the intention of the British troops not to cause the Massachusetts citizens any trouble and contends that the provincials fired first and provoked the fighting at Lexington and Concord, concluding that

232

"this unfortunate affair has happened through the rashness of a few people who began firing on the troops at Lexington." He also stresses the "scalping" incident at Concord's North Bridge and the fact that a resident of Concord struck Major Pitcairn, but downplays British losses (seventy-three killed and 174 wounded becomes "above fifty killed and many more wounded"). "He notes that Colonel Smith had executed his orders, by destroying all the military stores he could find" without revealing that Smith found practically nothing.

More interesting in many ways than Gage's official view are the letters written by the soldiers and junior officers of his garrison, who were less concerned with minimizing the shock they received on the 19th. One mentions the "incredible number" of provincials in the field, and adds, "they did not fight us like a regular army, only like savages, behind trees and stone walls. . . ." He tells his correspondent that the regulars "killed numbers of them," but writes, "I cannot be sure when you will get another letter from me, as this extensive continent is all in arms against us." Another soldier writes, in the same vein, "we could not fight as you did in Germany, as we could not see above ten in a body, for they were behind trees and walls, and fired at us, then loaded on their bellies." Throughout the extant letters there is a tone of surprise at the strength of the rebels and of righteous anger at their audacity.

For both sides, the night of April 19th and the morning of the 20th was a time of searching for the missing, caring for the wounded, and burying the dead. In Boston, the military surgeons had begun their work of bleeding the wounded and depriving them of food in order to effect cures according to the latest medical knowledge. (Ensign Lister later wrote that he surprised his doctors by taking a turn for the better after he broke the starvation diet imposed on him.) Some of the wounded regulars were not fortunate (or unfortunate) enough to reach Boston and the care of their own surgeons; they lay under guard in houses along the route of march, attended by the small-town physicians. There were several soldiers still at the Buckman Tavern in Lexington, and many in and around Menotomy. One anguished wife of a British soldier wrote from Boston, "My husband is now lying in one of their hospitals at a place called Cambridge, and there are now forty or fifty thousand of them gathered together; and we are not four thousand at most. It is a very troublesome time; for we are expecting the town to be burnt down every day, and

I believe we are sold, and I hear my husband's leg is broke, and my heart is almost broken."

And along the route of the retreat through Cambridge, the broken-hearted son of Moses Richardson stood by the large open grave where his father and some other dead soldiers were laid. As the first shovelfuls of earth were thrown in, he jumped down and covered his father's face with a piece of clothing so that the earth would not fall directly on it.

All along the road, men searched out the bodies of their companions who had fallen in the fields. Regulars and provincials alike were for the most part buried near the road or carried to cemeteries in the neighborhood. A furtiveness characterized some of the burials; the townsfolk were afraid that the King's troops might seek reprisal for the losses they had suffered. No one assumed that this would be the last of the marches from Boston into the countryside. Of the British regulars killed by provincial gunfire and left along the route of march by their companions, the location of only a few remains are known today. Most of the King's soldiers were stripped of their equipment and hurriedly buried in unmarked graves by provincials who knew only too well that Gage's troops would be thirsty for vengeance.

During the night of the 19th, Heath began the task of putting the Provincial Army into some kind of order. On the common near Charlestown Neck the provincial soldiers gathered and sought out their companies, and the companies reported to their regimental commanders. Within a few hours the several regiments that had fought through the day—Bridge's, Green's, Barrett's, Pierce's, Gardner's, Greaton's, Prescott's, and Davis's—were reorganized, and others who had not been able to march to the battle in time began to report in. Throughout the night they came into Charlestown and Cambridge in a continuous stream from all over Massachusetts. Colonel Fry's minute man regiment from the Andover area, like Pickering's Essex County men, never quite caught up with the British column but reported in to Heath only a few minutes after the regulars got over Charlestown Neck. Colonel Samuel Johnson, the man who had encouraged the soldiers of his own militia regiment to join the minute men under Fry, brought in his nine companies from Andover, Haverhill, Boxford, and Bradford. Four other partially formed Essex County regiments came in during the night, commanded by Colonels Samuel Gerrish, Isaac Merrill, John Baker, and Caleb Cushing.

General John Whitcomb of Lancaster arrived, according to General Heath, in time to participate in the last part of the battle. He was coming down with the minute man regiment he still commanded, and there is some evidence that the troop of horse from the regiment also arrived in Cambridge in time to attack the British. John Whitcomb and his brother Asa were regimental commanders in Worcester County; John led at least ten companies of minute men from Fitchburg, Harvard, Bolton, Lancaster, Leominster, Ashburnham, and Lunenburg, and Asa commanded eleven militia companies from the same towns. Both were veterans of many campaigns in the French and Indian War. During the night of the 20th, the road from Worcester toward Boston was filled with the men of these two units and of the other seven regiments from Worcester County (Warner's, Doolittle's, Learned's, Sparhawk's, Wheelock's, Artemas Ward's, and Jonathan Ward's). Coming down as a lieutenant colonel in Artemas Ward's minute man regiment was Joseph Henshaw, the man who was given credit for first suggesting the use of minute men at the Worcester County convention in the fall of 1774. Since Ward was to take over as commanding general of the forces confronting Gage, Henshaw was in effect the regimental commander.

Four regiments in old Suffolk County on the south side of Boston, commanded by Colonels Lincoln, Smith, Sargent, and Lemuel Robinson, were probably in Cambridge and on the far side of the river when Percy was marching along toward Charlestown. From Bristol County, farther south of Boston, Colonel John Daggett led in his mixed regiment of minute men and militia. Several of the companies from this regiment had participated ten days earlier in the little-known Assonet Expedition, a raid on the town of Taunton to capture "40 stands of arms and equipments" assembled there by a group of Loyalists.

The two far-western counties, Berkshire and Hampshire, had a total of seven regiments on the road to Boston (Pynchon's, Danielson's, Fellows's, Pomroy's, Patterson's, Williams's, Porter's, Woodbridge's, and Arnold's). Before morning there were parts of five regiments from Plymouth County (Thomas's, Mitchell's, James Warren's, Cotton's, and Bailey's) in Roxbury and Cambridge. The minute men of Colonels Bailey and Cotton were sent against Captain Balfour and his command of 100 British regulars isolated at Marshfield where they had been sent the previous January in order to assist Loyalist elements in controlling that town.

On the afternoon of the 20th Artemus Ward took command, relieving Heath. He called an immediate council of war in Cambridge, at which he designated Heath as the commander of the forces north of the Charles River, around Cambridge and Charlestown, and Thomas as commander in Roxbury, Brookline, and the towns south of the Charles. Thomas was assigned the regiments of Colonels Prescott, Warner, and Learned, giving him one Middlesex and two Worcester County regiments in addition to those of Suffolk, Plymouth, and Barnstable. The rest were assigned to Heath. As regiments, separate companies, and even individuals continued to pour into Cambridge (while at the same time more of the soldiers who had fought hard on the 19th arbitrarily decided to go home) Ward's command began to grow more and more confused. By the night of the 20th, there were an estimated 20,000 minute men and militia coming and going in the units surrounding Gage, and not one of them knew with any certainty what his official military status was. Those who returned to take care of their affairs at home probably felt that there had been no official order for them to stay—and besides, they were ready "on a minute's warning" to repeat their earlier performance.

In this crucial moment the Committee of Safety acted with characteristic sureness and speed to ease the confusion in the ranks and build an army out of the remains of a battle. On the 20th the committee drafted a circular letter to all the towns of the province, requesting them to "hasten and encourage, by all possible means, the enlistment of men to form the army, and send them forward to headquarters at Cambridge, with that expedition, which the vast importance and instant urgency of the affair demands."

The committee allowed itself as much leeway as possible. It did not request the units be formed, but merely that men be sent to Cambridge. On the following day the committee decided that the enlistment term would be from April to December, and the "eight months army" was created. The system that the committee used was a simple one: colonels who commanded partially formed regiments were permitted to enlist new companies to complete them. Each regiment was authorized ten companies, and after some disagreement the final size of each company was settled at fifty. Regiments were to be "commissioned" as soon as the committee was satisfied that they were up to strength. There were elements of at least forty regiments in the province, including both militia and minute men—enough to provide an organization capable of controlling 20,000 men—so there was no need to do more than request the towns to send troops, and to watch the regiments grow.

This was the plan and, in actuality, it was successful. Although the normal amount of selfishness, localism, and maneuvering for rank has been recorded in the months that followed, it did not stop the formation of the Provincial Army of Massachusetts. Other units from Connecticut, New Hampshire, Rhode Island, and Maine (then part of Massachusetts) arrived every day to take their places alongside the Massachusetts men. And in the organization of the new army, the minute men were to figure prominently.

Chapter 28

The Minute Men and the New Army

One of the reasons why Gage was unaware of the size and organization of the Massachusetts Provincial Army was the lack of information available even to the Provincial Congress on the number of men under arms. Gage had Dr. Church and perhaps other spies in the halls of the Provincial Congress and even on the Committee of Safety, where great exertions were being made by the provincials themselves to obtain just such information; fortunately, the confusion engendered by the changeover of officers in the militia and the establishment of the minute men obscured all such detail in the formation of the new army.

Beginning in December 1774, the Provincial Congress made several efforts to obtain returns of enrollment figures from the militia and minute men. By February, the committee established to procure the returns was still unable to report. A month later the returns had not come in. Early in April the Congress attempted to fix a figure as an overall goal for the strength of the army, meanwhile continuing the inventory to discover the existing number under arms. The march of the regulars to Concord interrupted this endeavor and made it necessary for the congress to come up with an army immediately. Under the pressure of impending attack a consensus was reached. The congress reconvened at Concord three days after the battle and passed a resolution on the following day creating an army of 14,600 men to form the largest contingent in a future New England army of 30,000. This gave the Committee of Safety a figure to guide it in building the regiments.

The minute man regiments, as well as the militia, were announced as eligible for enlistment, and since the officers of both were well known after the recent battle (and the winter of preparations preceding it), a large number of them came into the new army in the same positions they occupied in the old units.

All officers and men, of course, were volunteers. The momentum of the battle carried some whole companies into the new army under their old regimental commanders, but this was not always the case. A number of individuals and even companies were ready to fight Gage but not ready to join any army. These had to be persuaded, since there was no attempt to legislate any forced entry into the new regiments.

In order to encourage the rapid formation of regiments and also to make use of the leadership in the minute men, the Committee of Safety called all the field grade officers of the minute men (majors, lieutenant colonels, and colonels) to a conference in Cambridge to discuss the enlisting of the minute man soldiers and emphasize the need for them in the ranks of the new units. Presumably these officers were told of the opportunities that were open to them, as well as to the militia officers, in the reorganization.

To hasten the raising of the regiments, the congress pushed through legislation on May 4 providing an advance pay of twenty shillings for every soldier who enlisted, and the committee promised the men that "the utmost care will be taken to make every soldier happy in being under good officers." While the minute men and militia held to their positions around Boston, waiting to be relieved by the units of the new army, the committee sent an urgent request to all the towns, asking them to send temporary replacements for the men who had found it necessary to return home.

The old dangers still faced the province at this critical time; the army of militia and minute men had been organized in the shuffle that took place the previous fall under the noses of Gage and the regulars, and now the congress was attempting the same kind of shuffle again. There was a period, in the last weeks of April and during May, when the new army had not come into being but the old militia and minute men were fragmented and almost dissolved. If Gage recognized their inability to maintain themselves against him in the field for more than a couple of days of battle, he did nothing about it, and lost his opportunity forever.

The provincials did not need to be told of this weakness inherent in the reorganization. While the Committee of Safety waited impatiently for the regiments to come up to strength and get to Cambridge, it searched about for ways to fill the gap— and decided, once again, and not for the last time, on the employment of the minute man concept.

On April 29, ten days after the battle, all the towns around Boston were sent orders to send one half of their militia immediately to Cambridge to reinforce the pitifully small nucleus of the new army, and also were told to keep the remainder of the militia "in readiness to march on a minute's warning." The same day, a new company, raised in Medford for the army, but not yet committed to one of the new regiments, requested orders from the Committee of Safety and was instructed to hold itself "in readiness to march at a minute's warning, remaining in Medford till further orders."

On May 10, after receiving word from informers in Boston that the British might be planning another move against the countryside, the committee once more ordered that "Dorchester, Dedham, Newton, Watertown, Waltham, Roxbury, Milton, Braintree, Brookline, and Needham, immediately muster one-half of the militia, and all the minute men under their command, and march them forthwith to the town of Roxbury, for the strengthening of the camp there." When these troops arrived, bringing the total number of provincial troops on the Cambridge side of the Charles to a mere 2,200 men, General Putnam formed them in a column so widely spaced that they took up a mile and a half of road, and marched them from Cambridge to Charlestown and up on Bunker Hill, then down to the ferry-way and back to Cambridge again. The display was meant to deceive the British and to raise the confidence and morale of the provincial troops, and there is no reason to believe it was not successful in both. Gage, who forwarded to London in his reports the complaints of Lieutenant Colonel Smith and other regular officers that the provincials would not stand and fight, must have observed that the opportunity for such a confrontation was now present, but he did not take advantage of it.

The Committee thus far had employed the minute man concept

in a variety of adaptions, not only calling out some of the original minute men, but also using part of the militia as minute men and placing newly formed companies and regiments in a temporary status as minute men. The final conclusion was inevitable: rather than merely absorb the minute men back into the militia, the Committee decided to make every militia soldier a minute man.

On June 15, two days before the Battle of Bunker Hill, the Committee resolved "that all the militia in the colony be ordered to hold themselves in readiness to march on the shortest notice, completely equipped, having thirty rounds of cartridges per man." This resolution was approved and emphasized in the Provincial Congress on the 17th, the day of the battle; the congress changed the committee's words from "on the shortest notice" to "at a minute's warning."

All the time that the Committee of Safety was fighting to create the new army, it was also faced with the problems of justifying its own existence, of determining exactly what powers it was supposed to have, and of maintaining a proper relationship with the congress, from which it received its authority, and also with the militia, which it controlled in emergencies, and the new army, which it was supposed to create and direct (but not to command tactically in the field). It is no wonder that the committee often had trouble, during these fluid and fast-moving times, in determining its role.

The committee had many times requested the congress to reexamine and verify its position, and on May 19 the congress, noting that "there appears to be still a deficiency of power in said committee," approved a series of resolutions giving the committee more specific authority than before. The committee could keep the militia in the field as long as it judged necessary, and it could "direct" the new army (the generals and other officers of the militia and the army were "required to render strict obedience"). It was also to nominate all the officers to be commissioned by the congress.

The clarification of the powers of the committee tended to smooth out working relations between it and the congress, although there was no avoiding some differences of opinion as to the methods used in raising the army. In the confusion of the first days after the April 19 battle, too many promises were made to future regimental commanders and too many blank commissions for officers were given out. The result was that several regiments, none of them up to strength, found themselves competing with each other for men. It is to the credit of the committee that when the congress, early in June, inquired into the problem (under pressure from some of the regimental commanders concerned), the committee admitted the mistake, simply noting the exigencies of those first days after the battle, when "the committee not being able to prevail on the militia and minute men to tarry in camp, and there being but few men enlisted at the time, obliged us to issue further orders." The congress then set the number of regiments at twenty-three, and the contention was ended officially, if not otherwise, in the ranks.

A few days prior to the Battle of Bunker Hill, the provincials were able to muster in front of Boston the authorized force of twenty-three regiments, twelve of which were commanded by officers who had been minute men (Fellows, Cotton, Danielson, Fry, Nixon, Whitcomb, Bridge, Prescott, Ward, Doolittle, Woodbridge, and Gerrish). The over-all strength of the Massachusetts contingent did not, however, reach the goal of 14,600. The province had about 11,500 men actually in the field. Judged in terms of the state of the province at the time, the organization of the Massachusetts army was a great success, for all its minor difficulties, and one in which the minute man concept figured prominently.

Nor was this the end of the minute men. The Committee of Safety, on Sunday, June 18, the day after the Bunker Hill battle, prepared a form letter to be sent to all the towns in case of a march of the regulars into the countryside. Addressed to commanding officers of the town militias, it read: "Sir: as the troops under General Gage are moving from Boston into the country, you are, on the receipt of this, immediately to muster the men under your command, see them properly equipped, and march them forthwith to Cambridge. By order of the Committee of Safety." The letter was to be signed by the committee's chairman, at that time Benjamin White. The printing of such a letter had been recommended as early as the preceding February, but apparently was not printed at the time (possibly because Benjamin Church was one of the committee of three constituted to prepare it). Since Gage never attempted to go beyond Charlestown, the letter was not used.

The minute man concept extended beyond the confines of the province of Massachusetts, and had become part of the official correspondence of Connecticut, which in answer to the request for aid sent out by Massachusetts after the April 19 battle wrote, "Every preparation is making to support your province. . . . The colonels are to forward a part of the best men and the most ready, as fast as possible; the remainder to be ready at a moment's warning." In the Continental Congress in Philadelphia on July 18, that body, viewing the results achieved in Massachusetts two months earlier, recommended "that one fourth part of the militia in every colony be selected as minute men of such men as are willing to enter into this necessary service, formed into companies and battalions and their officers chosen and commissioned as aforesaid, to be ready at the shortest notice to march to any place where their assistance may be required for the defense of their own or neighboring colony." Thus the official sanction for the minute man concept was carried to the highest level of the newly forming nation.

Massachusetts continued to make use of the concept in its militia in order to provide a ready reserve during the time that so many of the men of the province were fighting far away with the Continental Army. In November 1776, the Massachusetts General Court passed an act providing that one-fourth of all the able-bodied men in the state over sixteen years of age (with certain exceptions) should, either by enlistment, lot, or draft, "be appointed and held in readiness, armed and equipped, to march at a moment's warning, serve for a term not exceeding three months from the time of their march from home, within and for the defense of any of the United States, when they should be called out to reinforce the continental army."

Chapter *29*

The Minute Men
in Perspective

When the 23rd Regiment was finally back in Boston after the ordeal of April 19, adjutant Frederick Mackenzie wrote in his diary, "I believe the fact is, that General Gage was not only much deceived with respect to the quantity of military stores said to be collected in Concord, but had no conception the rebels would have opposed the King's troops in the manner they did." Another officer mentions his surprise at "incredible numbers of the people of the country in arms," and Colonel Smith is convinced of a widespread plot; "Otherwise," he says, "I think they could not, in so short a time as from our marching out, have raised such a numerous body, and for so great a space of ground." It is not at all surprising that the British officers in Boston, even though they knew of militia musters and of the existence of the minute men, were quite unaware that an army of nearly fifty regiments was near completion at the time of the march to Concord; even today, this organization of the provincial forces is not generally known. The assertion that the minute men and militia were not an armed rabble but a well-organized, well-equipped, and relatively well-trained army of 14,000 men might provoke the same kind of smile now as it did on the eve of the British march, so many years ago. We have been content with the legend of the spontaneous rise and the one-day life of the minute men, a story pleasing to our sense of myth, and there are still many who, like Gage's regulars, will have to be convinced at musket-point that there is more to the minute men than first meets the eye.   It is ironic that the militia and the minute men, who together wrested their army from the control of the Crown, doubled it in size, equipped it with 20,000 muskets and 10,000 bayonets, and trained it secretly all one winter, are praised as an example of soldiers who fought well with no organization, no equipment, no training, and no planning. Though part of the misinterpretation is a result of the myth and its influence, much is also inattention to the facts of the battle: we stress the disorganization of the April 19 battle, which was in effect a twenty-mile running ambush, and conclude that the whole thing was a bit untidy, and that the embattled farmers had spirit, but little else.   One can only wonder what a minute man might comment if he could come back to see what we have said of his achievement.

A second factor of critical importance to an understanding of the April 19 battle is the minute man concept—its long and progressive development, its wide popularity, and its effective employment in the various wars before the revolution. Once the concept is isolated, it is fairly simple to trace it in such military organizations as the snow shoe men and the picket guards, and also to see it as a force modifying the militia organization in the early history of Massachusetts. The early militia was a rough Elizabethan model; then the alert system was superimposed on the practice of mustering; then the alert-muster-march techniques became merged with the older English system of levy from the regiments, and the embryo minute man appeared. He was a member of a designated levy, a fixed proportion of the militia, on call, responsive to a military committee, decentralized in his command structure, and prepared to march on very short notice whenever needed. From this minute man concept grew a number of adaptations, including not only the snow shoe men, the picket guards, and the April 19 minute men, but during the Revolutionary War, several other variations as well.

A third prerequisite to an analysis of the battle is a look at the activities of both sides in the months immediately before they met, to see what they knew about each other and what they did, tactically, in the preliminary sparring that occurred; that is, in the confrontations and near-confrontations at such incidents as Maddison's march to Quarry Hill, the march to seize cannon at

Charlestown, Leslie's visit to Salem, Balfour's occupation of Marshfield, and the frequent practice sorties into the countryside. In terms of these confrontations, the actions of Captain John Parker at Lexington Green, for so long subject to a variety of conjectures, do not seem at all illogical. He assumed that what had happened at every incident with the regulars in the immediate past would happen again, and that the regulars would not fire on him except under extreme provocation.

In a new evaluation of the battle from beginning to end, these three considerations—the relatively well-developed organization, the minute man concept, and the earlier confrontations—bring some light to areas that have been rather obscure. The first happy result is that some of the garbled anecdotes begin to make sense, but more important, several major events in the story of the day take on a new significance. The quick ease with which the minute men were established seems more reasonable, and their rapid assembly along the road of battle less surprising; the actions of not only Parker, but Barrett, Howe, Nixon, Tompson, Baldwin, Bridge, Brooks, Gardner, Heath, Warren, and many others take on new relevance; the relationship between minute men and militia becomes much clearer.

There is no way to separate the story of the minute men from the story of the militia. The battle caught many units still in a state of transition; some regiments contained both minute men and militia companies, and some militia companies considered their minute men as only temporarily detached and never carried them on separate rolls. In addition, several known companies were not picked up on any lists, and others belonging to militia regiments became minute men under the regulation of November 1776. On the Alarm Lists in the Massachusetts Archives, 473 companies are represented, of which 217 are minute men units. Of the forty-seven regiments (this figure is approximate) it appears that twenty-one were minute men, seventeen were militia, and nine were a mixture of both minute man and militia companies. This mixture occurred because some regiments had not yet relinquished their newly formed minute man companies to form new regiments. A good example is Colonel William Prescott's regiment from northwestern Middlesex County: ten companies are listed as militia, seven more as minute men, and another as militia but also containing nine minute men, making the regiment almost twice the size it should have been.

There is a great deal left to be done in the study of this, the least known of all American battles. Most of the missing information will concern the participants and, in the case of the Americans, will come from the kind of digging that the local historians of the New England towns are best situated to accomplish. There still remain to be studied not only the gaps in the military organization but the town Committees of Correspondence and Committees of Safety. The legends and anecdotes should be challenged one by one for the hidden information they contain.

In fighting the regulars the minute men fought their way into the hearts of Americans of all the following generations, and few are the calls to patriotic spirit that do not evoke the minute man as a symbol of preparedness. Perhaps if the minute man were better known for what he really was, it would be far easier to see that readiness means more than keeping one's musket close at hand. It means, as the minute men knew, that the ready force must be well organized, well equipped, well trained, and mentally prepared to fight. The minute men were not the exception to the rule; on the contrary, they are among the best examples of the importance of military preparedness that the country has provided.

Notes

Chapter 1: The Minute Man Concept
General references to early development: *Records of the Court of Assistants* (Noble, ed.), *Records of the Governor* (White, ed.), *The Colonial Laws of Massachusetts, The Compact with the Charter and Laws of the Colony of New Plymouth* (Brigham, ed.), *The Massachusetts Archives*. The best general guide to the military history of both the 17th and 18th centuries is Osgood. Early English militia: *Sources of English Constitutional History* (Stephenson and Marcham, eds.). The Ancient and Honorable: *History of the Military Company of Massachusetts* (Roberts), Ch. 1, 7-8. The Pequot War: the accounts of Mason, Underhill, Vincent, and Gardner, in *History of the Pequot War* (Orr, ed.). Plymouth arriving late: Leach, p. 350. Vincent in his narrative says (in 1637): "Hereupon the Council ordered that none should go to work, nor travel, no, not so much as to church, without arms. A corps of guard of fourteen or fifteen soldiers was appointed to watch every night, and sentinels were set in convenient places about the plantations, the drum beating when they went to the watch, and every man commanded to be in readiness upon an alarm, upon pain of five pound" (Orr, p. 101). This seems to be the earliest reference to the alarm and muster system.

Chapter 2: The Concept in Practice
The over-all guide is Bodge. Details of the various expeditions: *Massachusetts Archives*, LXVII and LXVIII. Decentralized control: *Colonial Laws*, pp. 110-11.

Chapter 3: The Snow Shoe Men
Phips's new regulations: *Massachusetts Archives*, LXX. Orders for early snow shoe men: *Archives*, XLXXI, and *Records of the Court*, VIII. The 1743 snow shoe men: *Archives*, LXXII, and *Records of the Court*, XI.

Chapter 4: The Picket Guards
From the *Massachusetts Archives*, the following: purchase of firearms, LXXIV, 200; thirty regiments, LXXIV, 508; levy of February, 1756, LXXV, 468-69 and 482-83; promise of land

249

for enlisting, LXXV, 700-06; lack of response, LXXV, 717-19 and LXXVII, 209-14.
Disconsolate provincial troops: Parkman, I, 400 (among other things, Loudoun refused to
recognize the commissions of the provincial officers and asserted that majors on regular
service would rank full colonels of militia. When the militia officers complained bitterly to
him, he let them know that they had two choices: serve or mutiny). Thompson's diary
entry: Sewell, p. 522. Pownall's call for minute men: *Records of the Court*, XIII, 284-85.
Money problems in the province: Parkman, II, 84-85. Feeling of impending disaster:
Parkman, II, 3; *Archives*, LXXVII, 313-18. 7,000 men for Ft. Ticonderoga: *Records of the
Court*, IV, 86-111.

Chapter 5: The Last Decade

Sedition from the pulpits: Gage used these same words twice in his correspondence, on
May 30, 1774 (I, 356), and on September 2 (I, 374). Town government: John F. Sly; Joel
Parker; Harry A. Cushing. Committee of Correspondence: *Boston Town Records*, XVIII, 93,
107. (In the committee system--Committee of Correspondence, Committee of Safety--there
is probably something drawn from Cromwell's Committee for the General Rising and
Committee of Safety. See Hexter pp. 58, 124, 144.) Fitchburg's answer: Davis, 1, 121.
Hard fight on Solemn League and Covenant: Rowe's diary for June 27, 1774. Rapid
compliance: Frothingham, p. 11. Temporal advice to flock: Cutler, p. 47. Thanksgiving
address refused: Hutchinson, *History*, III, 237. Mr. Stone's sermon: Hurd, *Middlesex*, I,
675. Committees of Correspondence a nuisance: *Massachusetts Gazette*, July 4, 1774.
Liberty Pole cut down: Sheldon, II, 677. Debate in Weston: *Massachusetts Gazette*,
January 24, 1774. Loyalists embarking: Sabine, II, 25.

Chapter 6: Showdown at Worcester

"In Worcester they keep no terms": Gage, I, 358. Details of Gage's life: Alden. The
Worcester County Convention: *Journals of Each Provincial Congress*. The Powder Alarm:
Massachusetts Gazette, September 5, 1774; Stiles, *Diary*, pp. 479-80; Frothingham, *Siege*, p.
14. Warren to Adams ("I doubt whether a man. . . .") Frothingham, *Warren*, p. 356. The
parallel to the British Civil War is interesting; Firth, p. 15, says: "All over England the
struggle began with an attempt to obtain possession of the county magazine in which the
powder and the arms of the local trained bands were stored." Gage decides not to march:
Gage, I, 370.

Chapter 7: The Birth of the Minute Men

Action at the Worcester County Convention and the First Provincial Congress: *Journals of
Each Provincial Congress*. Andrews letter: Mass. Hist. Soc. *Proceedings*, VIII, 316, Colonel
Johnson's call for minute men: Bailey, p. 298. Major Thomas Bourne: French, *First Year*,
p. 40 n. Colonel Isaac Williams: Sheldon, p. 398.

Chapter 8: Winter Preparations

Less than equal treatment for provincial soldiers; Osgood, *Eighteenth Century*, III, 501.
Low ebb of militia training: Pickering, I, 16. (In his letters to the *Essex Gazette*, January
31 and February 21, 1769, he says not one officer in five knew the manual of arms.)
Saluting by firing at commander's feet: Pickering, I, 26-7. Methuen muster roll: *Essex
Institute Historical Collections*, VII, 243. Parker and Munroe: Hudson, pp. 381-82. Nixon,
Gleason, Eames, Edgell: Temple, pp. 651 ff. John Wood; Sewell, pp. 348-50. British forces
in Boston organized as follows: Lt. Gen. Gage, Governor of Province of Massachusetts and
Commander in Chief of forces in North America; Maj. Gen. Haldimand, Commanding
Officer of troops in Boston; Brigadier Percy, 1st Brigade (4th, 23rd, 42nd, Marines);
Brigadier Pigott, 2nd Brigade (5th, 38th, 52nd); Brigadier Jones, 3rd Brigade (10th, 43rd,
59th, part of 18th, part of 65th); Lt. Col. Leslie, 64th (not brigaded--garrison of Castle
William). Information on the British regiments is from *Historical Records of the British
Army* (Cannon), augmented by other works as noted: 4th Regiment: Scotland 1746,

Minorca 1756, Guadeloupe 1759, Martinique 1762, England 1764, Scotland 1768, England 1773 (Fortescue, II, III). 5th Regiment: Ireland 1728-1758, combat in France 1758, campaigns in Germany 1760-1763, England 1763-1774 (Wood). 10th Regiment: garrisoned at Gibraltar 1730-1749, Ireland 1749-1767, North America 1767, Quebec, Niagara, Detroit, Michilimackinac, Oswegatchie 1772-1774. 18th Regiment: "returned to England in 1715. From that date till 1775 they were not engaged in any particularly important operations" (Richards, I, 265). 23rd Regiment: "After taking part in the expeditions against St. Malo and Cherbourg, their next great warlike achievement was at Minden, in 1759. . . . They fought at Kirch Denkern; they assisted in the victory at Graebenstein. Before peace was declared they were engaged in very many actions, and no regiment merited better the ten years' rest they enjoyed consequent to the Treaty of Fontainebleau" (Richards, II, 129). 38th Regiment: Five years after its formation (in 1702) the regiment went to the West Indies and served there "an unprecedented period of, it is said, nearly sixty years, during which detachments of the corps served at the capture of Guadeloupe in 1759, and of Martinique in 1762" (Richards, II, 100). 43rd Regiment: Ireland 1749-1757, Canada 1757-1760 (Quebec, Montreal), Barbadoes 1761, "Havannah" Campaign 1762, England 1764, Scotland 1770 (Levinge). 47th Regiment: Louisburg, Quebec 1750, Ireland 1763. 52nd Regiment: Organized 1775. 59th Regiment: Organized 1755, in England until 1774. 64th Regiment: Organized 1758, Ireland 1758-1768, Boston 1768, Halifax 1770 (Purdon). 65th Regiment: Organized 1758, Guadeloupe 1759, Havanna 1762. Troops "newly-raised": Stiles, p. 482. Light infantry trained in Indian-style fighting: Honyman, pp. 43-44. Major Hanger on the Brown Bess: quoted in Harold L. Peterson, "Brown Bess, the Standard Arm," *The American Rifleman*, April, 1854, p. 20. The contemporary expert on the Brown Bess: Donald B. Webster, in *Guns and Hunting*, March, 1965, p. 27. Returns of the militia and minute men: *Journals of Each Provincial Congress*, p. 756. Mittens on: Temple, p. 269. Clergymen learning manual of arms: Andrews letter, October 1, 1774. Field day at Concord: Tolman, p. 19. The Provincial Congress, on April 12, 1775, considered the feasibility of training the minute men in battalions, but "after a long debate" decided it would cost too much.

Chapter 9: Marches
The raid on Charlestown: Andrews letter, September 8, 1774. Haldimand's notebook: Mass. Hist. Soc. *Proceedings*, LXVI (1936), pp. 41 ff. False alarm of September 18: Andrews letter of that date; Stiles, p. 460. The marches out of town during the winter: diaries of Barker, Mackenzie; letters of Pitcairn, Percy. Loss of cannon from the common: Frothingham, *Siege*, p. 15. High death rate: Andrews letter of January 9, 1774. "upwards of a hundred," minor delinquencies: Barker, pp. 24, 30, 39. Balfour to Marshfield: Gage, I, 392. Brown and DeBerniere: Mass. Hist. Soc. *Collections*, Vol. IV, pp. 204 ff.

Chapter 10: The Salem Affair
Salem town meeting ignores Gage's troops: Force, 4-1, p. 730. "Minute's warning": Andrews letter of August 26, 1774. Accounts of Leslie's march: *Essex Gazette*, February 28, 1775, and March 7, 1775; *Massachusetts Spy*, March 2, 1775; recollections of William Ganett, Samuel Gray, Abijah Northey, Benjamin Jackson, Mrs. Story; memoir of Colonel Mason, written by his daughter; all of these appended to Endicott "Leslie's Retreat." Pickering's account: Pickering, I, 61-63. Gage's account: Gage, I, 394. Stiles's account: Stiles, p. 522 (contains a sketch of the area). "It is my firm belief": Pickering, I, 24, "Inflammatory": *Ibid.*, 26. Pitcairn's letter: Sandwich, p. 61. Hutchinson's comment: diary, p. 432. Diary of Caleb Prentice for February 27, 1775: Hurd, *Middlesex*, II, 478.

Chapter 11: Gage
Gage's changing view is apparent in his correspondence. "If you yield": II, 671-72. "Masters of the country": I, 387. "Not a Boston rabble": I, 371. "Moment's warning": I, 382. "Numbers will declare themselves": I, 387. Hopes are "not without foundation":

I, 390. "Humor to assemble," and "good effect" at Marshfield: I, 392. Gage's background: Alden. Monongahela: Alden, McCardell. Gage and Rogers: Cuneo. Gage and Church: French, *General Gage's Informers*, and the Church letters of April 3, 9, 11, and 15 in the Clements Library. Dartmouth's letter calling for action: Gage, II, 179-83.

Chapter 12: The Order
The selection of Smith and Pitcairn: "Lt. Col. Smith & Major Pitcairn are the two field officers first for duty, and the senior of each rank" (Mackenzie's diary for April 18). Pitcairn's point of view on the provincials is analyzed in Chap. 14. Gage's order and the rough draft: Gage MSS, Clements Library. Howe, Burgoyne, and Clinton on the way: Gage, II, 185. His prediction of the provincial style of fighting is quoted in French, *Day*, pp. 57-58. Donkin's comments: Donkin, p. 7. Mackenzie's analysis: Mackenzie, pp. 69-71.

Chapter 13: The March to Lexington
In the interleaved almanac of Rev. Mr. Marrett, pastor at Woburn: "1775, April 19. Fair, windy and cold. A distressing day. . . ." (Sewell, p. 363). In Paul Litchfield's diary, Mass. Hist. Soc. *Proceedings*, XIX (1882), 377: "Something blustering and cool." The embarkation: Lister, Sutherland, Mackenzie. The message to members of Provincial Congress: *Journals of Each Provincial Congress*, 147. Couriers: *Ibid.*, 513. Characterization of Mitchell, and other details of Revere's ride: Revere's deposition (Goss, I, 180 ff).

Chapter 14: Lexington
Dandelions: Lossing, pp. 10-11. Parker: Hudson, II, 512; Elizabeth S. Parker, "Captain John Parker." The Lexington company belonged to Gardner's militia regiment (see the analysis of regimental organization, Chap. 15). The Lexington town records for the early months of 1775 have been missing for years, and there is no official record specifically ordering the creation of any minute man company (just as there is no official record of Foster's Danvers minute men, though they are known to have been organized). On December 28, 1774, the town of Lexington voted to supply bayonets to one third of the company; this is the only official indication that there might have been minute men in Lexington. Parker and others, in their depositions, refer to themselves as militia. Mixed companies of minute men and militia were common. There were mixed companies in Lincoln, Danvers, Groton, Sudbury, and Marblehead, among others. "Alarm, muster, and cause to be assembled": *Journals of Each Provincial Congress*, p. 90. Depositions of the Lexington men: *Ibid.*, 662-78. "I don't know what to believe": Coburn, p. 62. "Loaded only with powder": Lossing, p. 7. The officers surrounding Pitcairn: Sutherland. Pitcairn's account: (French, *General Gage's Informers*, pp. 52-54). Gould: *Journals of Each Provincial Congress*, p. 676. Pitcairn's letter: Sandwich, pp. 60-61. It is only fair to add that Pitcairn's views were shared by most of the other officers, including Evelyn, who wrote: "Never did any nation so much deserve to be made an example of to future ages, and never were any set of men more anxious [than we] to be employed on so laudable a work. We only fear they will avail themselves of the clemency and generosity of the English, and by some abject submission evade the chastisment due to unexampled villainy, and which we are so impatiently waiting to inflict" (diary, December 6, 1774, pp. 43-43). British officer firing a pistol: Depositions and Rev. Clarke, quoted in Shattuck, p. 103. Drummer for "cease fire": Sutherland.

Chapter 15: The March to Concord
"So wild they could hear no orders": Barker, p. 32. Advising Smith to return: Mackenzie, p. 63. "Stop the slaughter": Clements MSS; Smith to Donkin, October 8, 1775: "I was desirous of putting a stop to all further slaughter of those deluded people." Wood and Lee: Shattuck, p. 117, and Sewell, pp. 363-64. Snipers firing on column: Mackenzie, p. 63. A five-mile circle: the main source of information on the organization of the provincial militia and minute men is the *Alarm Rolls* manuscript, bound in volumes 11, 12,

and 13 of the *Massachusetts Archives*. Captains of the companies each sent in to the Provincial Congress a list of the men who marched that day, with the number of miles marched, in order to receive payment for this service. About half the captains named the colonel commanding their regiment. Since the regiments were organized geographically (all companies within the same county; all companies in contiguous towns) the rest of the regimental organization can be traced. Town records, town histories, and the Provincial Congress records are also of help. Each of the minute man regiments was formed out of a militia regiment and thus came from the same cluster of towns as did the "parent" militia regiment. 14,000 men: this is probably too conservative, because it is based on the average strength of companies that marched on April 19. Records are complete for 473 companies, but the rolls list only the troops who actually marched, not the full complement. Where both lists are known for a single company, the figures are as might be expected on a day of alarm and confusion; from twenty percent to as many as fifty percent of the men for one reason or another were not present.

Chapter 16: The Regulars at Concord
Riders out to warn towns: Hurd, *Middlesex*, II, 585. Samuel Prescott continued on to warn Acton; William Parkman went to Sudbury. The Bedford flag: Mass. Hist. Soc. *Proceedings* (1885), pp. 166 ff. The arrival of the British, and movement: Amos Barrett, Sutherland, DeBerniere, Lister, Barker. List of supplies in the town: MSS, "account of the provisional stores sent to Colonel Barrett of Concord." quoted in Shattuck, pp. 97-99. Spectators complicate matters: Stiles, p. 551. Colonel Robinson's arrival: Hodgman, p. 105. Troop movements are from a comparison of the accounts previously mentioned. Most of these are conveniently grouped in French, *General Gage's Informers*.

Chapter 17: The Bridge Fight
Wooden ware: Shattuck, p. 97. Martha Moulton: from her petition, quoted in Frothingham, *Siege*, pp. 369-70. Amos Barrett's words: True, p. 33. Davis: Josiah Adams, p. 47. French also discusses at some length the controversy concerning the order of march at the bridge. "They are firing ball": Murdock, p. 67 n. Analysis of the terrain around the bridge was facilitated by the recent research there by the National Park Service. Formations and movements are from the accounts of Sutherland, Laurie, Lister, and Amos Barrett, and Thorp's deposition in Josiah Adams, p. 44.

Chapter 18: Concord Surrounded
Light companies up on the ridge: Lister. The movement of the Sudbury minute men across the South Bridge instead of the North Bridge: they were not engaged at Meriam's Corner, but came into the fight from south of the road at Hardy's (Brooks') Hill. Hudson (p. 374) has Nixon pass around to the North Bridge. "Not quite dead": Parsons' account. How, Nixon, and the Framingham and Sudbury men: Temple, p. 268-81, and Hudson, *Sudbury*, pp. 370-76. William Thompson: Hazen, pp. 142, 234, 237. Brooks: Charles Brooks, p. 134.

Chapter 19: Smith Marches from Concord
Foster's account: Hudson, p. 166. Lister wounded: Lister, p. 29. "Gave the rebels more confidence": Mackenzie, p. 66. Nixon: Temple, Hudson. Hardy's Hill probably was called Brooks' Hill at that time.

Chapter 20: The Bloody Angle
The name "Bloody Angle" was given to this spot some time after the battle. British bending down: Thompson's deposition, Hurd, *Middlesex*, pp. 390-91. Wilson killed: Brown, p. 24; Hazen, p. 236 (Stearns was from Billerica but was a lieutenant in the Bedford company, which had men from both towns). Loammi Baldwin: his diary excerpt in Hurd, *Middlesex*, pp. 445-47. Town of Woburn slow to conform: *Town Records*, IX; Sewell, p. 361. Baldwin's movements: his diary and Tay deposition, Frothingham, *Siege*, pp. 368-69.

The reconnaissance around Concord by Baldwin's men: Thompson in Hurd, *Middlesex*, p. 391. Baldwin says simply that the men "refreshed themselves," but this would not account for the amount of time that passed. Samuel Thompson: Sewell, p. 362; Hurd, *Middlesex*, p. 390. Men "from the clouds": Force, 4-2, p. 359.

Chapter 21: Parker's Revenge

Not one "gallant attempt": Smith's account. The boulders: Coburn: p. 103. Parker on Pine Hill: Nathan Munroe's deposition: "we met the regulars in the bounds of Lincoln, about noon." The horseman informing Parker is an assumption based on the several references to riders bringing news of the British actions. Conditions in the British column: DeBerniere, Lister. Pitcairn unhorsed: Foster. Noah Eaton's exploit: Temple, p. 276. James Hayward: Coburn, p. 108. Wounded regulars: *Ibid.*, 110.

Chapter 22: Percy's Relief Column

The town "a good deal agitated": Mackenzie, p. 52. "Utmost expedition": *Ibid.* Six pounders: Barker, p. 35. Percy pays to help soldiers' wives: Percy, p. 18. Andrews letter: August 21, 1774. Percy weak-eyed: Percy, p. 30. "I hope it will not be my fate.": *Ibid.*, 34. Cleaveland and the ammunition: Duncan, p. 302. Montresor: French, *First Year*, p. 18. Percy and Gould meet: Cutter, p. 81. The exempts: S.A. Smith, p. 28. Disposition of the captured articles: Hanson, pp. 106-108, 217-18; Cutter, p. 63. Gould captured: S.A. Smith, p. 31. Arrival at Lexington: Mackenzie, p. 59. Rooke: *Ibid.* "Sanguine hopes of our returning": Pope, p. 23. Percy's comment: French, *Day*, p. 233.

Chapter 23: Lexington Surrounded

"The battalions broke": Pope, p. 24. The British formations: Mackenzie. Burning the houses: Coburn, pp. 123-28; *Journals of Each Provincial Congress*, pp. 584-94. Baldwin: Hurd, Middlesex, p. 447. "Dispersed, tho' adhering": Stiles, p. 552. Tudor: Tudor, p. 51. Andover men: Bailey, p. 308. Faulkner "organizing his regiment": Hamblin, p. 6. Heath's activities and characterization are from his memoirs. Warren "perhaps the most active": Frothingham, *Siege*, p. 77 n.

Chapter 24: Percy Retreats

"As it began to grow pretty late": Percy's report to Gage. The formation leaving Lexington: Mackenzie; Sutherland; *Late News*. Lord Harris: Lushington, p. 49. Provincial horsemen: Chase, p. 156; Hudson, *Sudbury*, p. 382; S.A. Smith, p. 47; Cutter, p. 72. "Numbers of them were mounted": Mackenzie, pp. 26-27. Thirty-five companies waiting for Percy: see analysis in Chap. 15.

Chapter 25: The Menotomy Fight

Danvers Companies: Hanson, p. 108. Changing directions of march: Chase, I, 130. Amos Putnam dies: Danvers Soldiers' Record, p. 157. Captain Hutchinson warns Foster: Hanson, 107. "Obliged to force almost every house": Barker, p. 36. Looting houses: Coburn, p. 139. Foster's account: Cutter, p. 67. Lynn men: Wellman, p. 106. John Bacon: Chase, I, 140. Benjamin Pierce: *Ibid.*, 182. Dennison Wallis: Cutter, p. 67 n. Solomon Bowman: S.A. Smith, p. 47. Sam Whittemore: Cutter, p. 77; S.A. Smith, pp. 39-43. "Whoever looks upon them as an irregular mob": Percy, p. 52. "Having no shot to fire from our cannon": *Late News*, p. 24. "Moving circle of fire": Percy, p. 52. British casualties: Mackenzie, p. 61; DeBerniere's account.

Chapter 26: Charlestown

Major Gardner: Coburn, p. 147; Paige, p. 411. Heath halts the provincials: Heath, p. 22. Washington: quoted from Jared Sparks, *The Writings of George Washington*, II, 407, in Tourtellot, p. 202. Marblehead minute men: Pickering, I, 541 n. Pickering's march: Pickering, pp. 70-71. Heath does not remember: Heath, p. 72 n. Selectmen of

Charlestown to see Percy: DeBerniere's account. Charlestown refugees: Frothingham, *Siege*, p. 79. 10th Regiment company has eleven men left: Lister, p. 32. Montresor: French, *First Year*, p. 19.

Chapter 27: The Aftermath

Percy's brigade on Bunker Hill until the twenty-sixth: Barker, p. 39. Gage's account: *Journals of Each Provincial Congress*, pp. 679-81. "I cannot tell when you will get another letter.": *Ibid.*, 682. "We did not fight as you did.": *Ibid.*, 683. "My husband is now lying in one of their hospitals.": *Ibid.*, 684. Moses Richardson: Paige, p. 414. Assonet Expedition: Daggett, pp. 129-30. Twenty thousand minute men and militia: French, *First Year*, p. 721, gives the figure 19,875. "Hasten and encourage . . . the enlistment.": *Journals of Each Provincial Congress*, p. 518.

Chapter 28: The Minute Men and the New Army

Unless otherwise noted, references for this chapter are to *Journals of Each Provincial Congress*. Committee of Safety requests returns: pp. 552, 565, 574. Army of 30,000: p. 148. "Under good officers": p. 523. Temporary replacements: p. 526. Medford company, p. 528. Towns close to Boston to send men: p. 540. Putnam's ruse: Frothingham, *Siege*, pp. 107-108. Glover's regiment: pp. 562-63. Congress changes wording to "minute's warning": p. 348. Powers of Committee of Safety: pp. 241-42. Twenty-three regiments: p. 325. There was some difficulty involved in finding the correct command positions for all the minute man officers when the forty-seven regiments were compressed into twenty-three: James Warren wrote to John Adams (May 7, 1775), "We are embarrassed in officering our army by the establishment of Minute Men. I wish it had never taken place." The embarrassment must have been administrative, rather than tactical. Form letter calling out militia: p. 571. Connecticut minute men: p. 149 n. Continental Congress minute men: Upton, p. 8. 1776 minute men: Pickering, I, 77.

Bibliography

Abbott, John F. *History of King Philip*. New York: Harper, 1885.

Adams, Charles F. "Genesis of the Massachusetts Towns," Massachusetts Historical Society *Proceedings* (2nd Series, VII, 1892, pp. 172 ff.)

_____. (ed.). *The Works of John Adams*. 10 Vols. Boston, 1850-1856.

Adams, Herbert B. "The Germanic Origin of New England Towns." *Johns Hopkins University Studies in Historical and Political Science*, Vol. I, No. 2, pp. 8 ff.

Adams, Josiah. *An Address Delivered at Acton, July 21, 1835*. Boston: Buckingham, 1835.

_____. *Letter to Lemuel Shattuck, Esq.* Boston: Darrell and Moore, 1850.

Alden, John R. *General Gage in America*. Baton Rouge: Louisiana State University Press, 1948.

Andrews, John. "The Andrews Letters," Massachusetts Historical Society *Proceedings*, VIII (July, 1865), pp. 316 ff.

Bailey, Sarah L. *Historical Sketches of Andover, Massachusetts*. Boston: Houghton, Mifflin, 1880.

Barber, John W. *Historical Collections of Massachusetts*. Worcester: Dorr, Howland, 1841.

Barker, John. *The British in Boston* (Harold Murdock, ed.) Cambridge: Harvard, 1924.

Bates, Samuel A. (ed.). *Records of the Town of Braintree, 1640-1793*. Randolph, Mass.: Huxford, 1886.

Bodge, George M. *Soldiers in King Philip's War*. Leominster: Published by the author, 1896.

Boston, (City of). *A Report of the Record Commissioners of the City of Boston, Containing the Boston Town Records, 1770-1777*. Boston: Rockwell, Churchill, 1887.

_____. *Records of the Governor and Company of the Massachusetts Bay in New England*. 5 Vols. Boston: White, 1853.

Boyle, Col. G.E. "The 18th Regiment of Foot in North America," *The Journal of the Society of Army Historical Research*, II (January 1923), 65 ff.

Brattle, William. *Sundry Rules and Directions for Drawing Up a Regiment, Posting the Officers, etc.* Boston: Mills, Hicks, 1773.

Brigham, William (ed.). *The Compact with the Charter and Laws of the Colony of New Plymouth.* Boston: Dutton and Wentworth, 1836.

Brookline (Town of). *Muddy River and Brookline Records, 1634-1839,* Farwell & Co., 1875.

Brooks, Charles, and James M. Usher. *History of Medford.* Boston: Rand and Avery, 1886.

Brown, Abram E. *The History of the Town of Bedford.* Published by the author, 1891.

Buell, Augustus C. *Sir William Johnson.* New York: Appleton, 1903.

Butler, Caleb. *The History of the Town of Groton.* Boston, 1848.

Cambridge (Town of). *Town Records of Cambridge, 1630-1703.* Printed by the town, 1896.

Cannon, Richard. *Historical Records of the British Army.* London: Parker, Furnall, & Parker, 1850-1870.

Chase, Ellen. *The Beginnings of the American Revolution.* 3 Vols. New York: Baker & Taylor, 1910.

Church, Thomas. *Entertaining Passages Relating to Philip's War Which Began in the Month of June, 1675.* Boston: 1716.

_____. *The History of Philip's War.* Exeter, N.H.: J. & B. Williams, 1829.

Clenedenen, Clarence C. "A Little Known Period of American Military History," *Military Affairs,* Spring, 1955, pp. 37-38.

Coburn, Frank Warren. *The Battle of April 19, 1775.* 2nd ed. Lexington: Lexington Historical Society, 1922.

Crane, Ellery B. "The Early Militia System of Massachusetts." (A paper read before the Worcester Society of Antiquity, Oct. 2, 1888) Worcester: Private Press of F.P. Rice, 1889.

Cushing, Harry A. "Political Activity of Massachusetts Towns during the Revolution." *Annual Report of the American Historical Association.* 1895, pp. 105-13.

Cuneo, John R. *Robert Rogers of the Rangers.* New York: Oxford, 1959.

Cutler, Benjamin, & William. *The History of the Town of Arlington.* Boston: Clapp, 1880.

Daggett, John. *A Sketch of the History of Attleborough.* Boston: Usher, 1894.

Davidson, Philip. *Propaganda and the American Revolution, 1763-1783.* Chapel Hill: University of North Carolina, 1941.

Davis, Walter A. (ed.). *The Old Records of the Town of Fitchburg, Massachusetts, 1764-1789,* Vol. I, Fitchburg: 1898.

DeBerniere, John. "Narrative," Massachusetts Historical Society *Collections,* 2, IV, 215 ff.

Donkin, Robert. *Military Collections and Remarks.* New York: Gaine, 1777.

Drake, Francis S. *The Town of Roxbury.* Boston: Municipal Printing Office, 1905.

Draper, Richard. "A Plan of Exercise for the Militia of the Province of Massachusetts-Bay," extracted from *The Plan of Discipline for the Norfolk Militia.* Boston: 1772.

Dudley (Town of). *Town Records of Dudley, 1732-1754.* Pawtucket: Sutcliffe, 1893.

Duncan, Francis. *History of the Royal Regiment of Artillery.* 2 Vols. London: Murray, 1872.

Duxbury (Town of). *The Records of Duxbury, 1642-1770.* Plymouth: Avery & Doten, 1893.

Ellis, George & John E. Morris, *King Philip's War.* New York: 1906.

Endicott, Charles M. "Leslie's Retreat," *Essex Institute Proceedings.* XII.

Evelyn, William G. *Memoir and Letters of William Glanville Evelyn* (G.D. Scull, ed.). Oxford: Parker, 1879.

Firth, C.H. *Cromwell's Army.* New York: Barnes & Noble, no date (initially published in 1902).

Force, Peter & M. Clarke (eds.). *American Archives,* 4th Series, Vol. I, Washington, December, 1837.

Fortescue, J.W. *A History of the British Army.* London: Macmillan, 1902.

Freese, J.W. *Historic Houses and Spots in Cambridge, Massachusetts and Near-by Towns.* Boston: Ginn, 1897.

French, Allen. *General Gage's Informers.* Ann Arbor: University of Michigan, 1932.

_____. *The Day of Concord and Lexington.* Boston: Little, Brown, 1925.

_____. *First Year of the American Revolution.* Boston: Houghton, Mifflin, 1934.

Frothingham, Richard, Jr. *The History of Charlestown, Massachusetts*. Boston: Little & Brown, 1845.

_____. *History of the Siege of Boston*. Boston: Little, Brown, 1851.

_____. *The Life and Times of Joseph Warren*. Boston: Little, Brown, 1866.

Gage, Thomas. *The Correspondence of General Thomas Gage*. 2 Vols. (C.E. Carter, ed.). New Haven: Yale, 1933.

Gardiner, Samuel R. *The History of the [British] Great Civil War*. 4 Vols., New York: Longmans, Green, 1901.

Goss, Elbridge, II. *The History of Melrose*. Melrose: Published by the author, 1902.

_____. *The Life of Colonel Paul Revere*. Boston: 1891.

Hagen, Rev. Henry A. *History of Billerica*. Boston: Williams, 1883.

Hamblin, Rev. Cyrus. *My Grandfather, Colonel Francis Faulkner. . . .* Boston: Stanley and Usher, 1887.

Hanson, J.W. *History of the Town of Danvers*. Danvers: Published by the author, 1848.

Hatch, Louis C. *The Administration of the American Revolutionary Army*. New York: Longmans, Green, 1904.

Heath, William. *Heath's Memoirs of the American War*. New York: Wessels, 1904.

Hexter, J.H. *The Reign of King Pym*. Cambridge: Harvard University Press, 1941.

Hodgman, Rev. Edwin. *History of the Town of Westford, 1659-1883*. Lowell: Morning Mail Co., 1883.

Honyman, Robert. *Colonial Panorama, 1775/Dr. Robert Honyman's Journal*. San Marino, California: Huntington, 1939.

Hosmer, James K. (ed.). *Governor Winthrop's Journal*. Vol. I. New York: Scribners, 1908.

_____. *Samuel Adams*. Boston: Houghton, Mifflin, 1891.

Hudson, Alfred S. *History of Sudbury, Massachusetts*. Published by the town, 1889.

Hudson, Charles. *History of the Town of Lexington*. 2 Vols. Boston: Houghton, Mifflin, 1913.

Hurd, D.H. *History of Essex County, Massachusetts*. Philadelphia: Lewis, 1888.

_____. *History of Middlesex County, Massachusetts*. Vol. I, Philadelphia: Lewis, 1890.

Hutchinson, Thomas. *The Diary and Letters of His Excellency Thomas Hutchinson, Esq.* Boston: Houghton, Mifflin, 1884.

_____. *The History of the Colony and Province of Massachusetts-Bay* (L.S. Mayo, ed.). Cambridge: Harvard, 1936.

Jameson, J.F. (ed.). *Amherst Town Records*. Amherst: Williams, 1884.

Journals of Each Provincial Congress. See Lincoln.

King, Daniel P. *Address Commemorative of Seven Young Men of Danvers. . . .* Salem: Ives, 1835.

Kreidberg, M., and Henry Merton. *History of the Military Mobilization in the US Army, 1775-1945* (DA Pam. 20-212). Washington: Department of the Army, 1955.

Leach, D.E., *Flintlock and Tomahawk*. New York: Macmillan, 1958.

_____. "The Military System of Plymouth Colony." *New England Quarterly*, XXIV (September, 1951), 342-64.

Letters and Doings of the Council. Part of *Massachusetts Archives*. MSS notebook covering period April 9, 1774-April 21, 1776.

Levinge, Sir Richard G.A. *Historical Records of the Forty-Third Regiment, Monmouthshire Light Infantry*. London: Clowes, 1868.

Lewis, A. and James Newhall. *The History of Lynn*. Boston: Shorey, 1865.

Lincoln, William (ed.). *The Journals of Each Provincial Congress*. Boston: Dutton and Wentworth, 1838.

Lister, Jeremy. *Concord Fight*. Cambridge: Harvard, 1931.

Lossing, Benson J. *Hours with Living Men and Women of the Revolution*. New York: Funk & Wagnalls, 1889.

Lushington, Stephen R. *The Life and Services of General Lord Harris*. London: Parker, 1840.

Lyman, Phineas. *General Orders of 1757* (William S. Webb, ed.). New York: Gilliss, 1899.

Mackenzie, Frederick. *A British Fusilier in Revolutionary Boston* (Allen French, ed.). Cambridge: Harvard, 1926.

Massachusetts *Archives* (MSS). State House, Boston, Massachusetts.

Massachusetts. *The Colonial Laws of Massachusetts* (reprinted from edition of 1672). Boston: Rockwell and Churchill, 1890.

Massachusetts-Bay. *Acts and Resolves of the Province of Massachusetts-Bay, 1692-1780.* 21 Vols. Boston: Wright & Potter, 1869.

McCardell, Lee. *Ill-Starred General/History of Braddock's Expedition.* Pittsburgh: University of Pittsburgh, 1958.

McGuire, William (ed.). *Watertown Records Fifth Book, 1745-1769*; and *Sixth Book, 1769-1792.* Newton: Graphic Press, 1928.

Milton (Town of). *Town Records of Milton, 1662-1729.* Boston: Sherrill, 1930.

Murdock, Harold. *The Nineteenth of April, 1775.* Boston: Houghton, Mifflin, 1923.

Noble, John (ed.). *Records of the Court of Assistants of the Colony of Massachusetts-Bay, 1630-1692.* Vol. II. Boston: Suffolk County, 1904.

Nourse, H.S. *History of the Town of Harvard, Massachusetts, 1732-1893.* Harvard: 1894.

_____. *Military Annuals of Lancaster, Massachusetts, 1740-1864.* Lancaster: 1889.

Orr, Charles (ed.). *History of the Pequot War.* Cleveland: Helman, Taylor, 1897.

Osgood, Herbert. *The American Colonies in the Seventeenth Century.* New York: Macmillan, 1904.

_____. *The American Colonies in the Eighteenth Century.* Vols I & II. New York: Columbia, 1924.

Paige, Lucius. *History of Cambridge, 1630-1877.* Boston: Houghton, 1877.

Pargellis, Stanley. *Military Affairs in North America, 1748-1765.* New York: Appleton-Century, 1936.

Parrington, Vernon L. *The Colonial Mind.* New York: Harcourt, Brace, 1927.

Parker, Elizabeth S. "Captain John Parker." *Proceedings of the Lexington Historical Society,* I (1886-1889), 43 ff.

Parker, Joel. "The Origin, Organization, and Influence of the Towns of New England." *Massachusetts Historical Society Proceedings,* IX, p. 20.

Parkman, Francis. *Montcalm and Wolfe.* Boston: Little, Brown, 1889.

Parsons, Usher. *The Life of the Sir William Pepperrell, Bart.* Boston: Little, Brown, 1855.

Percy, Hugh. *Letters of Hugh, Earl Percy, 1774-1776* (Charles K. Bolton, ed.). Boston: Goodspeed, 1902.

Peterson, H.L. *Arms and Armor in Colonial America, 1526-1783.* Harrisburg: Stackpole, 1962.

Pickering, Octavius. *The Life of Timothy Pickering.* 4 Vols. Boston: Little, Brown, 1867.

Pope, Richard. *Late News of the Excursion and Ravages of the King's Troops on the 19th of April 1775.* Boston: Harvard, 1927.

Purdon, H.G. *An Historical Sketch of the 47th (Lancashire) Regiment and of the Campaigns Through Which They Passed.* London: Guardian, 1907.

_____. *Memoirs of the Services of the 64th Regiment (Second Staffordshire) 1758 to 1881.* London: Allen, n.d.

Records of the Governor and Company of Massachusetts-Bay in New England. Boston: William White, 1853.

Richards, Walter. *Her Majesty's Army.* London: Virtue, n.d.

Roberts, Oliver Ayer. *History of the Military Company of Massachusetts, 1637-1888.* Boston: Mudge, 1897.

Rowe, John. "Diary of John Rowe," *Massachusetts Historical Society Proceedings.* 2d Ser., X, 86 ff.

Sabine, Lorenzo. *Loyalists of the American Revolution.* Boston: Little, Brown, 1864.

Sandwich, Earl of. *The Private Papers of John, Earl of Sandwich.* London: Navy Records Society, 1932.

Sewell, Samuel. *The History of Woburn, 1640-1860.* Boston: Wiggin & Lunt, 1868.

Shattuck, Lemuel. *The History of the Town of Concord.* Boston: Russell, Osborne, 1835.

Sheldon, George. *A History of Deerfield, Massachusetts.* 2 Vols. Deerfield: 1896.

Shy, John. *Toward Lexington: The Role of the British Army in the Coming Revolution.* Princeton: Princeton University Press, 1965.

Simes, Thomas. *The Military Guide for Young Officers.* 3d Ed. London: J. Millan, 1781.

Sly, J.F. "A Critique of Town Origins." Chap. III, *Town-Government in Massachusetts, 1620-1930.* Cambridge: Harvard Press, 1930.

Smith, Charles F. *Proceedings of the Beverly Historical Society of Massachusetts on the Occasion of the Presentation of a Tablet Commemorating the Minute-Men of Beverly,* 1st Ser., no. 1, New York: DeVinne, 1896.

Smith, Lt. Col. Francis. "Report to Gage." Massachusetts Historical Society *Proceedings.* II, 2 (May, 1876), 350-51.

Smith, Samuel A. *West Cambridge on the Nineteenth of April, 1775.* Boston: Mudge, 1864.

Smith, S.F. *The History of Newton.* Boston: American Logotype Co., 1880.

Stephenson, Carl and Frederick G. Marcham (eds.). *Sources of English Constitutional History.* New York: Harper, 1937.

Stiles, Ezra. *The Literary Diary of Ezra Stiles, DD, LLD.* Vol. I, 1769-1776 (F. Dexter, ed.) New York: Scribner's 1901.

Stone, E.M. *The History of Beverly.* Boston: Munroe, 1843.

Sumner, William. *The History of East Boston.* Boston: Tilton, 1858.

Teele, A.K. *The History of Milton.* Boston: Rockwell and Churchill, 1887.

Temple, J.H. *The History of Framingham.* Published by the town, 1887.

Tourtellot, Arthur B. *William Diamond's Drum.* New York: Doubleday, 1959.

True, Henry. *Journals and Letters.* Marion, Ohio: Published by the author, 1906.

Tudor, William (ed.). *Deacon Tudor's Diary.* Boston: Spooner, 1896.

Upton, Emory, Bvt. Major General. *The Military Policy of the United States.* Washington: Government Printing Office, 1912.

Van Tyne, Claude. "Influence of the Clergy and of Religious and Sectarian Forces on the American Revolution." *American Historical Review,* XIX, pp. 44-64.

Wellman, T.B. *History of the Town of Lynnfield, Massachusetts, 1635-1895.* Boston: Blanchard & Watts, 1895.

Wenham (Town of). *Wenham Town Records, 1730-1775.* Wenham: Wenham Historical Society, 1940.

Weston (Town of). *Weston Town Records, 1754-1803.* Boston: Mudge, 1893.

Wheildon, William W. *A New Chapter in the History of the Concord Fight.* Boston: Lee and Shepard, 1885.

Winsor, Justin. *The Memorial History of Boston.* 4 Vols. Boston: Ticknor.

Wood, Walter. *The Northumberland Fusiliers.* London: Grant Richards, n.d.

Worthington, Erastus. *The History of Dedham.* Boston: Dutton & Wentworth, 1827.

Index